Harvard English Studies   11

Modernism Reconsidered

HARVARD ENGLISH STUDIES   11

Modernism Reconsidered

Edited by
Robert Kiely
Assisted by
John Hildebidle

Harvard University Press
Cambridge, Massachusetts
London, England
1983

Library of Congress Cataloging in Publication Data

Main entry under title:

Modernism reconsidered.

(Harvard English studies; 11)
1. English literature—20th century—History and criticism—Addresses, essays, lectures. 2. Modernism (Literature)—Addresses, essays, lectures. 3. American literature—20th century—History and criticism—Addresses, essays, lectures. I. Kiely, Robert. II. Hildebidle, John, 1946–   . III. Series.
PR478.M6M62 1983   820′.9′1   83-6152
ISBN 0-674-58065-6
ISBN 0-674-58066-4 (pbk.)

38,361

Preface

In reference to the "modern" qualities of a story by Chekhov, Virginia Woolf wrote: "The emphasis is laid upon such unexpected places that at first it seems as if there were no emphasis at all; and then, as the eyes accustom themselves to twilight and discern the shapes of things in a room we see how complete the story is, how profound, and how truly in obedience to his vision."

If we take the modern period to include the years between the late 1880s and the beginning of World War II, we can say with some confidence that our eyes have "accustomed themselves" to the light and that, as critics and scholars, we have kept very busy discerning "the shapes of things." The emphases are no longer unexpected. How could they be, since so many of them are of our own making? Modernism is no longer so simply associated with formalism, fascism, or dehumanization as it was by some critics in its earlier phases. Still, considering its proximity, the critical outlines and assumptions about it are surprisingly firm.

In many ways this is admirable, a sign both of the compelling nature of many modernist works and the extraordinary outpouring of scholarship and criticism they have inspired. Distinguished biographies, meticulously edited volumes of letters and journals, as well as hundreds of critical studies have mapped out the modern terrain with alacrity and sophistication. Yet like all important achievements, the critical and scholarly legacy has its burdensome side. The immortals have been named and the doors to the pantheon closed. Tendencies and theories have been noted and stressed and, quite naturally, works have been ranked.

What is to be done? Or, more precisely, what is *left* to be done? The broadside is useless. There have always been those who thought Joyce a fraud, Eliot a prig, Yeats mad, Woolf precious, Lawrence a fanatic, and Pound a savage. They have all been debunked, almost from the very beginning, and yet their reputations are more solid than ever. Part of the reason seems to be that there is enough

v

self-mockery in most of their work to have served as a form of immunization. Furthermore, attacks on these authors have a familiarity that makes them sound too quaint to be lethal.

If useful discussions of modernism are to continue, they must build on what has been done without taking it to be sacrosanct. The original texts themselves are not Scripture, though sometimes they are treated as such; and even the best commentaries are still far from Augustinian in authority. The work of the scholar and critic is never finished, not only because new information invariably can be found, but because each generation has its own experience, its own way of asking questions, its own way of reading.

The contributors to this volume were asked to reconsider authors who, for one reason or another, have been excluded by critics from the great modern constellation; to examine works by major writers that are not usually regarded as among their most typical or greatest achievements; or to explore some of the received opinions about modernist theories and the assumptions that inform the literature of the period. The response has produced a collection of essays that range widely over the era and the modes common to it. Inevitably, major works and writers have not all been included. Our purpose has not been "coverage," but the reexamination of texts and ideas. In the process, perhaps there will have been some slight shift in those emphases to which we may have grown almost too accustomed.

R.K.

Contents

JEROME H. BUCKLEY

Towards Early-Modern Autobiography:
The Roles of Oscar Wilde, George Moore,
Edmund Gosse, and Henry Adams

Fascinated by the masks he could fashion for himself, Yeats praised Oscar Wilde's ability to strike an unconventional pose, to sustain the "discipline" of a new role, and to observe public reaction to his performance. By contrast, he argued, Wordsworth was "often flat and heavy" because he had "no theatrical element" in his character but simply "an obedience to a discipline which he [had] not created."[1]

Setting aside the value judgment, we might apply Yeats's comment specifically to *The Prelude* and extend it to other nineteenth-century self-presentations. We might then agree that Wordsworth and the major Victorian autobiographers, however dramatic may have been their sense of discovery and commitment, however resourceful their rhetorical strategies, were all indeed untheatrical. Each, to be sure, recognized his role in life and played it effectively: Wordsworth as the dedicated poet, Darwin as the scientific observer, Ruskin as the critical spectator, Newman as religious leader, Mill as defender of intellectual liberty. But each assumed his role as something given by endowment, circumstance, and vocation, rather than as a part he himself was devising and staging for special effect. The question of sincerity in their autobiographies

---

1. W. B. Yeats, *Autobiographies* (London: Macmillan, 1973), pp. 469–470.

1

scarcely arises, for by the time of reviewing their careers, each of them had supplied ample objective evidence that the role claimed was his true and sufficient identity.

In the more "theatrical" late-Victorian generation, on the other hand, the author of a self-history was less confident of the truths of selfhood, and his self-presentation, or role playing, involved a different sort of self-consciousness. Though acutely aware of his audience, he felt alienated from the ordinary world and no longer accountable to it. "The egoistic note," Wilde remarked in 1897, "is . . . and always has been to me, the primal and ultimate note of modern art, but *to be an Egoist one must have an Ego.*"[2] The "personality," in other words, as opposed to the "nature" of a man that Edwin Muir would prize,[3] must validate itself by the uniqueness of private impressions and the individuality of personal style, the singularity of gesture and voice. If the self as a separate entity seemed elusive and amorphous, or if, perhaps, it did not exist at all, it must be invented, dressed up, and projected. It mattered little that the creation of a self-image might distort the masker's actual experience or willfully commingle fiction with fact.

In the most striking late-Victorian autobiography, Wilde himself rehearsed his boldest role. Though written as a letter from Reading Gaol and first published in full more than sixty years later, *De Profundis* reads like a long, carefully wrought monologue in an immediate cultural tragedy. Lord Alfred Douglas, the addressee, is cast as the ruthless, self-seeking antagonist who precipitates the hero's downfall; and many pages denounce his perfidy. But the letter must transcend diatribe, must destroy all bitterness of heart; it should prove, Wilde insists, "as important a crisis and turning-point" in Douglas's life as "the writing of it" proves in Wilde's own (p. 448). The writer, the speaker, is, of course, the real subject, the actor at center-stage. At frequent intervals he reminds us of his tragic credentials, of the greatness he has lost or betrayed. He

2. Letter to Lord Alfred Douglas, probably June 1897; italics Wilde's; in Rupert Hart-Davis, ed., *The Letters of Oscar Wilde* (New York: Harcourt Brace and World, 1962), p. 590. All further references to the *Letters* and to *De Profundis,* the title later applied to the letter of January-March 1897, are taken from this edition and are identified by page numbers in the text.

3. See Edwin Muir, *An Autobiography* (New York: Seabury Press, 1968), p. 181, where Muir celebrates his friend John Holms as a "nature," a selfless "soul" rather than a contrived "personality."

declares himself the scion of a noble and honored family, the master of every literary form he touched, "once a lord of language," an incomparable shaper of public thought and feeling: "The gods had given me almost everything. I had genius, a distinguished name, high social position, brilliancy, intellectual daring" (p. 466).[4] For every good reason, then, "I was a man who stood in symbolic relations to the art and culture of my age. I had realised this for myself at the very dawn of my manhood, and had forced my age to realise it afterwards" (p. 466).[5] Now that he has fallen, though he may revile Douglas, he must recognize the real tragic flaw in himself, since "nobody, great or small, can be ruined except by his own hand" (p. 465). Henceforth he must practice deep humility. The model he chooses in his grief is Christ, the Man of Sorrows, whom he refashions quite arbitrarily in his own image as the "artist in sympathy," the arch-individualist, the first Romantic, and the determined anti-Philistine. When released from prison, he will, he vows, go down to the sea for healing and a new baptism—he remembers Euripides' saying that the sea "washes away the stains and sins of the world." There Nature, he trusts, or at least fantasizes, will restore him: "She will hang the night with stars so that I may walk abroad in the darkness without stumbling, and send the wind over my footprints so that none may track me to my hurt; she will cleanse me in great waters, and with bitter herbs make me whole" (p. 510).

Whether or not, as Wilde once remarked, "one should always be a little improbable," the prose of *De Profundis* as here is often implausible, derivative, and self-indulgent. The actor himself is scarcely persuaded by his rhetorical compunction, and he can hardly expect his audience to be. In an earlier passage of confessed abasement, concluding with a quotation from one of his own plays, he declares, "I would not a bit mind sleeping in the cool grass in summer, and when winter came on sheltering myself by the warm close-thatched rick, or under the penthouse of a great barn, provided I had love in my heart. The external things of life seem to me now of no importance at all. You can see to what intensity of individu-

4. Jacques Barzun introduces a reprint of *De Profundis* (New York: Vintage, 1964), with an acute comment on Wilde's view of himself as a kind of tragic hero.

5. See also p. 458, on the family name, and p. 500, where he extols his comedies above Congreve's.

alism I have arrived, or am arriving rather, for the journey is long, and 'where I walk there are thorns' " (p. 467).[6] But the aesthetic, urban self-image he has presented throughout his career is too strong for him—or for us—to take his rural excursion seriously, and he at once seeks refuge in a self-conscious, ironic realism: "Of course I know that to ask for alms on the highway is not to be my lot, and that if ever I lie in the cool grass at night-time it will be to write sonnets to the Moon" (p. 467).

Nonetheless, despite splashes of false sentiment, Wilde seems truly to mean much of what he says. If his claim to honored family is somewhat shaken by what we know of his raffish parents, his estimate of his own literary prowess is not wholly unjustified. By virtue of *The Importance of Being Earnest* and *Intentions*, his achievement both as writer of comedy and as critic is unassailable. He was, indeed, as most cultural historians now see him, the representative man of letters of the English nineties. And fallen from his brief eminence, he did suffer cruelly for his indiscretion and folly. Few descriptions of humiliation could be more moving than his account of standing handcuffed, in conspicuous prison garb, for half an hour on the central platform at Clapham Junction, while successive trains poured forth a jeering mob.

But our sympathy wavers as soon as he shifts his rhetoric to extravagant hyperbole or precious metaphor, when he recalls his majesty as King of "that beautiful unreal world of Art" or strives to reproduce not just his sorrow but "the purple pageant of [his] incommunicable woe" (pp. 458, 463). At such moments the actor's mask is more apparent than the reality of the self behind it; we begin to wonder what sort of Ego, if any at all, the Egoist actually has. By the end, however, the jarring lines count for less than the virtuoso performance; we come to see the role as an act of courage, the necessary protection of a hurt self against a demeaning pity.

For most of his private life, lived as it was largely in public, Wilde avoided self-confrontation. To be sure, he had his own special insights, his "spots of time," and he even borrowed directly from Wordsworth when he discussed the problem of sustaining such vision: "One can realise a thing in a single moment, but one loses it in the long hours that follow with leaden feet. It is so difficult to

6. The last clause is quoted from *A Woman of No Importance*, Act IV.

keep 'heights that the soul is competent to gain' " (p. 474).[7] But he dreaded revealing the long dull stretches of commonplace routine, the emptiness of the "ordinary" Wordsworthian perception. In his art he repeatedly invoked epigram and apothegm to generalize or dismiss his personal experience, and abundant defensive wit to conceal his unruly sentiment. Some months after his release from Reading Gaol, once more seeking an adequate mask but now finding none, he wryly remarked, "A man's face is his autobiography; a woman's face is her work of fiction."[8] In his most characteristic writing from the beginning through *De Profundis*, he himself made no great distinction between the two genres.

George Moore, with a less immediate need for dramatic gesture, also created fictions of the self. At least eight of his books belong to the autobiographical mode as he conceived it, an amalgam of incident, impression, and invention, commingling records of private life, sometimes embarrassingly frank, often heightened or distorted, with long stretches of confident art criticism and much literary gossip, all calculated to demonstrate his intelligence, sophistication, and importance.

Moore's motivation as perpetual autobiographer is most apparent in his trilogy, *Hail and Farewell*, where he claims to have been woefully neglected by parents who from his early childhood persuaded him of his personal ugliness, incompetence, and stupidity. He is quite aware that he may have overcompensated for his "inveterate belief in [his] own inferiority." Nonetheless, he insists, "Within the oftentimes bombastic and truculent appearance that I present to the world, trembles a heart shy as a wren in the hedgerow or a mouse along the wainscoting."[9] His swaggering bravado, then, which the Yeats circle dismissed with contempt, was simply the "theatrical element" in a deliberate and often desperate self-assertion that Yeats elsewhere applauded.

Moore's first and most flamboyant self-advertisement, *Confes-*

---

7. The last words here are quoted (not quite accurately) from *The Excursion*, IV, 139.

8. Quoted in a letter of April 17, 1898, from Robert Ross to Leonard Smithers, *Letters*, p. 730n.

9. George Moore, "Ave," in *Hail and Farewell* (New York: Appleton, 1925), I, 73, 75.

sions of a Young Man, published in 1888, exploits some of the materials treated rather more discreetly in his later autobiographies but offers no explanation for the young man's rebellious behavior. The confessor is ostensibly one Edward Dayne, but the disguise is very thin; the author seems uncertain whether his first name is Edward or Edouard or Edwin (he uses all three forms), and in the French edition of 1889 he drops the alias altogether and calls himself George Moore. His inspiration, he says, is St. Augustine, but whereas that great exemplar told "the story of a God-tortured soul," he intends to tell for the first time "the story of an art-tortured soul."[10] He accordingly creates and maintains the pose of an expatriated aesthete living in Paris, producing no art but talking endlessly about it and enjoying the ambiance of artists. Even the possibility of a foolish duel poses no serious threat to his determined dilettantism: "We went out to dinner, we went to the theatre, and after the theatre we went home and aestheticised till three in the morning"; or, as a revised version reads, "After the theatre we went home and aestheticized till the duel became the least important event and Marshall's picture the greatest" (pp. 190, 231).[11]

The young man's opinions are expected to dismay and repel the respectable reader. Declaring himself bored with the "decencies of life," Dayne, or Moore, boasts of his faults and foibles, his willful hedonism and monstrous dissipations. He toys with sadistic emotion and the idea of decadence. He avows an "appetite for the strange, abnormal and unhealthy in art." He alleges "feminine depravities in his affections": "I am feminine, morbid, perverse. But above all perverse, almost everything perverse interests, fascinates me. Wordsworth is the only simple-minded man I ever loved, if that great austere mind, chill even as the Cumberland year, can be called simple" (p. 76). But he has, of course, none of Wordsworth's concern for the common man or the "ordinary sight." The pyramids, he contends, were well worth all the millions of wretched lives sacrificed to build them, if eventually they may "fill a musing hour with wonderment." His literary models, he boasts, are Gautier and Baudelaire, in whom he thinks he finds a defiantly pagan amor-

10. George Moore, *Confessions of a Young Man,* ed. Susan Dick (Montreal, McGill-Queens University Press, 1972), p. 35. All further citations are taken from this edition and are identified by page numbers in the text.
    11. The revised version dates from 1918.

ality and a rejection of Christian pity, which he himself dismisses as "that most vile of all vile virtues." Looking into the future, he deplores the coming victory of "pity and justice," the light he chooses to call darkness, "which is imminent, which is the twentieth century" (p. 124).

Moore has clearly no great gift of prophecy, and his flagrant irreligion plumbs no Nietzschean depths, nor carries any real conviction. It is largely an irrelevance, serving only to shock the pious and to sanction his own aesthetic autonomy and his release from moral and social concern. By the end, when his "exquisitely hypocritical reader" is asked, ironically no doubt, to accept the short and fragmentary record as "this long narrative of a sinful life," *Confessions of a Young Man* has become its own parody. Moore obviously prides himself on his wit, daring, and outrageous overstatement. But the part he plays lacks all real intensity; the noisy aesthete, far from being a genuinely art-tortured soul, can scarcely imagine the pains of aesthetic creation.

In his *Confessions* Moore twice disparages Edmund Gosse as the typical Philistine of literature, begotten in a London club by an overstuffed armchair (pp. 138, 228). Nonetheless, the two men remained close friends for nearly forty years, and Moore took credit upon himself for suggesting that Gosse write the personal history that was to prove his most enduring book.[12] Gosse's talent as "objective" novelist, at least as evinced by his one slight romance, was far smaller than Moore's, but his capacity for sustained autobiographical narrative was surely greater. *Father and Son* is a well-shaped chronicle of the self, as "theatrical" in presentation as Yeats could have wished. Begun in the early nineties and published anonymously after delays in 1907, it remains the best example of the movement of late nineteenth-century autobiography toward a self-consciously literary form, more intent on dramatic coloring than on verifiable factual accuracy, a genre in which ultimately the author may seem to create a self in the very act of writing and in

12. See Edmund Gosse, *Father and Son*, ed. William Irvine (Boston: Houghton Mifflin, 1965), p. xxxvii, and Evan Charteris, *The Life and Letters of Edmund Gosse* (New York: Harper, 1931), p. 307. All citations from *Father and Son* are taken from the Irvine edition and are identified by page numbers in the text.

which his existence in any other state of being may be questioned or denied.

At the outset of *Father and Son* Gosse warns the reader that his narrative will blend comedy and tragedy in odd, perhaps disturbing, proportions. He clearly aims at a tragic pathos, but he freely employs comic devices, the strategies of satire and irony, to lend dramatic edge and distance to his story. He designs the whole as a sort of *Bildungsroman* describing his lonely childhood, the restraints imposed upon him by his father's narrow fundamentalism, and eventually his liberation at seventeen, when he leaves his home, his village, and the religious Brethren to make his independent, agnostic way in the secular city. As the past unfolds in sharpened detail, many earnest episodes fall into comic perspective: the child experiments with idolatry by worshiping a chair; the child expresses dismay that his widowed father is about to marry a "pedobaptist"; the father fulminates against a Christmas pudding as the accursed relic of pagan ritual; the father prays with the son for guidance to refuse an invitation to a tea party, and the son rises from his knees to declare that the Lord has granted him permission to attend; at the party itself the son shocks his audience by reciting morbid "graveyard" verses he himself only half-understands. Throughout the narrative minor figures among the servants and the "Saints" appear with comic heightening; the son's governess, Miss Marks, in particular, emerges as "somewhat grotesque . . . a kind of Dickens eccentric, a mixture of Mrs. Pipchin and Miss Sally Brass" (p. 69). But the "tragic" note intrudes upon the comedy. The boy's mother dies a sad, solemn death, her last gesture dedicating him irrevocably to the Lord and a life of perfect piety. The narrator evokes the pathos of the scene but then moves at once from object to subject, from the dying woman to himself and self-pity: "But what a weight," he comments, "intolerable as the burden of Atlas, to lay on the shoulders of a fragile child" (p. 53).

Gosse casts himself as the protagonist of this tragi-comedy, the innocent victim of repression driven to subterfuge and deceit in order to preserve his selfhood. Like Mill's *Autobiography*, his narrative describes a rigorous education supervised by a well-meaning parent of sorely limited vision. But the spiritual or intellectual distance between parent and child in Gosse's book is immeasurably greater than in Mill's. Whereas Mill eventually assimilates, deepens, and enriches his father's philosophy, Gosse questions the "Great Scheme" of enforced dedication, comes to repudiate his father's creed as a wholly untenable fanaticism, and sharply dramatizes, in a fashion quite alien to Mill, his escape from stifling commitment. Subtitling his story "A Study of Two Temperaments," he announces in his first sentence that the "struggle," the clash of the two, is to be his theme and that final "disruption" will be the inevitable result of the conflict. As in earlier autobiographies, an epiphany prepares the self for decisive conversion, but here it is deliberately contrived and placed as a climax in a novelistic structure. The son at boarding school, just before beginning his apprenticeship in London, contemplates the setting sun in the hope of a great apocalypse, the Lord's opening of the heavens to carry him off to Paradise. But when he discovers that no assumption is about to take place, he is half-ashamed of what he recognizes as a "theatrical attitude," in which perhaps he has never really believed. The anticlimax, at all events, is cruelly crushing:

The tea-bell rang,—the last word of prose to shatter my mystical poetry. "The Lord has not come, the Lord will never come," I muttered, and in my heart the artificial edifice of extravagant faith began to totter and crumble. From that moment forth my Father and I, though the fact was long successfully concealed from him and even from myself, walked in opposite hemispheres of the soul, with "the thick o' the world between us." (p. 210)

The epiphany, whatever its origin in actual experience, has the effect of fiction; the "mystical poetry" invites its immediate ironical reduction to the commonsensical, though still highly literary, "prose."

Throughout his narrative Gosse so molds his materials that they seem less remembered than invented, or at least embellished for the occasion. Nonetheless, he expects us to accept his story as "scrupulously true," in all respects "a genuine slice of life," for, he insists, "this record can . . . have no value that is not based on its rigorous adhesion to the truth" (pp. 3, 4, 194). The preface offers us a "document," the "diagnosis of a dying Puritanism," and the text is intended to have large implications, to depict the struggle not just of "two temperaments" and "two consciences" but also of "two epochs." Yet its truth as representative cultural history is debatable. At times it reads like yet another generalized Edwardian indictment of Victorianism. But to most Victorians, who enjoyed a measure of conviviality and folk ritual, including Christmas and plum pudding, the austerities of the Brethren would have seemed eccentric and repulsive. Few Victorian children suffered the son's almost total deprivation of imaginative literature, and no Victorian scientist, as even Gosse admits, was prepared to endorse the father's egregiously theologized biology. For the more convincing aspects of the record we must turn to the uniquely personal relationship between father and son, and even there our estimate of the "truth" will rest on our response to a skillful blend of fact and special pleading.

Father and Son is designed as the son's apologia, his self-defense against intransigent principle. But the unintended irony of the book—its strength as well as its weakness—lies in the fact that we may find ourselves ultimately more sympathetic with the father than with the son. Whatever his narrowness of view, his literalism, his fear of art and artifice, his misplaced ingenuity in the attempt to forestall the heresies of Darwin, the father remains a strong character, a man of unimpeachable integrity, loyal though mistaken in some of his loyalties, sincerely committed to his faith. He survives the son's descriptions weighted against him, efforts to read his unspoken thoughts, insinuations that he was unduly fond of the sound of his own voice lifted in private prayer or that he delighted in gymnastic gesticulation as he made his devout entreaties. The son, by comparison, is disingenuous and evasive. When as a youth alone in the city, overcome "by an invincible *ennui*," he breaks his promise to his father to keep up daily Bible readings and conceals his deception: "The dilemma was now before me that I must either deceive my Father in such things or paralyse my own character" (p. 216). It does not occur to him that another alternative might be possible—the honest disclosure of his own changing attitude. In the long run the father, not deceived, is strong enough in love to forgive. The son, for all his declared devotion to Truth, cares most for his own comfort and his final escape from the burden of "dedication." As a boy he found, he claims, an inner resource: "Through thick and thin I clung to a hard nut of individuality deep down in my childish nature" (p. 142). As a liberated young man he is able at last to exercise "a human being's privilege to fashion his inner life for himself" (p. 227). Of the child's secret resistance, we have indeed some distinct notion. Of the sincerity and strength of the selfhood to be shaped by the liberated adult, we have no such clear assurance.

The Education of Henry Adams, which appeared, privately printed, in the same year as *Father and Son,* records no religious conflict at all comparable to Gosse's and no repudiation of a repressive background. Though uncomfortably aware that much might be expected of him, Adams finds no occasion to proclaim his spiritual independence of a more fully committed father. Nor, on the other hand, does he feel any need to magnify, as Wilde did, his heritage and the social standing of his parents. His early rationality was cool and collected; his credentials of birth and station were impeccable; his position as an Adams was assured. Yet as autobiographer he is in his own way even more "theatrical" than Gosse or Wilde, readier, that is, to assume diverse roles and to fit his life story into a rigid mold of artifice. Despite an obvious endowment of intellect and sensibility and an unusually wide and privileged view of experience, both in America and abroad, he chooses to consider his "education" a series of melancholy failures and himself its disillusioned product. Wilde in the depths of Reading Gaol remains capable of the brave gesture, never quite so defeated as Adams imagines himself to have been, at liberty, in the highest circles of polite society.

Concentrating on that "education," however broadly he construes the theme, Adams deems himself free to exclude large segments of his career, most conspicuously, perhaps, any reference to his tragic marriage. But the story he tells retains enough variety of setting and observation, travel, episode, and reflection to belie the bleak judgments he has determined to impose upon it. Chapter after chapter, even when animated by incidents and impressions a less jaundiced memory would have cherished, ends with the refrain of failure. Harvard College fails to educate. Berlin disappoints. Rome and Paris offer nothing permanent. Five years in London, crowded with political excitement and social event, prove only "a false start." Washington brings repeated disenchantment. "Failure" labels the account of an apparently successful academic career, followed by a dismal foray into journalism: "Thus it turned out that of all his many educations, Adams thought that of school-teacher the thinnest. Yet he was forced to admit that the education of an editor, in some ways, was thinner still. "[13] In spite of a self-protective, chilly reserve, he eventually does warm to two close friends, Clarence King and John Hay, both of whom, like himself, he decides, are undervalued and misunderstood. For the most part, however, personal emotion yields to cold critical appraisal. Unlike Wordsworth or C. S. Lewis, he is never to be "surprised by joy." As "one of his eminent uncles or relations" remarks, even his Class Oration on graduating from Harvard is "singularly wanting in enthusiasm" (p. 68). At the beginning of his narrative he declares his preparation for the game of life and then almost immediately announces his withdrawal: "As it happened, he never got to the point of playing the game at all; he lost himself in the study of it, watching the errors of the players" (p. 4).

Adams the autobiographer remains aloof and ironic as he watches himself watching the mistakes of others, crediting them with few successes, and reluctant, either as the narrator or the subject, to admit the value of his own achievements. The third-person narration enhances the detachment, and the past tense, without any sense of an ongoing later present, establishes an irrecoverable, disjunctive distance. The result is our impression not of a career, as in most autobiographies, still in process while being recorded, but of a life already over and done with, a completed dramatic script for a box-set behind a proscenium arch. Again and again the tone suggests a long, closed history, seen in remote perspective:

To his life as a whole he was a consenting, contracting party and partner from the moment he was born to the moment he died.   (p. 4)

[The notion that Boston had solved the world's essential problems] seemed to him the most curious social phenomenon he had to account for in a long life.   (p. 34)

[Harvard undergraduates] were . . . the most formidable critics one would care to meet, in a long life exposed to criticism.   (p. 56)

Many a shock was Henry Adams to meet in the course of a long life.   (p. 108)

13. *The Education of Henry Adams*, Sentry Edition (Boston: Houghton Mifflin, 1961), p. 307. All further citations are taken from this edition and are identified by page numbers in the text.

In a long experience, before and after, no one ever approached [the brilliance of Swinburne's talk]. (p. 140)

The summer of the Spanish War began the Indian summer of life to one who had reached sixty years of age, and cared only to reap in peace such harvest as these sixty years had yielded. (p. 362)

Watching the watcher, as if from beyond life, the narrator concedes that the "identity" he is attempting to describe and define is no more than "a bundle of disconnected memories" (p. 209). Yet he is able to see in sharp enough outline the figure he himself recalls—or half-remembers and half-invents. (For he is not quite sure of the status of his impressions. Of an early train trip he writes: "This was the journey he remembered. The actual journey may have been quite different, but the actual journey has no interest for education. The memory was all that mattered," p. 43.) The Henry Adams presented in the narrative has become a sort of "manikin" (the image clearly borrowed from *Sartor Resartus*), draped in the costumes that are his successive "educations," and, if a manikin may be animated sufficiently to act several parts, he is assigned his successive roles: the private secretary, the dilettante, the editor, the professor, the speculative philosopher who likes to consider himself "the Virgin's pilgrim." Only in this last role does an individual rather than a type emerge, the character of a man born a century too late, alienated in the modern "multiverse," obsessed with a vision of vertiginous acceleration as his own spent life slows to a complete stop.

Yet the finished chronicle is by no means as dreary as the fixed expression on the manikin's face. *The Education of Henry Adams,* which remains, I should think, the most impressive of American autobiographies, rises repeatedly above its declared negations. Its power lies not only in the precision and color of its prose but also in the very devices that reduce its protagonist: the imposition of a shaped confining pattern, the attention to a range of external things, the skill in capturing the ambiance of great cities and cultures, the sophisticated satiric commentary, the portraits of memorable people—Lincoln and General Grant, Swinburne and Thackeray, Gladstone and Earl Russell—the sharp reactions of a gifted ironic witness, who seeks no reflected glory in eminent acquaintance. The record, to be sure, includes some mistakes and contradictions; the narrator chides Harvard College in the 1850's for ignoring Karl Marx's *Capital,* the first volume of which was actually not published even in German till near the end of the following decade; and he claims in one breath that no "education" could equal the Embassy life in London, and in another that "the private secretary" gained no real "education" at all in England. But factual consistency here matters less than the larger truths of fiction, and overstatement helps neutralize too-frequent confessions of defeat. Key scenes, such as the meeting with Clarence King in Estes Park or the splendid dinner given by Monckton Milnes at Fryston, are prepared and presented with the care and calculation of an accomplished novelist. The most moving episode of all, Henry Adams' visit to his sister Louisa, stricken in Italy with fatal tetanus, is elaborately set against the soft, sensuous beauty of the Apennines in mid-summer. And the epiphany which reveals the dynamo as a "symbol of infinity" and a portent of the frightening speed of the new century is timed deliberately as the climactic moment of a progress through the Gallery of Machines at the Paris exposition of 1900. From the beginning the narrator is aware of the ironies, comic or cruel, as in a Hardy novel, that may mock the protagonist's impressions or aspirations. But in the end, in the last sentence of *The Education,* the ironist can scarcely suspect an even greater irony in his suggestion that, were Henry Adams able to return to earth on his hundredth birthday, he might possibly find at last "a world that sensitive and timid natures could regard without a shudder." Henry Adams' centenary year was 1938.

As readers of *The Education,* however, we ought not to be swayed unduly by a misjudgment reaching far beyond the closed design created by Adams' expressive style. As in the autobiographies of Wilde, Moore, and Gosse, we must accept the author's need of a controlling fiction and even a considerable degree of "theatricality" if we are to approach an understanding of the temperament he seeks both to mask and to reveal. Though the method of each of these writers in presenting specific scenes is highly circumstantial, to none of them do the precise details of a vocation or mental history matter as they did, say, to Newman or to Mill. All four are centrally concerned with the elusive identity of the self and the parts it has played. In the work of each we see autobiography moving toward

one of its most characteristic twentieth-century forms, the autobiographical novel.

A Portrait of the Artist as a Young Man, to cite only the most
distinguished example of that modern genre, presents a hero drawn
closely from its author's own experience and in certain attitudes not
unlike the disaffected aesthetes or intellectuals we have met in the
self-histories of Wilde, Moore, Gosse, and Adams. Though Joyce
knew nothing of *The Education,* his *Portrait* apparently owes something to the legend of Wilde's personality, if not to the abridged text
of *De Profundis,* and it may be more specifically indebted to Moore
and Gosse. Moore, at any rate, claimed to have done "the same
thing, but much better, in *The Confessions of a Young Man.*"[14]
The claim does not, of course, require our serious consideration, but
we should note one signal advantage of Joyce over Moore and the
others. Joyce presents himself as the novelist rather than the autobiographer, and as such, no matter how subjective the materials he
chooses to exploit, he must create an independent protagonist,
whose role we as readers will appraise quite apart from any question
of the author's "theatricality" or any right to demand a true reflection of his real life and character.

14. Moore, quoted by Richard Ellmann, *James Joyce* (New York: Oxford University Press, 1965), p. 544. Ellmann also suggests that Gosse and Moore were possible
influences on Joyce's *Portrait* (p. 153n). It is interesting to note that Gosse and
Moore were among the select few to whom Joyce sent copies of the first edition of
the novel; see Stuart Gilbert and Richard Ellmann, eds., *Letters of James Joyce* (New
York: Viking, 1966), II, 386.

DONALD D. STONE

The Art of Arnold Bennett: Transmutation and Empathy in *Anna of the Five Towns* and *Riceyman Steps*

*The poet does not repeat old wives' tales. He has no
past, but lives in a world that is new. As regards the past
and the affairs of this world, he has realized absolute
sublimation.*

    Gaston Bachelard, *The Poetics of Space*

*. . . the Usual miraculously transformed by Art into the
Sublime.*

    Arnold Bennett, *The Truth about an Author*

Among the more agreeable events of the 1980's have been the
ceremonies of homage paid to, or being planned for, both those
masters of nineteenth-century literature who died approximately a
hundred years ago (for example, George Eliot, Carlyle, Trollope)
and those giants of modernism who were born in the 1880's (Joyce,
Virginia Woolf, Kafka). The cultural eclecticism of our time per-
mits us to appreciate eminent Victorians and modernists alike, with
the happy result that, in the field of fiction for example, it is no
longer considered necessary to defend Woolf at the expense of Eliot
or to dismiss Trollope if his aims and methods differ from Joyce's.
However, the novelists writing between these two classic periods
have fared less well. What are we to make of H. G. Wells or George

17

Gissing or Arnold Bennett, writers who seem neither Victorian nor modern, although by turn rejecting and partaking of the artistic and social values of each period?

The case of Arnold Bennett is particularly interesting. A defier in the name of "absolute realism" of the conventions and attitudes of Victorian fiction, he found his "new novel" criticized by Henry James on the grounds of its excessive "saturation" in "his own body of reference" (the everyday materials of Bennett's native Potteries), while a younger generation, led by Virginia Woolf, accused him of materialism, in both senses of the word, and of an excessive conventionalism which overlooked the "essential thing" ("call it life or spirit, truth or reality") necessary to the novelist's art.[1] Woolf's denunciation of Bennett remains, sadly, better known than those major achievements of Bennett which give the lie to the thesis of "Mr. Bennett and Mrs. Brown": "He is trying to make us imagine for him; he is trying to hypnotize us into the belief that, because he has made a house, there must be a person living there. With all his powers of observation, which are marvellous, with all his sympathy and humanity, which are great, Mr. Bennett has never once looked at Mrs. Brown"—Woolf's embodiment of "human nature"—sitting in her railway carriage corner.[2]

To be assailed by the old guard and the new was unfortunate for Bennett's posthumous reputation; yet Bennett's historical position as a transitional figure, looking back and looking forward, combined with his characteristic dualism of outlook, is a contributing factor to his success as a novelist. Absorbing many of the new artistic tenets of the 1880's and 1890's while also working within the mainstream of English fiction, aiming at complete fidelity to material reality while also probing the mystery of human identity, Bennett is perhaps the most richly contradictory of early modern English novelists. He is a cosmopolite from the provinces, a good-humored stoic, a romantic realist, a combination, in his dedication and practicality, of the contrasting protagonists of Gissing's *New*

1. Henry James, "The New Novel," *Notes on Novelists* (New York: Scribner's, 1914), pp. 319–320; Virginia Woolf, "Modern Fiction," *The Common Reader* (New York: Harcourt, Brace, 1953), p. 153.

2. Virginia Woolf, "Mr. Bennett and Mrs. Brown," *The Captain's Death Bed* (New York: Harcourt, Brace, 1950), pp. 109–110. The best commentary on the Woolf–Bennett feud is in Samuel Hynes, "The Whole Contention between Mr. Bennett and Mrs. Woolf," *Novel,* 1 (Fall 1967), 34–44.

Grub Street, Edwin Reardon and Jasper Milvain—capable of turning out self-help manuals or "frolics" and "fantasias" like *The Grand Babylon Hotel* in a few weeks, but also devoting five years to the writing of *Anna of the Five Towns.* The author of *The Old Wives' Tale* is surely the finest literary realist of his generation, yet his best novels draw upon more than realism, are indebted to something beyond the realist's world of time and place and causality. For Bennett is also, by Gaston Bachelard's definition of the title, a poet—a phenomenological poet who, through force of empathy, the ability to see the world through his characters' eyes, transmutes the everyday material reality that is his starting point into something rich and strange.

Bennett's chief character trait is his dualism, a habit of perception and self-perception nurtured by his Staffordshire background. "We are of the North," he noted in his *Journal,* "outwardly brusque, stoical, undemonstrative, scornful of the impulsive; inwardly all sentiment and crushed tenderness."[3] Such an individual might be obliged to conform outwardly to a sense of oppressive reality, but inside he harbored a romantic sense of unlimited human potentiality. In discovering his vocation as an artist, Bennett was to resolve the tension implicit in that dualism. Despite the tendency to self-repression in his personal life which his biographers and friends have pointed out, Bennett allowed his romantic side an outlet in his novels—in his depictions of "cards," for example (enterprising individuals who bend circumstances to their ends in defiance of reality), but also in his portraits of bleakly-situated protagonists who employ their imagination to remake the world they live in. For all the authorial fidelity to objective reality, nothing and no one are as they initially appear in a Bennett novel. To this sense of the doubleness of identity and things we owe Bennett's continual insistence on the beauty that is to be found in commonplace reality and on the bravery that underlies the daily lives of ordinary people. "To find beauty, which is always hidden," he told himself; "that is the aim . . . My desire is to depict the deeper beauty while abiding by the envelope of facts." As an artist, this seemingly unpoetic writer was able to create a world of remarkable beauty using the most intransigently mundane materials: that world of "valorized space"

3. Arnold Bennett, *Journals,* ed. Frank Swinnerton (Harmondsworth: Penguin, 1971), p. 27.

which Bachelard has eloquently described as the poet's created world—a space for which, "whether sad or ponderous, once it is poetically expressed, the sadness is diminished, the ponderousness lightened."[4]

James was not inaccurate when he stressed Bennett's "saturation" in the world of the Potteries, but he might have added that Bennett, like James himself, was also saturated in the world of literature. Near the start of his *Journals* Bennett describes himself as "the latest disciple of the de Goncourts"—not only in the keeping of a notebook but in his early adherence to "that passion," imported from France through the works of the Goncourts, Flaubert, and Maupassant, "for the artistic shapely presentation of truth, and that feeling for words as words." Like another disciple of the French, James Joyce, Bennett in 1898 avowed that "an artist must be interested primarily in presentment, not in the thing presented." Any subject would seemingly do if only the artist depicted it with candor and art. From the beginning, however, Bennett was concerned with more than technique or the habit of taking notes in a detached manner. Even while he was seeking to emulate the methods of the French (his first novel, he says waggishly, "was to be a mosaic consisting exclusively of Flaubert's mots justes"[5]), Bennett was being fired by the example of two novelists who united firm technical control and absolute fidelity to life with an impassioned sense of characterization: George Moore and Ivan Turgenev.

Moore's *A Mummer's Wife*, part of which is set in Bennett's own Five Towns region, inspired Bennett (as he later admitted) to become a writer himself. Bennett saw in Moore's realism a "protest against the long-accepted methods of English novelists: a superb and successful effort to show that from life at its meanest and least decorative could be drawn material grand enough for great fiction."[6] Viewing himself as an English Flaubert, Moore nevertheless succeeded in what is perhaps his finest novel, *Esther Waters*, in

4. Ibid., pp. 53–54; Gaston Bachelard, *The Poetics of Space*, trans. Maria Jolas (Boston: Beacon Press, 1969), pp. 201–202.

5. *Journals*, pp. 17, 45; Bennett, *The Truth about an Author* (London: Constable, 1903), p. 90.

6. Arnold Bennett, "Mr. George Moore" (1901), reprinted in *The Author's Craft and Other Critical Writings*, ed. Samuel Hynes (Lincoln: University of Nebraska Press, 1968), pp. 147–148. And see Bennett, *The Evening Standard Years*, ed. Andrew Mylett (London: Chatto & Windus, 1974), pp. 139, 318.

being true to life while also, in an unFlaubertian manner, depicting the nobility of his heroine—a feat Bennett was to duplicate in his first great novel, *Anna of the Five Towns*. In the work that preceded *Anna, A Man from the North* (1898), Bennett made the mistake of copying too slavishly the pessimism fashionable in the 1890's: "Life being grey, sinister, and melancholy, my novel must be grey, sinister, melancholy. As a matter of strict fact, life deserved none of these epithets."[7] The thwarted hero of Bennett's first novel is, curiously, a novelist lacking in will and imagination. That the heroine of *Anna*, inhabiting a similarly grey world, manages to transcend her milieu is largely the result of the lessons in characterization Bennett learned from native and Russian sources.

From Turgenev, Bennett learned not only how to concentrate his materials into "the simplest, most straightforward form" but also how to develop a characterization from within, allowing the reader to appreciate the character's point of view. Bennett admired Turgenev's habit of keeping dossiers for his fictional characters so that he could imagine what and how Bazarov, of *Fathers and Sons*, would think and feel on any given occasion. Where the French novelists had stressed form and authorial detachment, Turgenev exhibited a tenderness toward his characters, and by extension toward all mankind; and this emboldened Bennett, even at the height of his "Gallic" phase, to declare that the "essential characteristic of the really great novelist" is "a Christ-like all-embracing compassion."[8] In later years Dostoevsky would supplant Turgenev in Bennett's affections because of his superior capacity for empathy, but Bennett's pioneering enthusiasm for Dostoevsky (and Chekhov) was an elaboration, not a rejection, of his early enthusiasm for Turgenev. Bennett may have claimed Turgenev as the literary deity presiding over *Anna of the Five Towns* and Dostoevsky for *Riceyman Steps;* yet, for all that, both books are unmistakably Bennett novels in their combination of acutely realized description and intensely conveyed compassion.

7. *The Truth about an Author,* pp. 90–91.

8. Arnold Bennett, *Letters,* 3 vols., ed. James Hepburn (London: Oxford University Press, 1966–1970), II, 38; *Journals,* p. 24. And see *The Evening Standard Years,* p. 32: "The Russians have no qualms about disgusting you with human nature, for they are not themselves disgusted with it. They understand; they forgive; they love. They compel you to do the same. There is a Christ-like quality in the finest Russian fiction."

It is these two marvelous but lesser-known Bennett novels, one written at the outset of his career, the other at a time when his reputation was sagging, that I wish to focus on in this essay, for in them one can see how Bennett absorbed the tenets of modernism while keeping within the mainstream of English fiction. Compact in design, scrupulously realistic as well as symbolic in detail, gently ironic in tone, the two novels illustrate Bennett's thorough grounding in French craftsmanship. However, as a result of his compassion toward his characters, his desire to raise them above their limited natures and restrictive surroundings to the level of the heroic without losing sight of their ordinary reality, Bennett simultaneously joins the company of the Russians and enters an important mainstream of Romantic-inspired Victorianism. From the French Bennett learned to sharpen his powers of observation, but he affiliated himself with another literary tradition when he insisted that the novelist must promote "kindliness." As he wrote in *The Author's Craft*, "Observation . . . is a moral act and must inevitably promote kindliness . . . Observation endows our day and our street with the romantic charm of history, and stimulates charity—not the charity which signs cheques, but the more precious charity which puts itself to the trouble of understanding." The "modern" in Bennett had determined to show that anything the artist turned to was capable of being transmuted to art, but the "Victorian" element (which surfaces in his later criticism) argued that the novelist could do nothing of value without "fineness of mind"—a quality he found increasingly absent in both the French naturalists and his own contemporaries. "A great novelist must have great qualities of mind," he contends. "His mind must be sympathetic, quickly responsive, courageous, honest, humorous, tender, just, merciful. He must be able to conceive the ideal without losing sight of the fact that it is a human world we live in."[9]

Although the young Bennett seems to have felt that little of good could be said about the Victorian novelists, the developing author began to find a growing number of resemblances between himself and his predecessors. As a writer notable for his candor, even to the point of self-deflation, and notable for astonishing prolificacy, Bennett was bound to prize Anthony Trollope, whose novels and auto-

---

9. *The Author's Craft*, pp. 8, 18. (This work first appeared in 1914.)

biography reveal these same qualities. (Who but Bennett would have viewed Trollope's life as "extraordinarily romantic"?[10]) And he found the full-blown romanticism of Disraeli and the Brontës a bracing experience. But it is in his shift of attitude toward George Eliot that Bennett displays his awareness of his literary roots. Whereas the young apprentice novelist chastised Eliot for her technical clumsiness, her lack of candor, and her intrusive moralizing, the older Bennett was surprised to find himself recommending the *Scenes of Clerical Life.* Yet Eliot, all along, had been the main English exponent of compassionate realism; Bennett's contention in *The Author's Craft* that the novelist must both write out of sympathy and show how "all physical phenomena are inter-related"[11] is borne out by *Middlemarch* no less than *The Old Wives' Tale.* Though he was not an admirer of *Middlemarch,* his praise for *Scenes* is noteworthy—for Eliot in her first work of fiction had endeavored, as Bennett would do in *Anna of the Five Towns* and *Riceyman Steps,* to point out "the poetry and the pathos, the tragedy and the comedy, lying in the experience of a human soul that looks out through dull grey eyes, and that speaks in a voice of quite ordinary tones." Missing in Bennett is the occasional sense of authorial condescension and the pervading judgmental tone in Eliot. Even so, what Bennett held up as the rightful aim of the modern novelist in his early (1899) essay on Gissing, he would later recognize in the practice of at least one Victorian novelist: "To take the common grey things which people know and despise, and, without tampering, to disclose their epic significance, their essential grandeur—that is realism, as distinguished from idealism or romanticism."[12]

That such "realism" was not disconnected from romanticism Bennett soon discovered—in the figure of Eliot's poetic mentor, Wordsworth. To admit to a love for Wordsworth in 1904 amounted to "heresy," yet Bennett declared himself "ready for the thumb-

10. *The Evening Standard Years,* p. 156. And see Bennett, *Books and Persons* (New York: George Doran, 1917), pp. 148–149.

11. *The Author's Craft,* p. 9. For Bennett's changing opinion of Eliot, see, for example, *Journals* (1896), p. 19; "My Literary Heresies" (1904), "George Meredith" (1909), and "On Re-reading the English Novelists" (1927), the last three reprinted with *The Author's Craft,* pp. 237, 121, 260.

12. George Eliot, "Amos Barton," *Scenes of Clerical Life,* 2 vols. (Edinburgh: Blackwood, n.d.), I, 67; Bennett, "George Gissing," *The Author's Craft,* p. 161.

screw" in defense of his favorite. In *Literary Taste: How to Form It* (1909), Bennett recommends Wordsworth's "unsurpassed" criticism, along with such poems as *Michael,* to the novice in search of taste.[13] The protagonist of a late Bennett novel, *Accident* (1929), finds solace amid various crises in reading *The Prelude.* Many of the sentiments echoed in *The Author's Craft* and embedded in Bennett's novels may be found in the 1800 preface to *Lyrical Ballads*: the attempt to be faithful to the facts and figures of ordinary life, while also "to throw over them a certain coloring of imagination, whereby ordinary things should be presented to the mind in an unusual aspect; and, further, and above all, to make these incidents and situations interesting by tracing in them, truly though not ostentatiously, the primary laws of our nature." Bennett seems to have discovered Wordsworth in 1901, while he was at work on *Anna of the Five Towns,* and he admits that *"Michael* quite overcame me by its perfect simplicity & power." The power of that poem he described as "disturbing" rather than "pleasing";[14] yet the poet's transmutation of simple, rugged life into a stoic epic struck Bennett as similar to his intention in *Anna,* the epigraph to which he took from *Michael*:

> Therefore, although it be a history
> Homely and rude, I will relate the same
> For the delight of a few natural hearts.
>
> (ll. 34–36)

Bennett's avowed intention in *Anna of the Five Towns* (1902) was twofold: to write "a sermon against parental authority" (a supremely modern theme) and to show the fictional possibilities of his native Five Towns. His detailed study of a small industrial town—*"mœurs de province* it will be"—would be painstakingly French in manner, with the technique of the Goncourts applied to a subject reminiscent of Balzac's *Eugénie Grandet* (with its dutiful daughter

13. Arnold Bennett, "My Literary Heresies," *The Author's Craft,* p. 232; Bennett, *Literary Taste* (New York: George Doran, 1909), pp. 75–77. See *Letters,* III, 50: "It is quite possible to be romantic & truthful at the same time . . . There is no opposition or mutual-excluding between romance & realism." Walter Wright examines Bennett's dualism in this respect in *Arnold Bennett: Romantic Realist* (Lincoln: University of Nebraska Press, 1971).

14. Bennett, *Letters,* II, 158; *Literary Taste,* p. 75.

victimized by her lover and her miser-father).[15] The novel would show all the ugliness and oppressiveness of life in a Potteries town, complete with a guided tour of one of the factories, and would show the few ways in which the inhabitants dealt with their lot—through Wesleyan revival meetings, church functions, walks through the park, sewing meetings, and, for the lucky, occasional flights from the town in the form of vacation or reverie. Yet while Bennett's French admirer Georges Lafourcade noted the French influence in the book's concrete depictions of provincial life ("It would have won a literary prize in France," he remarks condescendingly), he was annoyed to find a less honorable literary ancestor: "The book has all the sluggishness and something of the atmosphere of a novel by George Eliot."[16] Written long before his revaluation of Eliot, *Anna* does reveal that Bennett, for all the modernism of his technique, was less than modish in his insistence on the atmosphere of "beauty" to be found in his ugly setting and especially in his affection for his heroine—indeed, for all the major characters in the book. One might call *Anna* a French novel undermined—or saved—by authorial love.

Turgenev provided Bennett with the inspiration here. The Russian novelists received his highest praise throughout his life: "They are not frightened by any manifestation of humanity," he affirmed in 1927.[17] Moreover, the author of *Fathers and Sons, On the Eve,* and *The Sportsman's Notebook* was the first to show Bennett how ordinary life could be transformed through art and love. In his description of the ramshackle Kirsanov estate, near the beginning of *Fathers and Sons,* for example, Turgenev indicates how what the peasants mock as the "Will-o'-the-wisp Farm" is seen as something

15. *Letters,* II, 75, 36. For the connection between Bennett and Balzac, see Louis Tillier, *Studies in the Sources of Arnold Bennett's Novels* (Paris: Didier, 1970), pp. 26–31; and Margaret Drabble, *Arnold Bennett* (London: Weidenfeld and Nicolson, 1974), p. 95.

16. Georges Lafourcade, *Arnold Bennett: A Study* (London: Frederick Muller, 1939), pp. 98–99. The reviewer of *Anna* in the *Staffordshire Sentinel* admits having "always had a decided leaning towards George Eliot, and on more than one occasion we have, we believe, expressed a hope that a novel of the 'Mill on the Floss' type treating of the Potteries might some day be forthcoming. We are very well satisfied to regard 'Anna of the Five Towns' as fulfilling that desire." (Reprinted in *Arnold Bennett: The Critical Heritage,* ed. James Hepburn [London: Routledge and Kegan Paul, 1981], p. 156.)

17. *The Evening Standard Years,* p. 31.

Arcadian by its inhabitants. Similarly, the force of authorial affection transforms Bazarov from a boorish, self-righteous medical student into a heroic figure whose fate is profoundly moving. In Bennett's novel, too, an unheroic, submissive young woman is proved capable of heroism and an ugly world is made to seem picturesque and even beautiful. In 1898, while working on *Anna,* Bennett expressed himself "convinced that there is a very real beauty underneath the squalor & ugliness of these industrial districts"; and in the novel he writes thus of the Five Towns:

> They are mean and forbidding of aspect—sombre, hard-featured, uncouth; and the vaporous poison of their ovens and chimneys has soiled and shrivelled the surrounding country till there is no village lane within a league but what offers a gaunt and ludicrous travesty of rural charms. Nothing could be more prosaic than the huddled, red-brown streets; nothing more seemingly remote from romance. Yet be it said that romance is even here—the romance which, for those who have an eye to perceive it, ever dwells amid the seats of industrial manufacture, softening the coarseness, transfiguring the squalor, of these mighty alchemic operations.

Bennett's characteristic dualism runs through the entire passage (of which the quotation above is a small section). He is both objectively modernist in his description of the "prosaic" ugliness and romantic in his evocation of a mysterious nature which sends forth "sooty sheaves" in defiance of man's efforts to "disfigure" her. Nature and man are involved in an "unending warfare," Bennett contends in the manner of a French naturalist, whereby each disfigures the other; but the imagination allows one to "transfigure" both.[18] The key phrase is "romance is even here . . . for those who have an eye to perceive it": one is irresistibly reminded of Wordsworth's view of the imaginative mind which half creates what it perceives. Thus, when Anna Tellwright expresses delight at her first sight of Liverpool harbor—"it was all too much, too astonishing, too lovely"—Bennett by no means intends us to look down on his seemingly naive heroine. ("They call Liverpool the slum of Europe," her prospective suitor, Henry Mynors, responds, p. 183.) From Turgenev Bennett learned to cherish the point of view that

18. *Letters,* II, 114; *Anna of the Five Towns* (New York: George Doran, 1910; originally published in 1902), pp. 14–15. All further quotations from *Anna,* identified by page numbers in the text, are from this edition.

sees beauty where others see it not. Bennett's first great novel pays
tribute to Anna's poetic sensibility, her ability to transform the
world through vision in opposition to that world's attempt to contain
her spirit.

Like Eliot's Dorothea Brooke, Anna is initially described as
having been born out of her time and in the wrong place: hers
"seemed a face for the cloister, austere in contour, fervent in expression, the severity of it mollified by that resigned and spiritual
melancholy peculiar to women who, through the error of destiny,
have been born into a wrong environment" (p. 6). The habit of
submission is ingrained in Anna, not as a result of her religious
ardor (it is a sign of Anna's integrity that she cannot give herself
over to a religion she does not fully believe in), but as a result of her
father's hold on her. Ephraim Tellwright belongs to what Bennett
sardonically describes as "the great and powerful class of house-
tyrants, the backbone of the British nation" (p. 153); yet Anna's
reaction to him is dual. Up to her twenty-first birthday, at the point
the novel begins, he has been the "chief figure" in her life, "that
sinister and formidable individuality, whom her mind hated, but her
heart disobediently loved" (p. 22). Anna's native Bursley is dominated by patriarchal figures, whether they be parental autocrats,
industrial masters, or a Methodistically-inclined heavenly Father;
and Anna's main action in life (as we see it in the novel) is to leave
her father's house and marry Mynors, the ambitious industrialist.
On the way to that act, however, she is required to assert herself in
two unforeseen ways: against her faith and against her father. Incapable of giving way to the emotional fervor of the Methodist
revival meeting, Anna blames herself for her sinful pride; but Bennett lets us see that Anna is in fact saved by her "just and un-
shakeable self-esteem" (p. 12), by her honesty in regard to herself
and her situation. After the revival meeting she wishes that she had
been able to make the public leap of faith, "yet knew well that such
an act would always be impossible for her." By denying herself the
comfort of a transcendental realm proferred by religion, she feels
that she is doomed to a world that is "mean, despicable, cheerless,"
containing "nothing to inspire. She dreamed impossibly of a high
spirituality which should metamorphose all, change her life, lend
glamour to the most pitiful surroundings, ennoble the most igno-
minious burdens—a spirituality never to be hers" (pp. 80–81).

But in refusing to accept through religion the means of transcending Bursley, Anna allies herself with her antireligious creator, who points to other means by which relief is to be attained. The symbolic center of the novel is Anna's kitchen, her refuge from Bursley and its grim religion, its narrow materialism, and its ugly surroundings. Bennett devotes three pages of description to this single "satisfactory apartment in the house" with its atmosphere of order and tradition. Half his description is devoted to the oak dresser, which "a dynasty of priestesses of cleanliness" had polished to such a smoothness that its "surfaces were marked by slight hollows similar in spirit to those worn by the naked feet of pilgrims into the marble steps of a shrine" (p. 123). In this respect Anna is a surrogate artist, the Bachelardian housewife who shines her cherished household objects until they attain "a new reality of being, and . . . take their place not only in an order but in a community of order."[19] Poets and women, suggests Bachelard, build houses from within, shelters of civilization that provide refuge against the world of disharmony and discontent lurking outside.

Bennett was annoyed when a friend, charging that *Anna* had been written in too detached (that is, French naturalist) a spirit, cited the kitchen scene as a proof that his characters were treated like "animals at the Zoo."

The book is impassioned & emotional from beginning to end [Bennett replied]. Every character . . . is handled with intense sympathy. But you have not perceived the emotion. Your note on the description of Anna's dresser is a clear proof of this. The whole thing, for some reason or other, has gone right past you. You are looking for something which you will never get in my fiction, or in any first-rate modern fiction—the Dickens or Thackeray grossness. I "let myself go" to the full extent; but this does not mean that I shout and weep all over the place.[20]

And, in fact, the kitchen scene reveals, with brilliant economy, the poignance of Anna's situation; her refuge is also a kind of prison. The irony of Mynors' remark to Anna that he associates her with her

19. "From one object in a room to another," Bachelard continues, "housewifely care weaves the ties that unite a very ancient past to the new epoch. The housewife awakens furniture that was asleep" (*The Poetics of Space*, p. 68).

20. *Letters*, II, 175. Bennett adds that his friend had "said just the same things about Turgenev when [he] first read him."

kitchen becomes apparent at the end of the novel when she leaves her father for a man she realizes to be a kindlier and younger version of Tellwright. However, for Bennett's reader to realize the poignance of her situation—indeed, for the reader to feel the heroism of Anna's position when she reacts against father and religion—that reader must become as observant as Anna or Bennett. The majority of people, as Bennett contends in *The Author's Craft,* are incapable of such feats of perception: "We all go to and fro in a state of the observing faculties which somewhat resembles coma. We are all content to look and not see."[21] Bennett's friend who failed to see the author's force of sympathy—kindliness based on observation, to repeat the maxim from *The Author's Craft*—is not unlike those holders of the "general opinion" in the novel to whom Anna seems "a cold and bloodless creature" (p. 267). One recalls George Eliot's mention, at the end of *Middlemarch,* of those inhabitants of the town, denied the author's and reader's knowledge of Dorothea, who assume "she could not have been 'a nice woman,' else she would not have married" Casaubon or Ladislaw. But then, as Eliot says early in the novel in words that could stand as epigraph to Bennett's finest novels: "That element of tragedy which lies in the very fact of frequency, has not yet wrought itself into the coarse emotion of mankind."

What distinguishes Anna from the other members of the Five Towns is the quality of her perception, a perception that deepens in the course of the novel. Anna alone seems aware of "the repulsive evidences of manufacture" (p. 80)—not just the material ugliness but, more important, the materialist codes of Bursley society which prize money above all things and which support a religion designed to keep workers and women in their place. Anna initially idealizes Mynors for his good qualities, and she especially envies him "his sex. She envied every man. Even in the sphere of religion, men were not fettered like women" (p. 82). She discovers in time that the possession of such mastery involves the loss of something precious. When, on her twenty-first birthday, her father signs over to her her mother's property, Anna is baffled by her enormous wealth. The Bursley banker predicts that the "naive and unspoilt" young woman will "harden like the rest" (p. 44); but Anna keeps her distance from

21. *The Author's Craft,* p. 6.

the world of getting and spending. Unlike her father, for whom "the productivity of capital was . . . the greatest achievement of social progress," Anna, who has "some imagination" (pp. 128–129), is troubled by the money. She refuses to see it as something of importance despite its obvious value to her father, to Mynors, or to the wretched father and son, Titus and Willie Price, whom Anna learns to be the defaulting tenants of a ramshackle factory she now owns. In *Clayhanger* Bennett speaks of "the vast unconscious cruelty which always goes with a perfect lack of imagination";[22] but Anna, with her kindly imagination, finds herself disturbingly allied with the "rich, powerful, autocratic" hounds, and she realizes, when she sees the effects of her father's harassment of the Prices, the human implications of the text, "Blessed are the meek, blessed are the failures, blessed are the stupid, for they, unknown to themselves, have a grace which is denied to the haughty, the successful, and the wise" (p. 100).

The plots of Bennett's novels are usually inconsequential: two sisters grow old, two misers marry, a young woman moves from her father's tutelage to her husband's. In the case of *Anna*, Bennett's heroine learns the value of love when she discovers the truth of her maternally inspired feeling for Willie Price, yet is obliged to renounce it. She has a "revelation of the loveliness of the world" (p. 192) on her visit to the Isle of Man, but is forced to settle down in ugly Bursley. She does renounce her inheritance, in effect, by passing it from fatherly to husbandly control; and, most important, she does stand up to her father when she destroys the forged note which Willie has given her in lieu of his rental payment. The result of that "audacious and astounding impiety" in her father's eyes (p. 254) is that she is cut off forever from him. Joseph Conrad was especially impressed by the beginning of chapter 12 in which Anna contemplates the magnitude of her deed:[23]

She was not to be pardoned: the offence was too monstrous, daring, and final. At the same time, the unappeasable ire of the old man tended to weaken his power over her. All her life she had been terrorised by the fear of a wrath which had never reached the superlative degree until that day. Now that she had seen and felt the limit of his anger, she became aware that she could

22. Arnold Bennett, *Clayhanger* (London: Methuen, 1910), p. 148.
23. Reginald Pound, *Arnold Bennett* (London: Heinemann, 1952), p. 126.

endure it; the curse was heavy, and perhaps more irksome than heavy, but she survived; she continued to breathe, eat, drink, and sleep; her father's power stopped short of annihilation.   (p. 256)

Anna stoically resigns herself, since "experience had taught her this: to be the mistress of herself" (pp. 265–266). Estranged from her father and Willie Price, she marries Mynors. "She who had never failed in duty did not fail then. She who had always submitted and bowed the head, submitted and bowed the head then. She had sucked in with her mother's milk the profound truth that a woman's life is always a renunciation, greater or less" (p. 297). For the sympathetic reader, however, Anna's fortitude and acts of bravery, her "generosity of spirit" (in John Lucas' phrase), make her at once a notable inhabitant "of" the Five Towns, as the title implies, and also enable her to escape Bursley's narrowness and squalor.[24]

    D. H. Lawrence's reaction to *Anna of the Five Towns* is perhaps better known than Bennett's novel: "I hate Bennett's resignation. Tragedy ought really to be a great kick at misery. But *Anna of the Five Towns* seems like an acceptance—so does all the modern stuff since Flaubert."[25] Yet *Anna,* as I have been suggesting, is not so "modern" as Lawrence, and even Bennett at one point, thought. Instead of being a detached examination of wasted lives in the Potteries, the novel is about the small forms of heroism permitted people in impossible positions, and it is about the transforming power of imagination and love. For Anna, the discovery of love's existence is momentous: "She saw how miserably narrow, tepid, and trickling the stream of her life had been, and had threatened to be. Now it gushed forth warm, impetuous, and full, opening out

    24. John Lucas, *Arnold Bennett: A Study of His Fiction* (London: Methuen, 1974), p. 52. And see Drabble, *Arnold Bennett,* p. 94 ("she fails more heroically, against greater odds, and with fewer concessions," than the hero of *A Man from the North*); and Wright, *Arnold Bennett,* pp. 146–147.
    25. D. H. Lawrence, *Collected Letters,* 2 vols., ed. Harry T. Moore (London: Heinemann, 1962), I, 150. Lawrence drew upon *Anna* and *The Old Wives' Tale* for his *Lost Girl;* yet his heroine's fate, escape to Italy with a mindless lover, may offer less in the end than Anna's fate. "How interesting it is," writes Drabble, "that Bennett, who could write with dull banality about masters and slaves and submission, should have made all his true heroines fight till the end, with an inner indestructible core, whereas Lawrence's women find themselves only in submission and destruction" (*Arnold Bennett,* p. 253).

new and delicious vistas. She lived; and she was finding the sight
to see, the courage to enjoy" (p. 30). Anna's initial sense that
Mynors will liberate her from the worst of her serflike status under
her father is not entirely unjustified: Mynors is capable of appreciating the "picturesque" perspective from outside his factory window (p. 148), and he is romantic enough to cherish the plate Anna
paints when he shows her around his factory. But her inability to
love him as she loves Willie is based on her knowledge that he too
belongs among the hounds, not the hares. The fact that Mynors is
one of the successful of Bursley ("that symbol of correctness and of
success") makes him one of the masters, one of the "Pharisees,"
who will never be able to feel with the weak and downtrodden on
their level (pp. 247–248). Anna's feeling for Willie, by contrast,
puts them on the same level, although only in her eyes as it turns
out. For Willie is incapable of being saved through love, and the
discovery that his love for Anna is reciprocated pushes him over the
edge. Although Anna is sustained, in the end, by a "vision" of
Willie "pursuing in Australia an honourable and successful career"
(p. 297), Willie has in fact followed his father's example. Titus
Price's suicide—a "theatrical effect," as Bennett calls it, and which
Anna sees as "something grand, accusing, and unanswerable" (pp.
233, 229)—is one form of confronting one's fate; but Anna eschews
such dramatic gestures. Her heroism rests in her ability to accept her
lot and thereby transcend it.

Anna accepts because she is a loving character, and in a similar
manner Bennett regards his creations with boundless generosity of
affection. Paying tribute to Bennett's "insatiable appetite for life,"
Rebecca West declared, "What he saw he loved."[26] The Sutton
family, Anna's upper-crust friends, are treated with amused affection rather than the satire which Bennett's friend H. G. Wells would
surely have employed—and at the other end of the social spectrum,
the Prices' overworked servant, Sarah Vodrey, is allowed her moment of glory. But it is, above all, in the figure of the surly miser
Tellwright that we see Bennett's ability to write with candor as well
as authorial fondness. Tellwright is a monster, but he is also a
superb comic creation. Like Balzac, Bennett loves his monsters,
although he humanizes them in a manner that Balzac was incapable

26. Rebecca West, *Arnold Bennett Himself* (New York: John Day, 1931), p. 13.

of. One can see why Anna both loves and fears her father, not why Eugénie should love old Grandet. Typically, for a Bennett novel, Tellwright is perceived by others in a mistaken fashion: "To the crowd . . . he was a marvelous legend" (p. 27). Up close, he is a tyrant to his family, a tyrant not by independent choice or system but out of habit and failure of imagination. "If you had told him that he inflicted purposeless misery not only on others, but on himself, he would have grinned . . . vaguely aware that he had not tried to be happy, and rather despising happiness as a sort of childish gewgaw." Lacking all capacity for "joy" and thus creating "a melancholy gloom" at home (which Anna and her sister Agnes seek to assuage by means of polish or a potted mignonette), Tellwright fails to notice "that his heart lightened whenever he left the house, and grew dark whenever he returned; but he was incapable of the feat [of self-analysis]. His case, like every similar case, was irremediable" (p. 153). Anna's terror when she forgets to buy bacon for her father's breakfast is vividly conveyed—and indicates the momentousness of her later act of defiance. Nevertheless, Bennett, in giving the most significant stage directions and the best bits of dialogue to Tellwright,[27] creates a figure who makes the reader, no less than Anna, reluctant to make moral judgment in the miser's presence. And we are never allowed to forget that we are seeing Tellwright, most of the time, through Anna's eyes. It is her mixture of fear and reverence that makes him so forbidding a character, but that also makes his rejection of her so poignant an event.

Bennett's focusing on the characters and events in Bursley as seen through Anna's point of view is the most distinctive aspect of his art: in *Anna of the Five Towns,* as in the more famous novels *The Old Wives' Tale* and *Clayhanger,* these things have significance because the characters invest them with significance. Once we step away from Constance Povey, we see her from the point of view of others, "a stout old lady with grey hair and a dowdy bonnet." But in her

27. In adapting *Anna* to the stage (retitled *Cupid and Commonsense*), Bennett allowed the comic aspect of the father to dominate the proceedings. Anna's request for money for her wedding trousseau is met with a punch line, "Art naked?" (The line appears in the novel in a tenser context.) Bennett created a genial counterpart to Tellwright in James Ollerenshaw in *Helen with the High Hand* (1910). Ollerenshaw, the richest man in Bursley after Tellwright, is subdued by women and forced to abandon his miserly habits. In Henry Earlforward, of *Riceyman Steps,* the comic and grim aspects of miserly life come together.

mind, and in that of the reader, Constance remains youthful, resourceful, romantic—albeit in less obvious ways than the
self-conscious romanticism of her sister Sophia. (A source of irony
in *The Old Wives' Tale* is the fact that the "romantic" sister who
goes to Paris becomes a model of good sense, while the stolid sister
who stays home has an adventurous streak which is finally the cause
of her death.) In Bennett's second novel we are shown the father,
the suitor, and the simple-minded lover from Anna's point of view,
and this allows them qualities that could scarcely be projected sympathetically in a French naturalist novel where the point of view is
invariably flawed or misguided.[28] For what a feeling heart sees has
its own validity: a tyrannical father is still one's father, and the
uncouth lover is the man one loves. In this way, Bennett reveals his
Romantic origins and provides the premise for the most extraordinary of his novels, *Riceyman Steps*.

   With its sympathetic portrait of Anna and vivid characterization
of Tellwright, its fine sense of place, interrelationships, and point
of view, all presented in a narrative succinct enough to have pleased
Turgenev, *Anna of the Five Towns* demonstrates that Bennett was
capable of great things to come; and for most subsequent readers and
critics, *The Old Wives' Tale* (1908) and *Clayhanger* (1910) have
represented the fulfillment of that promise. Marvelous as these
novels are, it is a comparatively late novel, *Riceyman Steps* (1923),
written when he had fallen "under the whips of les jeunes" (as he
observed to his friend André Gide),[29] that reveals, I think, the fullest
measure of Bennett's genius. Here he drew upon his mastery of the
uses of point of view and upon his considerable generosity of spirit
to produce a *tour de force:* the sordid world of a miserly bookseller
who starves his wife and himself to death is transformed into a prose
poem in celebration of the human and artistic spirit. In this book the
underlying theme of *Anna, The Old Wives' Tale,* and *Clayhanger*
reaches its ultimate expression: the world redeemed by love and
imagination. There is no need, he shows, for one to go to the Isle

   28. *The Old Wives' Tale* (New York: George Doran, 1909), p. 569. One thinks
of Flaubert's sardonic treatment of Charles Bovary's infatuation for his wife or his
wife's misguided infatuations for Rudolphe and Léon.
   29. *Letters*, III, 213.

of Man or Paris or even the Imperial Palace Hotel in search of romance; romance exists in the most unlikely of places, in the heart of Gissing's "nether world," Clerkenwell.

Coming from a novelist who was tagged, early in his career, as a documentary realist, *Riceyman Steps* is an uncommonly literary book. Bennett's original idols, Turgenev and the French naturalists, have given way to Stendhal, Chekhov, and, above all, Dostoevsky; and one can detect traces of the psychologist of love, the master of "absolute realism" (Bennett's description of Chekhov),[30] and the most probing and forgiving of the Russians in Bennett's novel. To Gide, Bennett expressed his ambition of "getting so near the truth, and getting there beautifully," as had Stendhal and Dostoevsky, although he felt that he "could never do anything equal to that." In *Riceyman Steps* he came very close indeed to a Dostoevskian richness of empathy. Bennett viewed the author of *The Brothers Karamazov* as the "greatest sympathiser of all"; his "nature had for human imperfections that universal, Christ-like, uncondescending pity which should be the ideal of all novelists." Along with the Dostoevskian power of empathy in *Riceyman Steps* there exists a measure of Dostoevsky's humor.[31] Henry Earlforward, Bennett's miser-hero, is related to one of those Dostoevskian comic monsters—Marmeladov in *Crime and Punishment,* for example— who is never denied our sympathy in spite of his worst excesses. Furthermore, the book's subplot, which involves the charwoman Elsie's wait for the return of her wayward lover Joe, recalls Dostoevsky's "White Nights."

There is also a strong element of literary self-parody in the book: Elsie's amazing devotion to her employers, the Earlforwards, makes Anna's devotedness to her father seem trifling by comparison; and in place of Anna's theft and destruction of Willie Price's forged document, Bennett gives us Elsie's theft of sixpence

30. Arnold Bennett, *Books and Persons* (New York: George Doran, 1917), p. 118. Bennett was one of the first English critics to call attention to Chekhov's genius—first as a writer of stories, later (with the first professionally staged production of a Chekhov play in England, *The Cherry Orchard*) as a dramatist.

31. *Letters,* III, 131; "The Progress of the Novel" (1929) and (for Bennett on Dostoevsky's humor) "Some Adventures among Russian Fiction" (1916), both reprinted with *The Author's Craft,* pp. 95, 116–117.

from the Earlforward safe—an act which destroys the miser's "foundations of faith"[32] and precipitates his death. In the miserly couple's clinging to the "mystery" of one another, Bennett seems to be burlesquing the sentimental excesses of the Edwin Clayhanger–Hilda Lessways relationship; and in Earlforward himself, descendant of a line of misers in Bennett's fiction, Bennett appears to be indulging in a parody of his own proneness to inflated rhetoric and to be mocking certain of his own weaknesses: his meticulousness, his orderliness, and his faith in willpower. James Hepburn has provocatively argued that in *Riceyman Steps* Bennett goes beyond documentary realism—despite the novelist's claim that the miser and his shop were based on actual Southampton models which he transplanted to Clerkenwell. Although he read up on Clerkenwell and studied a book about misers for various details, Bennett ultimately turned to his imagination for the main points.[33] In doing so, however, he also returned to the world of nineteenth-century English fiction. Elsie, for example, inevitably reminds us of one of Gissing's dutiful characters. His comment that "in some magic way she had vanquished the difficulties of a most formidable situation by merely accepting and facing them" (p. 270) echoes Bennett's description of Gissing himself, made over two decades earlier: "He is neither gay nor melancholy; but just, sober, calm, and proud against the gods; he has seen, he knows, he is unmoved; he defeats fate by accepting it."[34]

Bennett, in the 1899 essay on Gissing, paid special tribute to *The Nether World* for the depiction of Clerkenwell with its toiling workers and stoical lovers. Thanks to the novelist's art, Clerkenwell is "no longer negligible. It has import. You feel the sullen terrible pulse of this universe which lies beneath your own." Gissing's accomplishment would be Bennett's own aim in *Anna of the Five Towns* (which he was then writing) and, above all, in *Riceyman Steps:* exercising "the artist's prerogative as an explorer of hidden

32. Arnold Bennett, *Riceyman Steps* (London: Cassell, 1923), p. 298. All further quotations from the novel, identified by page numbers in the text, are from this edition.

33. See James Hepburn, "Some Curious Realism in *Riceyman Steps,*" *Modern Fiction Studies,* 8 (Summer 1962), 116–126; Hepburn, "The Notebooks for *Riceyman Steps,*" *PMLA,* 78 (June 1963), 257–261; and Bennett, "Back to Riceyman Steps," *The Evening Standard Years,* p. 383.

34. "George Gissing," *The Author's Craft,* p. 164.

and recondite beauty in unsuspected places."[35] In this modernist manifesto, Bennett was also, unknowingly, allying himself with the greatest of all masters of the "poetry of fact," Dickens. The grimness of *Riceyman Steps* may suggest Gissing, but the quirky humor of the book is Dickensian, as are certain significant details in the book. Earlforward's cluttered bookstore, for example, is a reincarnation of that "dark greasy shop" in Clerkenwell where Mr. Venus accumulates his precious junk, while Earlforward himself is akin to the fantastic misers whom Boffin enjoys reading about in the same novel, *Our Mutual Friend*. (Dickens might have written Earlforward's bizarre query to the vacuuming crew that has removed the dust from his shop: "Do you sell it? Do you get anything for it?" [p. 102]. The heaps of dust have obvious symbolic value in both *Our Mutual Friend* and *Riceyman Steps*.) Bennett, nonetheless, expressed a lifelong dislike of Dickens, citing his ignorance, exaggerations, and lack of a sense of art or beauty. The modern critical sense that certain Bennett characters—such as Earlforward or Tellwright—are Dickensian in their comic grotesquerie would have horrified him. One is speaking, hence, not in terms of influence but of temperamental affinities—above all, in the two novelists' mutual determination to recreate the world according to the whims and needs of the imagination.[36]

Imaginary recreation of the world is not only Bennett's object in *Riceyman Steps* but also the occupation of his major characters. However, while he is aware of the terrible squalor overlying the strange beauty of his subject, they are blind to all but what their limited perspectives perceive as beautiful. The fortyish bookseller Henry Earlforward and his stolid cleaningwoman Elsie are described initially in terms of their mixture of insensitivity and extravagance: "An enchantment upon these two human beings, both commonplace and both marvelous, bound together and yet incurious each of the other and incurious of the mysteries in which they and all their fellows lived! Mr. Earlforward never asked the meaning of

35. "You may even," Bennett adds (in a phrase that also appears in *Anna of the Five Towns*, p. 100), "envy the blessedness of the meek, and perceive in the lassitude of the heavy laden a secret grace that can never be yours" ("George Gissing," *The Author's Craft*, p. 161).

36. *Our Mutual Friend*, chap. 6. See Wright, *Arnold Bennett*, on the Bennett-Dickens connection (pp. 93–95). For Bennett on Dickens, see, for example, "My Literary Heresies," *The Author's Craft*, p. 235.

life, for he had a lifelong ruling passion. Elsie never asked the meaning of life, for she was dominated and obsessed by a tremendous instinct to serve" (p. 16). Earlforward's "strange passion" and Elsie's "tremendous instinct" are the contending values of the novel, as they were in *Anna of the Five Towns:* the malignant power of money and the saving power of love. But Bennett refuses to bring the book down to earth by intruding moral judgments. Elsie and Earlforward and Violet Arb, the widow whom Earlforward marries and locks up within his shop, see life from a narrow but magical perspective that lifts them above their Clerkenwell setting. What they don't know, oddly enough, saves them.

As middle-aged lovers, Henry and Violet regard one another with an incomprehension that is romantic rather than pathetic. From the beginning, we learn that he is "subject to dreams and ideals and longings" (p. 16); at the sight of Violet, he is attracted to her embodiment (in his eyes) of "life, energy, downrightness, masterfulness" (p. 22). She is, to be sure, a "sensible" woman (sensible in her sharing of many of his frugal habits), but she is also magnificently "feminine." "Forceful, she could yet (speaking metaphorically) cling and look up. And also she could look down in a most enchanting and disturbing way" (p. 58). From her point of view, the miser's defects are a source of delight: "His slight limp pleased and touched her. His unshakable calmness impressed her. Oh! He was a man with reserves, both of character and of goods. Secure in these reserves he could front the universe. He was self-reliant without being self-confident. He was grave, but his little eyes had occasionally a humorous gleam . . . In brief, Mr. Earlforward, considered as an entity, was nearly faultless" (p. 40). In her state of presumed helplessness, he seems "a rock of defence, shelter, safety!" (p. 73). Earlforward, smitten, yearns to "share with her sympathetic soul his own vision of this wonderful Clerkenwell," where they have neighboring shops. He wishes to tell her the romantic history of the district, including the fact that here, in the Middle Ages, "the drama of Adam and Eve [was] performed in the costume of Adam and Eve to a simple and unshocked people. (Why not? She was a widow and no longer young.) And he would point out to her how the brown backs of the houses which fronted on King's Cross Road resembled the buttressed walls of a mighty fortress, and how the grim, ochreish unwindowed backs of the houses of Riceyman Square (behind him) looked just like lofty, mediaeval keeps" (p. 3). One can no more mock these curious fancies and romantic descriptions than one can mock Anna's astonishment at the sight of Liverpool harbor: in Bennett's novel, Clerkenwell becomes a kind of Eden and the middle-aged lovers reenact the story of Adam and Eve. Under their unprepossessing exteriors, they are primal beings.

To Violet, Henry is a chivalrous protector (she sees "chivalry" even in his choice of wedding present to her, a safe for her securities), while to the inexperienced bachelor she is "the most brilliant, attractive, competent, and comfortable woman on earth; and Mr. Earlforward was rapidly becoming a hero, a knight, a madman capable of sublime deeds. He felt an heroical impulse such as he had never felt" (p. 25). Presuming to know the characters better than they know each other, the sagacious reader is likely to remember the prenuptial blindness of Lydgate and Rosamond in *Middlemarch*— "Each lived in a world of which the other knew nothing"—and suspect that grave disillusionment is in store. But the Earlforwards married are not altered by experience; their points of view remain colored by their original romantic preconceptions, and no realization of annoying discrepancies can change them: "Simple souls, somehow living very near the roots of happiness—though precariously!" (p. 126). The characters' inability to see that the security they find in one another is delusive makes their situation comic at times, but it also lends them a form of Quixotic bravery as they approach the brink.

The most extreme case of redemptive blindness in the book is that of Elsie, who becomes the Earlforwards' maidservant after their marriage. Victimized by her employers and by her occasionally brutal boyfriend Joe (who has been traumatized by his experience in the war), Elsie is the most downtrodden example of the "priestess" class mentioned in *Anna of the Five Towns;* yet she sees nothing wrong with her situation. For the first time in her life having a bedroom and a bed to herself, Elsie is unable to see the room as the "cold," "bare," and "small" thing that it is: "It was ugly, but Elsie simply could not see ugliness." For her, possession of the room affords a delusive security equivalent to that which the Earlforwards have found in one another. Unaware of the injustice of her circumstances, Elsie has "no glimmer of realization that she was the salt of the earth! She thought she was in a nice, comfortable, quiet house, and appointed to live with kindly people of superior excellence" (pp. 86–88). Elsie's role in the novel gives her a superficial resemblance to the legion of devoted servants in English fiction, but the deliberately exaggerated nature of her devotedness (Bennett was annoyed at the sentimental public which saw in her the domestic servant of its dreams),[37] plus her too-obviously symbolic function as life force—each morning she "breathed the breath of life into the dead nocturnal house" (p. 123)—lift her above mere sentimentalism. She is at once archetype and self-parody. With her voracious appetite and her masochistic streak, she incarnates the opposing pulls of the novel, simultaneously toward and away from life. Rather than serving as an "innocent" foil to her employers, she embodies *in extremis* their own dual natures.

To see Elsie as the life force opposed to the Earlforwards' death instinct does an injustice to Bennett's remarkable achievement in *Riceyman Steps*. Just as she has her perverse strain (her clinging to Joe parallels Violet's clinging to Henry in defiance of her own early advice to Elsie: "What do you want with men?" [p. 56]), so too do Henry and Violet have a life force and romantic streak that survive all the horrors of their self-imposed penury. The reader's first glimpse of Henry Earlforward—a man "in the prime of life," whose "vitality" is suggested by his "rich, very red lips" (p. 1)—is the image that Violet never loses sight of. Similarly, for him she always remains the "girlish" yet "masterful" woman who has sexual "experience" (p. 24) on her side to bring him. During the course of their marriage, which lasts barely over a year, both husband and wife waste away, of cancer and undernourishment respectively; yet he sees in her, even when emaciated, a "romantic quality perceptible in no other woman," while she, despite grievances against him, "wanted to fondle him, physically and spiritually; and this desire maintained itself not without success in opposition to all her grievances, and, compared to it, her sufferings and his had but a minor consequence" (p. 223). From their point of view, they alone are safe—unlike the "pathetic creatures" whom they see thronging the streets in search of vain pleasures, "sheltered in no strong fortress" such as theirs. Neither Henry's miserliness nor his in-

37. *Letters*, III, 213.

creasingly withered features can alter her vision. After pondering the fate of the helpless outsiders, Violet, unaware of her own helplessness, regards her good fortune in having such a protector in a manner which invests her with grandeur as well as pathos. " 'Come. Come to bed,' she said. 'It's very cold here after the office!' " (p. 166). And when Violet lies dying in the hospital, Henry, who is dying himself, sends her a letter of remarkable tenderness and self-deception concerning his own health. (Characteristically, he refuses to allow Elsie sixpence to have the letter delivered; hence her theft.) "He thought that he alone had mysteriously remained young among his generation," Bennett observes a few pages earlier (pp. 222–223). Bennett's novels are not about the effects of time on his characters—despite the oft-cited remark of E. M. Forster that the real hero of his work is time.[38] Rather, they are about how characters transcend time through their obstinate and ignorant, but also imaginative and loving, natures.

And it is thus that the author of *Riceyman Steps* transmutes and transcends realism: by focusing on his characters' reworking of reality, he enables us to see with their eyes and accept as beautiful what to an objective outsider can only seem sordid or comic-pathetic. Bachelard's insight into the poet's recreation of reality applies both to Bennett as novelist and to his characters as surrogate poets. Among the strongest images of permanence which the poetic imagination clings to, notes Bachelard, are images of the house as nest: a secure world built from within, whereby "facts" are altered by the "values" which the poet applies to them.[39] Violet's initial impression of Earlforward's home (over the bookshop) fills her with doubts and fears concerning the man she will marry. The "gloomy shop" has "the air of a crypt"; "the dirt and the immense disorder almost frightened her" (p. 68). Yet she is "fascinated" as well as filled with "terror" by the house and its revelation of Earlforward; and she is attracted by the challenge of bringing order and life and warmth to the house and its master. "What could she not do with him? Could she not accomplish marvels?" (pp. 72–73). Her associ-

---

38. Forster's comment on *The Old Wives' Tale,* in his *Aspects of the Novel* (New York: Harcourt, Brace, 1927; p. 62), has occasionally been extended to Bennett's entire work. Cf. Walter Allen, *Arnold Bennett* (Denver: Alan Swallow, 1949), pp. 64–65.

39. Bachelard, *The Poetics of Space,* chap. 4 ("Nests").

ation of husband and house ironically echoes Henry Mynors' link-
ing of Anna with her kitchen: the male admires the woman who will
bring order to his life; the woman is delighted by the challenge to
bring order to her husband's life.[40] However, despite an initial brave
attempt to transform the house (as her wedding present to Henry,
Violet arranges to have it vacuumed), all returns to its original state.
A year after the marriage the dust has resettled in place, and even
Elsie is dimly aware that something must be done. "The atmosphere
of the sealed house," notes Bennett, "was infected by the strange-
ness of the master, who himself, in turn, was influenced by it. Fresh
air, new breath, a great wind, was needed to dispel the corruption.
The house was suffocating its owners" (p. 174).

Like Woolf's Mrs. Ramsay, Violet makes a valiant effort to
impose order upon disorder; but her husband is intractable, life is
intractable, and corruption conquers in the end. Nevertheless, she
does make an impression on her husband—his romantic letter to her
is proof of that—and he in turn confirms her in the view that they
are safe within the house. Once out of that delusive safety she dies;
and Henry, tormented by the loss but incapable of realizing his
contribution to it, makes a pathetic and heroic effort to disregard his
own frail state. "Animated by the mighty power of his resolution to
withstand fate he felt strong—he *was* strong" (p. 296). Before his
final collapse, he dresses himself in one of his new blue suits and
returns downstairs to his business: "Work! Work! The reconstruction of his life!" (p. 298). (His work ethic is a wry parody of
Bennett's own obsessiveness.)[41] Henry dies a surrogate artist, and
much of the shock of the ending comes from the intrusion, after the
Earlforwards' deaths, of the outside world offering a commonplace
version of, and passing conventional judgment on, the characters
and events the reader has absorbed through unconventional and
unmoralistic eyes. "What a dreadful face!" observes a good-
natured but unperceptive neighbor. "White, blotched, hairy skin
drawn tightly over bones and muscles—very tightly. An expression
of torment in the tiny, unseeing eyes!" (p. 306). One recalls, sadly,

40. In a similar but more successful manner, Hilda plots to remake Edwin Clayhanger's life in *These Twain*.

41. James Hepburn explores the connections between Bennett and Earlforward in
The Art of Arnold Bennett (Bloomington: Indiana University Press, 1963), pp.
43–44.

Violet's reaction to the "humorous gleam" in those "little eyes."

"The amazing aspect of [Earlforward]," marveled a contemporary reviewer (who compared Bennett's hero to King Lear), "is that you are forced to love him, not because he is a miser, but because he is a human being." Bennett's accomplishment is to make the reader share the vision of his characters—and hence to regard as impertinent the attempts of the outside world to make its judgment on the basis of physical appearance or to evaluate the story with conventional complacency. For once, the hackneyed headlines of the London newspapers, in their attempt to make an affair of "world-glory" out of the Earlforwards for an hour or two, approach the truth: "Astounding Story of Love and Death," "Midnight Tragedy in King's Cross Road" (pp. 308–309).[42] Within Clerkenwell, however, it is only in "Elsie's heart" that the Earlforwards survive beyond the evening headlines; and Elsie herself, despite her heroism in tending after Joe, appears no more worthy of attention to Clerkenwell than had Anna to Bursley: "A dowdy, over-plump figure, whom nobody would have looked twice at" (p. 312). Together with Joe, she carrying his suitcase which he is too weak to lift, Elsie passes out of the shop and disappears into the crowd. "Nor were people shocked at the spectacle of the woman lugging a heavy grip-bag while the man carried naught," the novel concludes. "Such dreadful things were often witnessed in Clerkenwell" (p. 319).

"Every scene, even the commonest, is wonderful," Bennett proclaimed early in his career, "if only one can detach oneself, casting off all memory of use and custom, and behold it (as it were) for the first time; in its right, authentic colours; without making comparisons." The artist's goal should be to see with the eyes of a baby "who lives each moment by itself and tarnishes the present by no remembrance of the past." Poetry liberates, as Bachelard reminds us, because it takes us out of the causal and material world we know and into a recreated world of the imagination in which everything

42. Early in the novel, Earlforward, seeing a newspaper announcement "Death of a well-known statesman," dismisses the hyperbole: "As an expert in interpretation, [he] was aware that 'well-known' on a newspaper placard meant exactly the opposite of what it meant in any other place; it meant not well-known" (p. 19). James Douglas, *Sunday Express* (28 Oct. 1923), reprinted in *The Critical Heritage*, p. 411.

appears fresh and significant. The poet avoids "old-wives' tales. He has no past, but lives in a world that is new. As regards the past and the affairs of this world, he has realized absolute sublimation."[43] Bachelard urges the phenomenologist to learn from the poet in order to transfigure the ordinary world into images of safety and beauty. In this respect, *Riceyman Steps* may be seen as Bennett's ultimate piece of phenomenological poetics: the world is remade from within; a prison becomes a nest; the main characters transform themselves into knights and ladies and loyal subjects; and the life force persists despite all the material evidence to deny it nourishment. The final effect of the book, hence, is exhilarating rather than bleak. A potentially ugly subject has been transformed into something remarkable through the power of Bennett's compassionate artistry; and in the Earlforwards and Elsie, Woolf's elusive Mrs. Brown has found three of her most memorable incarnations in modern fiction.

To Gide, Bennett described *Riceyman Steps* as follows: "Type: réaliste. Old-fashioned, of course. C'est plus fort que moi. We have several young novelists here [for example, Woolf, with whom Bennett was having a literary feud] who are trying to invent a form to supersede Balzac's. *They are not succeeding.* I also am trying, and almost succeeding." Bennett's sense of himself as both "old-fashioned" and innovative is correct; as a realist he was, as he had come to realize, a companion of George Eliot as well as George Moore. But he was also aligned with his younger contemporaries—with Joyce, for example, who was similarly transforming ordinary individuals into figures of epic significance; or with Woolf, "making of the moment something permanent." And he has remained a source of inspiration for recent novelists like Margaret Drabble, John Wain, Angus Wilson, and Alan Sillitoe—"dealing with material that," as Drabble declares, "I had never before encountered in fiction, but only in life."[44] In his best work Bennett demonstrates that it is possible to achieve the "absolute realism" desired of

43. *Journals* (1897), p. 28; Bachelard, *The Poetics of Space*, pp. xxv, 169.

44. *Letters*, III, 201; Drabble, *Arnold Bennett*, p. xi (Drabble observes that Bennett, like Woolf, "writes magnificently of the little movements of the spirit in its daily routine"; p. 294).

modern fiction without abandoning the humanistic perspective to be found in the great nineteenth-century novels.

It is the fate of literary realists to be attacked periodically by critics who hanker after grander subjects and grander styles. Just as Lawrence objected to Bennett's "acceptance" of reality, so too did Ruskin, a hundred years ago, condemn the "English cockney school, which consummates itself in George Eliot." In a memorable and misguided assessment, Ruskin described the characters in *The Mill on the Floss* (those "insignificant people, whom you pass unnoticingly on the road every day," but who, as Eliot adds, "have their tragedy too") as the "sweepings out of a Pentonville omnibus." When Frank Harris, complaining of the lack of "romance" in *The Old Wives' Tale,* quoted Ruskin to support his case, Bennett accepted the charge. He admitted to being a realist; but, as in the case of the creators of Maggie Tulliver and Daniel Deronda and Mrs. Ramsay, his was a realism broad enough to encompass the romantic longings and visions of an Anna Tellwright and a Henry Earlforward, and his was an artistry capable of bringing to light the "deeper beauty" underlying reality. No less than Virginia Woolf in her determination to capture Mrs. Brown in her railway compartment, Bennett aimed (as he wrote in *The Author's Craft*) at the depiction of "life," concrete and mysterious, taking the form of "the woman next door" or "the man in the train." "At bottom I am proudly content with the Pentonville omnibus," he told Harris. "Why not? If I cannot take a Pentonville omnibus and show it to be fine, then I am not a fully equipped artist. (And I *am*.)"[45]

45. John Ruskin, *Fiction, Fair and Foul,* in *Complete Works,* 39 vols., ed. E. T. Cook and A. Wedderburn (London: George Allen, 1903–1912), XXXIV, 377–378; *The Mill on the Floss,* bk. III, chap. 1; Frank Harris, review in *Vanity Fair* (9 Dec. 1908), reprinted in *The Critical Heritage,* pp. 219–224; Bennett, *Letters,* II, 239; *The Author's Craft,* p. 8.

LISA RUDDICK

William James and the Modernism of Gertrude Stein

Parallels between William James's theory of the "stream of consciousness" and certain stylistic developments in twentieth-century fiction have long been evident. But to think of James's *Principles of Psychology* as prophetic of modernist literary practice is to lose sight of its place as a transitional document. The ambiguity of James's relationship to modernism is suggested by his impact on the writings of Gertrude Stein. As has long been suspected, James's theory of consciousness had an influence on Stein. Moreover, this influence has something to do with the "modern" quality of her work. But even those writings that owe most to James show Stein subtly distorting his emphases. For Stein accepted the descriptive elements of the *Psychology* but was unsympathetic to its values, which were a part of James's inheritance from the mid-Victorians.

Stein took psychology courses from James in the 1890's, as an undergraduate at Radcliffe. By her own account, James was the one figure from her college years who had a lasting intellectual effect on her.[1] I believe that she was specially receptive to James's theories of consciousness because they gave her a language to apply to certain idiosyncracies in her own nature.

1. See *The Autobiography of Alice B. Toklas,* in *Selected Writings of Gertrude Stein,* ed. Carl Van Vechten (New York: Vintage, 1962), p. 73; Gertrude Stein, *Wars I Have Seen* (New York: Random House, 1945), pp. 63–64.

The autobiographical pieces Stein produced in college suggest the quality of her emotional life during the period.[2] They dwell on the figure of a divided young woman in whom a strongly sensual nature competes with an exacting need for self-mastery. "In the Red Deeps" is an account of a morbidly erotic temperament. Its speaker recalls a period during childhood when she experimented with the "exquisite delight" of self-inflicted pain, and diverted herself by thinking up tortures she might inflict on others. But she has an attack of conscience, characterized by a "terrible and haunting fear of loss of self-control" (p. 108).

In "The Temptation," illicit pleasures again alternate with self-reproach. The heroine, an indistinct surrogate for Stein, finds herself in church one day with a strange man who leans heavily against her. She enjoys the "sensuous impressions," but again has a "quick revulsion," and asks herself, "Have you no sense of shame?" Yet still "she did not move." The conflict leaves her immobilized; she vaguely indulges herself, but only by passivity (pp. 154–155). Later her sexual inclinations stigmatize her; her companions, who have missed nothing, upbraid her, and she becomes "one apart" (p. 151).

When these characters are not oppressed by conscious fears of impropriety, they have vague inhibitions which are no less paralyzing. Stein writes a theme about a boy who is both frightened and interested when a pretty girl asks him to help her across a brook. Once again, "he . . . could not move" (p. 146). Finally he accommodates her, only to flee in alarm. These characters never pass beyond the faintest stimulation; they prefer emotional and physical barrenness to the risk of losing themselves.

Nothing, of course, distinguishes this as an unusual mental type. But the fact that tensions like these preoccupied Stein during her late teenage years helps to account for her ready embrace of Jamesian psychology.[3] James too sees a duality in human nature, one that

---

2. The "Radcliffe Themes," written for a composition course in Stein's junior year, are anthologized in Rosalind S. Miller, *Gertrude Stein: Form and Intelligibility* (New York: Exposition Press, 1949), all references to which will appear in the text. I use "The Temptation" to refer both to the piece of that name and to its earlier, untitled version.

3. The text for Stein's first course with James was *Psychology: The Briefer Course,* an abridgment of *The Principles of Psychology.*

traps us between eagerness and self-control. In his view, moreover, the self-division is a sign not of deviance but of mental health.

Every mind, by his account, has a promiscuous and a repressive element. In normal perceptual life, we are torn between two ways of admitting phenomena to consciousness. Part of us is welcoming and indiscriminate; we have an impulse to respond to every stray sensation, and to notice every object that crosses our path. But if we indulged this impulse exclusively, we would lose our way in the world; so many impressions crowd in on us from moment to moment that to accept each one would result in a fatal inability to lay hold of anything in particular. Our practical life, and ultimately our survival itself, depend on an ability to attend to some things at the expense of others. We must limit the field of vision by noticing only what bears on our particular interests.

Every mind, then, has a faculty of "selective attention" that works against the impulse to take everything in.[4] The selective function is automatic, but we may manipulate it at will; there is nothing to prevent our choosing where to direct our attention. The business of locating what is practically important is aided by a mass of stable concepts; we have an intellectual pigeonhole, and a name, for each object that normally interests us, and whatever does not fit one of these we ignore (p. 273).

But selective attention must not be exercised to excess. If we allowed our concepts to control us, nothing new would ever reach our awareness—and this itself would be harmful from a practical standpoint. We would be blind to everything but what we had already seen. The way to remain responsive to facts is to continue to admit some perceptions that have nothing to do with our preconceived interests or our categories. These alien data force revisions in the categories themselves; our labels for the world broaden by accommodating unforeseen phenomena. Mental life proceeds by a perpetual "compromise" between the selective tendency, which commits us to a fixed conceptual framework, and the promiscuous tendency, which welcomes impressions for which we do not yet have labels (p. 753).

As I have argued elsewhere, this view of consciousness is metic-

4. William James, *The Principles of Psychology,* 3 vols., in *Works of William James,* ed. Frederick Burkhardt (Cambridge, Mass.: Harvard University Press, 1981), p. 273. All further references to this work will appear in the text.

ulously reproduced in Stein's early fiction.[5] It is easy to imagine
what she found attractive in James's theories. They alleviated a
certain amount of guilt about her own troublesome appetites, and at
the same time suggested a means of forgiving herself her inhibitions. For by James's account, the mind naturally has its thirsty
or revolutionary half, a menace but also a source of life. We would
stagnate if we lost the taste for raw sensation. Stein welcomes the
parallel; the unruly libidos of the Radcliffe heroines are identified
in her mature fiction with perceptual openness. Melanctha Herbert
in *Three Lives,* for example, is at once sexually promiscuous and
perceptually indiscriminate, "always wanting new things just to get
excited."[6]

The inhibitions too are later validated, by an equation with selective attention. Jeff Campbell, Melanctha's lover, is physically timid
and also incapable of focusing his senses on "new things." Indeed,
the very struggle between yielding and self-control that immobilizes
the characters of the Radcliffe themes comes, with an infusion of
Jamesian psychology, to be judged a creative part of consciousness.
Three Lives and *The Making of Americans* abound in pairs of characters who embody the two mental poles and who, through a kind of
"struggle" or Jamesian compromise, help one another to achieve a
proper focus on the world.[7]

In the process of assimilating James, Stein finds a way beyond
paralyzing self-scrutiny. In the Radcliffe themes, and in her first
novel, *Q.E.D.,* she struggles tediously with her own moralism and
cannot write without "revulsion" about the bodily yearnings that
preoccupy her.[8] Her first Jamesian narratives, on the other hand, by
shifting the focus to ethically neutral perceptual themes, free Stein
to consider various types of experience without questioning whether

5. See Lisa Ruddick, "Fluid Symbols in American Modernism: William James,
Gertrude Stein, George Santayana, and Wallace Stevens," in *Allegory, Myth, and
Symbol,* Harvard English Studies, no. 9, ed. Morton W. Bloomfield (Cambridge,
Mass.: Harvard University Press, 1981), pp. 335–353, and " 'Melanctha' and the
Psychology of William James," *Modern Fiction Studies,* 28 (Winter 1982–83).

6. Gertrude Stein, "Melanctha," *Three Lives* (New York: Vintage, 1936), p. 119.
All further references to this work will appear in the text.

7. See "Melanctha," p. 153; *The Making of Americans; Being a History of a
Family's Progress* (New York: Something Else Press, 1966), p. 438. All further
references to the latter work will appear in the text.

8. "Radcliffe Themes," p. 155.

they are acceptable or evil. In *Three Lives*, Stein's first narrative written under the stimulus of Jamesian psychology, Mrs. Lehntman and Melanctha Herbert are sexual "wanderers," but their lack of self-restraint is not subject to judgment because it is a symptom of indiscriminate habits of attention.

As it happens, this relaxation of ethical judgments is also largely responsible for the modern quality of *Three Lives*. It has often been noticed that "Melanctha," the central story in the volume, is a reworking of *Q.E.D.*;[9] little effort, however, has been made to explain the difference between the two stories. The later version, unlike the first, is unmistakably a product of the twentieth century. This impression is created partly by the story's lack of moral focus. In a gesture typical of her generation, Stein leads us forward with a dimsighted innocence, reluctant to interpret or persuade. *Q.E.D.*, written before the Jamesian period, has a strident moralism; it is about lapses from innocence and problems of conduct. *Three Lives* offers us conformists and troublemakers, but never suggests that one form of existence is more excellent or debased than another. As Jeff Campbell learns, no experience is "bad to be having" (p. 158).

The Jamesian apparatus contributes to Stein's modernism in another sense: the very decision to emphasize the minute operations of consciousness is characteristic of her generation. With such contemporaries as Woolf, Joyce, and Proust, Stein in her Jamesian period locates at the center of her narratives moments in which a character fixes his or her attention on things in a peculiar way. Fanny Hissen in *The Making of Americans* and Jeff Campbell in *Three Lives* experience major crises simply by making the transition from selective attention to sensational fullness. Jeff learns painfully to stop "think[ing] . . . in words" and instead to accept experience as a mass of "new things, little pieces all different" (pp. 155, 158); Fanny Hissen relinquishes "right thinking" for "important feeling" (pp. 57–58, 67). What these characters accomplish in the public sphere—how they behave, or what happens to them—is left out of focus. The "point of interest," to borrow from Woolf's character-

---

9. Carolyn Faunce Copeland, *Language and Time and Gertrude Stein* (Iowa City: University of Iowa Press, 1975), p. 10; Leon Katz, Introduction to Gertrude Stein, *Fernhurst, Q.E.D., and Other Early Writings* (New York: Liveright, 1971), p. viii.

ization of modern fiction, "lies . . . in the dark places of psychology."[10]

Yet for all the likenesses between James's theory of consciousness and the forms of mental experience delineated in twentieth-century novels, one has to apply James in a somewhat distorted way to use him as the basis for fiction like Stein's. In the first place, James's account of experience is itself directed by an intense moralism. His universe is one in which "the powers of light" are forever meeting "those of darkness."[11] Even in the largely descriptive *Psychology,* he does not hesitate to express values. His popular chapter on "Habit," for example, is unabashedly prescriptive. It offers "practical maxim[s]" of the following sort: *"Keep the faculty of effort alive in you by a little gratuitous exercise every day.* That is, be systematically ascetic or heroic in little unnecessary points" (p. 130).

Not surprisingly, James's own tastes in literature favored works with implicit moral applications.[12] It is understandable, then, if ironic, that when Stein sent him a copy of *Three Lives,* in certain respects her purest Jamesian narrative, he found little in it to lure him beyond the first forty pages.[13] Stein's ethical neutrality is the result of a long and conscious effort. Her earliest preserved pieces, the Radcliffe themes, are charged with ideals (James's own ideals of "effort" and "heroism"). A brief tribute to James himself captures her characteristic tone: "Is life worth living? Yes, a thousand times yes when the world still holds such spirits as Prof. James . . . He stands firmly, nobly for the dignity of man. His faith is . . . that . . . of a strong man willing to fight, to suffer and endure."[14]

This is Gertrude Stein in a vein unfamiliar to most of us. She is groping, at this stage, with whatever postures come to hand. *Three*

10. Virginia Woolf, "Modern Fiction," *The Common Reader,* First Series (New York: Harcourt, Brace and World, 1925), p. 156.

11. William James, "What Makes a Life Significant," *On Some of Life's Ideals* (New York: Henry Holt, 1899), p. 57. All further references to this work will appear in the text.

12. See Ralph Barton Perry, *The Thought and Character of William James,* 2 vols. (Boston: Little, Brown, 1935), II, 259–260.

13. Donald Gallup, ed., *The Flowers of Friendship: Letters Written to Gertrude Stein* (New York: Knopf, 1953) p. 50. James warmly acknowledges receipt of *Three Lives,* but admits having put it down after a brief sitting.

14. "Radcliffe Themes," p. 146.

Lives is the first sign of dislocation; here moral absolutes give way to the impartial norms of psychology, and Stein abandons questions of virtue and vice to ask whether a character is interesting, or perceptually alive. There is a conspicuous index of upheaval: in reworking the material from *Q.E.D.*, she shifts the sympathetic center of the story from the scrupulous Adele (who becomes Jeff Campbell) to the dissolute but undeniably exciting Melanctha Herbert.

Stein never reverts to a voice of judgment. Her silence has a partial source in a growing discomfort with ethical questions, but it also owes something to an emerging aesthetic bias. For the loss of moral definition is part of a greater disturbance. Beginning with *Three Lives,* Stein's technique shows signs of a progressive disintegration of focus, another indication of her distance from James.

Q.E.D. moves between its various crises with firmness and ease. By comparison, *Three Lives* seems curiously unable to advance or to build to a pitch. The dramatic outlines, like the moral contours, are flattened; there is an aimlessness, indeed a backward drag. Stein resists theatrical moments, beginnings and summations; she fails to take proper hold even of the most genuine crises, reducing for example the deaths of her heroines (as she does again in *The Making of Americans*) to casual data: "They sent [Melanctha] where she would be taken care of, a home for poor consumptives, and there Melanctha stayed until she died" (p. 236). "While [the baby] was coming, Lena had grown very pale and sicker. When it was all over Lena had died, too, and nobody knew just how it had happened to her" (p. 279).

Stein withholds the normal emphases. The effect is reminiscent, some have thought, of cubist painting, with its "sameness" and its "lack of focal point."[15] One also thinks of Cézanne, whom Stein claimed as an influence from the period of *Three Lives* on. Cézanne was important, Stein told an interviewer, because he "conceived the idea that in composition one thing was as important as another thing. Each part is as important as the whole, and that impressed me enormously."[16]

15. L. T. Fitz, "Gertrude Stein and Picasso: The Language of Surfaces," *American Literature,* 45 (1973), 231.

16. Robert Bartlett Haas, "Gertrude Stein Talking: A Transatlantic Interview," *Uclan Review,* 8 (Summer 1962), 8.

It is possible, then, to associate Stein's emerging technique with artistic movements in early twentieth-century Paris. Yet—to offer what seems at first a paradox—the apparently aimless manner might also seem a direct development from the *Principles of Psychology*. James himself claims that we coarsen experience by our emphases and designs; each act of selection has its cost in lost perceptual abundance. Stein, in embracing aimlessness, undoes the work of selective attention; she makes a copious record of existence without exalting special objects to dominance. She reminds us of the quality our perceptions have before we limit and rearrange them to suit our customary interests.

The dispersion of attention in *Three Lives* is incomplete; the stories are hardly so indiscriminate in focus as even to belong to the normal class of "stream of consciousness" narratives. But the drift of Stein's mind is suggested by the fact that within six years she would be composing *Tender Buttons* in as aimless a style as would still have a use for words. Even apart from subsequent developments, the early works show what seems a conscious attempt to capture the Jamesian "stream" of experience in fiction.

James's chapter on "The Stream of Thought" (retitled "The Stream of Consciousness" for the abridged *Psychology*) is a reply to associationist psychology. Associationists had pictured sensations and ideas as discrete links in a chain. James claims that it is artificial to think of consciousness as atomized; our psychic life looks like a clean succession of thoughts only when we limit our account of it to those mental states that we inwardly name—that we fix our attention on. But between these sharp foci, there is a "free water of consciousness," an indistinct, mingling body of associations and connections that occupies us between one halting place and the next and suffuses even our clearest perceptions (p. 246). We notice these in disinterested moments, when selective attention is relaxed. Consciousness "is nothing jointed; it flows" (p. 233). Each thought casts ripples before and after, and when we are not fixed on something distinct we have at least a remote "consciousness of whither our thought is going" (p. 247).

Now these reflections may be viewed as containing a prophecy of Gertrude Stein's style. If Stein seems to let her focus wander, it is because she has no thought of moving forward in clean strides as if life fell jointedly. She strains against habits of attention that select and divide—also outmoded literary habits that parcel experience into "a beginning and a middle and an end."[17] This is consistent, of course, with a revulsion in the period against Victorian literary practice. Stein abandons conventional peaks or halting places for the continuous flow of dying and beckoning thoughts.

The orthodox *Q.E.D.* expresses ideas singly: " 'You are wrong, you are hideously wrong!' Adele burst out furiously."[18] "Melanctha" shows how a thought like this dissolves, on inspection, into a mingled succession of thoughts, each suffused with echoes from the last: " 'Oh Jeff dear,' said Melanctha, 'I sure was wrong to act so to you. It's awful hard for me ever to say it to you, I have been wrong in my acting to you, but I certainly was bad this time Jeff to you. It do certainly come hard to me to say it Jeff, but I certainly was wrong to go away from you the way I did it' " (p. 202).

In spite of the repetitive content, no two of these phrases are identical. In *Three Lives* especially, Stein is scrupulous on this point. Each pulse of experience brings a configuration not quite the image of what preceded it. For as James notes, once one dips into the "stream" of mental life one finds an extraordinary fact. Habitually we think of a particular object or sensation as identical each time we encounter it; the great labor of attention is to recognize. But one free look about, and it is evident that the mass of peripheral thoughts endlessly changes, conspiring with an unstable context to produce a different constellation of experience each time an object is encountered. "However we might in ordinary conversation speak of getting the same sensation again, we never in strict theoretic accuracy could do so; . . . [in] the river of elementary feeling . . . we never descend twice into the same stream" (p. 227). For Stein to allow herself exact repetitions would be to falsify the intricate mutations of consciousness.

I add these observations to what others have said on the subject of Stein and the "stream."[19] But again Stein's application of James involves a distortion. Partly because James originated the phrase

---

17. Gertrude Stein, *The Geographical History of America* (New York: Random House, 1936), p. 218.

18. *Q.E.D.*, in *Fernhurst*, p. 131.

19. See Richard Bridgman, *Gertrude Stein in Pieces* (New York: Oxford University Press, 1970), p. 102; Wendy Steiner, *Exact Resemblance to Exact Resemblance: The Literary Portraiture of Gertrude Stein* (New Haven: Yale University Press, 1978), pp. 46–49; Miller, *Gertrude Stein*, pp. 22, 90.

"stream of consciousness," critics have assumed that something in the *Psychology* could be construed as support for a diffuse or wandering literary style. But this is to force James artificially into a modernist mold by confusing his descriptive purposes with his values. James's chapter on the stream of thought is meant to describe a little-recognized form of mental experience, not to champion it; he urges us to open our eyes to the fluid periphery of consciousness, not to immerse ourselves in it at the expense of our rational grip on things. The last thing he would recommend would be for us to give up our habits of conception and consign ourselves to the flux of momentary impressions.

No one who had read the *Psychology* with unmixed sympathy would be led by it to a style like Stein's. A strict Jamesian would find some descriptive value, to be sure, in a literary portrayal of the stream of impressions; but to fashion entire novels from it must be judged a distortion of the proper work of consciousness. Wandering without a distinct purpose is for James the meanest possible use of the mind. It is a species of rest—something that occupies us between one focus and the next, or overcomes us when attention is tired. Whoever declines to rise from it has little to distinguish him from the infant or the brute.[20]

For the crises and essential moments of consciousness fall, for James, precisely where aimlessness terminates and attention finds its object. These are the instants that summon all our acts into being. "The whole drama of the voluntary life hinges on the amount of attention" (p. 429); "attention and effort" are indeed "two names for the same psychic fact" (p. 130). Nor is there any value in a life that never finds its focus in volition and action—in the "manly concrete deed" (p. 129).

James as the advocate of the "manly deed" is closer to the Victorians—to Carlyle, for example—than to any major twentieth-century author. A mind fully congenial to James could not fail to catch the force of these considerations. It must be judged unwholesome in the extreme to wrap the reader in vagrant impressions so that he is prevented from halting, grasping, and rising to a decisive or serviceable thought.

---

20. See *Principles of Psychology*, p. 129. The references that follow in the text are to *Psychology* as well.

James's voluntarism is inconsistent with an art that never seems to announce its point. Thus if we are inclined to view Stein's style as an outgrowth of his theories, we must recognize that she has altered the focus. She places exclusive emphasis on a part of consciousness that he views as secondary and, when exercised in isolation, debased.

Now there is an old argument for poetic indirection that might partially restore Stein to a Jamesian light. It is not out of the question to think of Stein's early style as issuing from the romantic notion that vagueness or incompleteness serves to mobilize the reader's own synthetic powers. If Stein leaves us in a dark place, it might be in order to exercise us in manufacturing light. The fact that consistent ideas emerge at all from *Three Lives* or *The Making of Americans* is evidence that special rewards are laid for the reader's cooperation.

All this strikes a note that James's own romanticism could only have approved. He applauded a certain amount of indeterminacy in his brother's fiction, perhaps on grounds like these.[21] To draw the reader through mingling impressions to his own act of synthesis is to promote a "compromise" between intellectual control and the flux of perceptions. For James there is no finer mental discipline than one that wrests harmonies from confusion.

But these considerations only force us back upon prior questions. If such indeed is an account of Stein's early program, it seems inadequate to explain what follows *The Making of Americans.* *Tender Buttons* and the portraits of the same period certainly use every device to lead conception astray, but it would be absurd to cast about in their pages for a hidden means of integration. "Hope in gates, hope in spoons, hope in doors, hope in tables, no hope in daintiness and determination"[22]—the purpose of such a sentence seems to be to foil synthesis altogether and accustom us to a special variety of chaos.

Here there is no mistaking a serious break with Jamesian formulations. Paradoxically, *Tender Buttons* is one of Stein's works that regularly inspire analogies with James. If we read these pieces as inventories of "the immediate data of . . . consciousness," they do

21. Perry, *Thought and Character,* I, 270–271.
22. *Tender Buttons,* in *Selected Writings,* p. 480.

seem close transcripts of the stream of thought.[23] But James himself
scarcely sympathized with an art that made the field of impressions
so hostile to conception; he deplored what he called literary "wandering."[24] Confusion exists for him as a ground for our partial
intellectual triumphs. It is surely a sign of a Jamesian training but
also a sign of insurrection that Stein comes to discourage whatever
in us makes sense of the shapeless succession of phenomena.

Thematically as well as stylistically, Stein is moving, in these
early years, from a narrative of intellectual synthesis to one of
confusion. One reason *The Making of Americans* is so long is that
it is the record of Stein's slow and difficult emancipation from
inherited methods of framing her perceptions. Time and again she
asks herself, to what extent may intellect extract formulas from the
data that move its way? *The Making of Americans* begins as an essay
in characterology; Stein sets out—optimistically—to make a record
of every type of person that has ever existed. That her gener-
alizations about human nature sustain her for most of the novel is the
mark of heroic effort. But she is constantly forced to ward off chaos,
and finally welcomes the chance to abandon the struggle.

In a characteristic moment of assurance early in the novel, Stein
explains the dialectic by which her impressions of people are
formed. "There is," she believes, "a bottom nature in every one";
as that bottom nature slowly reveals itself, a complete image of the
individual emerges. When that picture is inadequate, Stein is alerted
to the fact by conflicting data. But the alien elements slowly come
"to have meaning"; gradually the person takes shape again as "a
whole one to me" (pp. 309–310). In short, "each one is sometime
a whole one to me . . . It settles down inside me . . . Sometimes it
is disturbed . . . and then again it settles down in me . . . Always
I am then learning more and more" (p. 323).

This is a version of the compromise James describes between
stable ideas and novel impressions. But into these reflections Stein
throws a troubled note. Certain people, it appears, never quite
crystallize as "a whole one"; whenever Stein thinks she has fixed
them, they "go to pieces again inside me," leaving the suspicion
that even omniscience would be helpless to find a unity (p. 311). It

23. Michael J. Hoffman, *The Development of Abstractionism in the Writings of
Gertrude Stein* (Philadelphia: University of Pennsylvania Press, 1965), p. 195.
24. Perry, *Thought and Character*, II, 271.

is not long before this misgiving widens into a thoroughgoing loss of certainty. Perhaps everyone, not only the eccentric few, is "in pieces"; there is little reason to suppose that even our fittest formulations really capture their objects. "Every one was a whole one in me and now a little every one is in fragments inside me . . . Perhaps not any one really is a whole one" (p. 519). The most meticulous categories may prove to be nothing but fictions.

This surmise that all her science has missed its object inspires a number of panicky monologues. By the end of the novel Stein is thoroughly discouraged with formulas, and makes what proves to be a lasting break with science. What began in an ambitious vein of characterology ends on a tentative and strangely interior note.

It seems plausible to suppose that Stein took some encouragement, in her gradual abandonment of abstractions, from the epistemology of Bergson, which was circulating among the French avant-garde in the years around 1910.[25] James himself, actually, would not have discouraged whatever private instincts led Stein to distrust generalizations. But the direction in which these thoughts led her was radical and idiosyncratic.

Once modernists formed their judgment on the artificiality of intellectual categories, they reorganized their values in a number of ways. James, like Stein, sees science as a set of partial truths that never entirely captures a complex reality. His pluralism even inclines him to suspect that the world itself has no absolute form—that it is (to reapply Stein's term) "in pieces."[26] But for him this is hardly a reason to abandon science or concepts. As a pragmatist, he values ideas not for their ultimate truth but for their usefulness as "working hypotheses" to get us from one place to the next. We cling to them for practical reasons: if they fall short of omniscience, they still enable us, miraculously, to bestride the world, to control it instrumentally, to accomplish in it special tasks. The fact that it is impossible to grasp the last mysteries of the universe does not prevent the engineer from harnessing natural powers, or the moralist from mobilizing forces for the good.

Yet Stein has nothing of the temperament of pragmatism. If

25. See Bridgman, *Gertrude Stein in Pieces*, p. 134.

26. See William James, *A Pluralistic Universe*, in *Works of William James*, ed. Frederick Burkhardt (Cambridge, Mass.: Harvard University Press, 1977), pp. 20, 25–26.

theories are only fictions born of our practical natures, she sees no
reason to linger in that blindness. By the end of *The Making of
Americans* she is left with a theoretical apparatus sadly eroded by a
complicated world; yet no remnant of speculative interest prompts
her to apply patchwork and bring back the old characterology as a
merely serviceable framework for surveying the confusion. She is
interested not in instrumental half-truths but in essences or "bottom
natures," and if the conceptual net she has flung before her has
failed to draw up realities, she chooses to give over theories
altogether.

Her notebooks, preserved at Yale, show that during this period
she was in the midst of a prolonged debate with her brother Leo
about pragmatism. While Leo remained a staunch Jamesian, the
entries register Stein's increasing alienation from pragmatism. The
disagreement hangs precisely on the question of how one is to
approach the essential "reality" beyond the intellect—through formulas or through direct intuition. "When Leo said that all classi-
fication was teleological I knew I was not a pragmatist. I do not
believe that, I believe in reality as Cézanne or Caliban believe
in it."[27]

Stein sets out in *The Making of Americans* to chart her perceptions
of that "reality." As the novel progresses she becomes less interested in her initial quasi-scientific categories, and more in her immediate or private reflections. "I was seeing one to-day who reminded me very much of another one"; "This is now a little more
history of me and the kind of suffering I can have" (pp. 607, 573).
Generalizations continue to multiply, but are undercut by a new
form of verbal play that exposes them as hollow. Spates of contradictory statements, for example, appear: "He certainly was one
wondering about such a thing. He was certainly one not wondering
about such a thing. He certainly was one being existing inside him
to him, he was certainly one being not existing inside him to him"
(p. 811). "This was all true and this was all not true of this one" (p.
559). Or Stein may create meaninglessness not by contradiction but

27. Quoted by Leon Katz in "The First Making of *The Making of Americans:* A
Study Based on Gertrude Stein's Notebooks and Early Versions of Her Novel
(1902–8)," Ph.D. dissertation, Columbia University, 1963, p. 291. See Katz's
discussion of this entry. My analysis of the end of *The Making of Americans* is
indebted to Mr. Katz's dissertation.

by tautology: "When one is a young one one is a young one" (p. 806). In either case the effect is to undercut any impression of a genuine hypothesis or formula.

The same may be said of the many straightforward gener-alizations that do fill these later chapters: as interpretations of ex-perience, they are worthless. It is hardly an insight or even a thought to say that "Old ones come to be dead. Any one coming to be an old enough one comes to be a dead one. Old ones come to be dead ones" (p. 923). Stein is purifying language of its instrumental features. She uses words no longer as vehicles for findings or beliefs—the function pragmatism gives them—but as a means of communicating the mood or dim preoccupation of the moment.

Stein's displeasure with pragmatism is not hard to explain. Pro-visional concepts have value only if we prize the actions or exercises of will that they make possible. James would have been disturbed, had he lived further into the century, to find that while his psychol-ogy found echoes in literary quarters, the ideal of work attached to it lost force. James's voluntarism leads him to prize synthesis, attention, the useful postulate; he cannot embrace action as an ideal without exalting along with it whatever instrumental concepts help us to cut a path through the world. Stein is free to yield to the pressure of irrational experience because she finds no nobility in preparing a footing for the will; consciousness is not for her what it is for James, "a *fighter for ends*" (p. 144).

The same growing antipragmatism affects Stein's treatment of characters. *Three Lives* and *The Making of Americans* have an oblique Darwinism; they form themselves about issues of "suc-ceeding and failing," or the ways in which people "fight to win out" in the world.[28] The word "struggle" is ubiquitous. But there is an increasing ambivalence about the battle for success. Jeff Campbell in "Melanctha" knows how to survive (and to accomplish good works) by being cautious and selective—by using consciousness, in James's words, as a "fighter for ends." But Stein finds her center of value moving toward the unfit and irrational Melanctha, a vehicle for a "religion" of indiscriminate, selfless perception (p. 138). While James champions humanity's fighters and laborers, Stein is quietly passing over to the idle side of experience.

28. *Making of Americans*, p. 695; "Melanctha," p. 223.

The conversion is complete in *Two*, when Stein casts an uni-
dentified "she" as a passive vehicle for divine revelation: "She and
the water trickling . . . she with diminishing attention . . . She with
elucidating self-abnegation . . . she with anticipating praying . . .
she is the anticipation of expression having immaculate conception
. . . She is the complication of receiving, she is the articulation of
forgetting, . . . she is the inroad of releasing."[29] Illumination, here,
is a consequence of "self-abnegation." And "self-abnegation" is
one thing with "diminishing attention": when private interests are
renounced, attention ceases to perform its selective function. Stein
sees in aimlessness an escape from hardened self-regard. The same
considerations will later generate her opposition between "human
nature"—that part of us that proliferates vulgar hopes and
anxieties—and "the human mind," which is impersonal and
visionary.[30]

Among modernists, the project of "fighting for ends" that was so
warm an ideal for the nineteenth century sometimes seems to
amount to a mere spasm of egotism; and there is a revulsion against
will, activity, and the tyranny of habit that makes us blindly indus-
trious. It is not Stein's shapelessness in particular that makes her
modern; it is the ideal of disinterestedness that underlies it.[31]

The purpose of this essay has been to identify points of contact
between James's psychology and Stein's fiction, and to draw attention to the ambiguities and tensions that characterize their intel-

29. Gertrude Stein, *Two: Gertrude Stein and Her Brother and Other Early Portraits (1908–1912)* (New Haven: Yale University Press, 1951), pp. 107–108. Much
is elided here. I am informed by Leon Katz that the subject of this passage is Stein's
sister-in-law, Sarah Stein.

30. See *Geographical History*, pp. 134–135.

31. Indeed, one may be a formalist, superficially the antithesis of Stein, and share
the same ideal. For if the stream of impressions may be contemplated apart from its
relevance to our practical existence, so may an idea or a construct of the intellect.
So, for instance, argued Santayana, who like Stein reacted against James but whose
rebellion led him in a different direction—perhaps the more common direction for
modernists. In James's view, practical life advances by a perpetual "compromise"
between crude impressions and ideas or intellectual forms. Stein and Santayana
challenged pragmatism with a claim that aesthetic experience releases us from the
pressures of practical existence, and thus from the "compromise." Each singled out
a different part of mental life for disinterested contemplation; Stein devoted herself
to the flux of impressions, Santayana to the intellectual forms. See the exchange
between James and Santayana in Perry, *Thought and Character*, II, 319–320.

lectual relationship. Stein's attachment to James was more complex than that of a disciple, and had paradoxical consequences. His theories helped her to develop as a "modern" novelist, but she used him in ways he would not have anticipated. Her very modernism is finally what distances her from him. If she accepted his model of consciousness, she had her own notions as to the uses to which consciousness should be put.

Her rebellion may be summarized as a form of antipragmatism. Yet—to introduce a final ambiguity—James himself was capable of exhibiting an antipragmatist streak which anticipated the "disinterested" ideal of his modernist students. It is to be found not in his *Psychology* but in his religious writings. In his quasi-mystical vein, he celebrates mental idleness as a source of revelation.

The mystical tendency, and its tension with pragmatism, are evident in the two lectures published as *On Some of Life's Ideals*. In the first of these James considers the merits of a life of random and disinterested perception. "Your mystic, your dreamer, or your insolvent tramp or loafer" has no practical existence; yet his very failure to conceive interests widens his field of vision. Whitman, for example, James's favorite "tramp," approaches the mere spectacle of the universe "rapt with satisfied attention" (pp. 25, 33). By suspending selective attention, and the corresponding ability to act, Whitman achieves the fullest possible contact with a world that "never did . . . contain more of essential divinity, or of eternal meaning" than in the details of the present moment (p. 32).

There is little to distinguish this image of Whitman from Stein's Melanctha, or from the woman Stein describes in *Two* who becomes "the inroad of releasing" by exercising "diminishing attention." Yet James does not indulge this Steinian strain long. In the companion address, his pragmatism reasserts itself; the mystical element of experience moves out of view. James makes a more characteristic plea for a life shaped by ends, and directs strong words against people who fail to conceive ideals and to act on them. As if in half-conscious apology for the celebration of aimlessness in the first lecture, he shifts the focus back from the play of perception to the "manly" virtues that accompany the exercise of the will (p. 85).[32]

32. I wish to thank Robert A. Ferguson, Paul Goldstein, Janet Silver, and Robert von Hallberg for helpful comments on an earlier draft of this chapter.

Contrived Lives: Joyce and Lawrence

No one is bad enough for this world.

This Brechtian formulation from the *Three Penny Opera* is specifically a justification for a rogue hero,[1] but some comparable assumption informs much, perhaps most, of the imaginative literature to
which we give serious attention. A simple shift—the world isn't
good enough for anyone—makes the formulation instantly more
familiar but does not really change it substantively. Either way, we
have a working assumption that man and the world to which he is
born and in which he must find both himself and his way are
essentially incompatible. As an assumption, this inevitably tends to
bend the novel toward the irony that Georg Lukacs has called its
"objectivity" and the "normative mentality" of the attempt to make
extended narrative of "the contingent world and the problematic
individual."[2] By now though, I think, irony is assumed to be the
"normative mentality" of all modern art and not just of the novel;
and yet there is also a significant alternative strain in modern story-

1. "Denn für dieses Leben / Ist der Mensch nicht Schlecht genug" (Bertolt
Brecht, "Das Lied von der Unzulänglichkeit Menschlichen Strebens," in *Die Drei-
groschenoper* [Berlin: Suhrkamp, 1955], Act III, Scene 7).
2. Georg Lukács, *The Theory of the Novel*, trans. Anna Bostock (Cambridge,
Mass.: MIT Press, 1971), pp. 90, 84, and 78.

making in which existences better than any readers are likely to have
experienced are not simply implied but substantially created. These
fictions—I use the less restrictive term because the example to
which I will give most space is a play—cannot perhaps quite banish
irony, but they can stringently limit its immediate presence.

This other vein is found in the work of both Joyce and Lawrence.
For a long time these two great writers of the early part of this
century were cast only as polar opposites and antagonists, a view
encouraged too by the expressed attitudes of each toward the other.
Now, when the noise of those battles has grown dim, it has become
possible to think of them as interilluminating,[3] though what I see in
that particular light still reveals difference for me more vividly than
it does communality. And yet in their very different ways, Joyce
and Lawrence are our two great monogamous imaginations. This
puts them in some common critical relation to the modern temper,
not least because monogamy posits duration for a relationship notoriously subject to attrition, and duration makes inexorably for the
multiple view that is the defining condition for irony. Each of these
imperious writers takes it upon himself in certain works to oppose
this compounded tendency—that is, to thwart what is supposed to
be man's nature and, in the process, to limit the domain of irony.
Each—Joyce in *Exiles* and then in very different but consequent
fashion in *Ulysses* and Lawrence most directly in *Women in Love*—
imagines a monogamy that is an arduously arrived at, extreme

3. F. R. Leavis recalled that at the time of Lawrence's death in 1930 "if you took
Joyce for a major creative writer, then, like Mr. Eliot, you had no use for Lawrence,
and if you judged Lawrence a great writer, then you could hardly take a sustained
interest in Joyce" (*D. H. Lawrence Novelist* [London: Chatto and Windus, 1955] p.
10). In a letter to Aldous and Maria Huxley, Lawrence wrote that he found in the
early portions of *Finnegans Wake* published in the journal *transition* "nothing but old
fags and cabbage-stumps of quotations from the Bible and the rest, stewed in the
juice of deliberate journalistic dirty-mindedness" (*The Collected Letters of D. H.
Lawrence,* ed. Harry T. Moore [New York: Viking Press, 1962], II, 1075). There is
no real evidence that Joyce ever read Lawrence, but he did express pique that the
efforts to lift the ban on *Ulysses* should be confused with similar efforts on behalf
of *Lady Chatterley's Lover,* "a piece of propaganda in favour of something which
outside of D. H. L.'s country at least, makes all the propaganda for itself" (*Letters
of James Joyce,* ed. Stuart Gilbert [New York: Viking Press, 1966], I, 309). Robert
Kiely in his *Beyond Egotism* (Cambridge, Mass.: Harvard University Press, 1980)
has amply and particularly demonstrated some of the interilluminations afforded by
comparisons of Joyce, Lawrence, and Virginia Woolf.

contrivance to serve as a bulwark against the inadequacy of the world as given. In each case too, the arduousness of the effort is the measure of a necessity which everything suggests is known to the author and not simply ascribed to his created characters. The monogamy imagined by each author, however, and the means imagined to bring it to fictive existence, are profoundly dissimilar. Neither the similarity nor the difference between Joyce and Lawrence in these regards can be fully appreciated without appropriate attention to *Exiles,* the odd play that Joyce wrote in the interval between *A Portrait of the Artist as a Young Man* and *Ulysses* and in which he dealt more directly with some aspects of his own character than he did in either of those better-known works.

The Joycean version of durable monogamy requires betrayal. It also assumes that happiness is not repeatable, which gives critical importance to memory and places past time and present time in a relationship in which past always has primacy over present in value as well as in order of occurrence. Moreover, or even consequently, the Joycean monogamy has the imagination as its most active, in fact its nearly exclusive, realm. These convictions and characteristics, best known as the givens of the marriage of Leopold and Molly Bloom in *Ulysses,* are arrived at by stages in the work that precedes *Ulysses*—*Dubliners, A Portrait of the Artist as a Young Man,* and most particularly *Exiles.* The irony of *Dubliners* (the irony particularly of the three opening stories, each in the first person, which Joyce called stories of "my childhood" presumably to signify their autobiographical provenance)[4] and the irony of *Portrait* is, in each case, in significant and sometimes brutal part an irony against self. This might be called impure irony, since it suggests that the multiple view on which it depends is not inevitable, that one of the two or several views of what is happening is more correct or healthier than the others. Impure irony is interested irony—it has a corrective purpose or concern which pure irony will not entertain.

Recurrently, the irony of *Portrait* and of *Dubliners* is a form of protection for the reader (and presumably for the author) from the confusions suffered by the fictive characters. Irony is always distancing, but the sanitizing element in the irony of these early Joy-

4. See my "*Dubliners* and Erotic Expectation," *Twentieth Century Literature in Retrospect,* ed. Reuben A. Brower, Harvard English Studies no. 2 (Cambridge, Mass.: Harvard University Press, 1971), pp. 3–26.

cean fictions is not merely a matter of distance. A curative impulse is palpably at work here, based presumably on a conviction that the exercise of irony can heal or perhaps even prevent injury. The very different irony of *Ulysses* implies no such reductive notion.

This difference between early and later Joycean irony is immense. In *Ulysses,* Stephen, Bloom, and Molly are each informed with aspects of Joyce's own character. By apportioning himself thus among all three of his principals, he assigns constituent parts to the sensibility at war with itself and allows each part then to achieve its own extravagance, an incomplete but vivid realization. That very division can perhaps also be thought of as a form of irony; but an earlier version of it, probably formative for *Ulysses,* is found in *Exiles,* and *Exiles* is the least ironic as well as the least known work in the Joyce canon.

This odd play dramatizes what is presumably a version of Joyce's understanding of his own inner conflicts by creating, somewhat as in a morality play, two male characters, Richard Rowan and Robert Hand, who represent, both emblematically and actively, conflicting dispositions. Their opposition manifests itself particularly in erotic terms, as a contest for possession of the same woman and the opposition of very different terms of possession. The ideal conception of the contest creates opportunities for something very like formal debate[5]—an ideal formality that is but one of the distinct matters that are neglected when *Exiles* is dismissed as Joyce's tribute to Ibsen, his imitation of *When We Dead Awaken.*

The three women of the play—Beatrice, Brigid, and Bertha—are also variant and complementary types. They too are components of an impossible whole, and each is defined both by what she is and by what she is not in relation to the others. Joyce's intention is signaled when he gives them, as he does the men, names each beginning with the same letter. Of the three, though, Bertha is by all odds the most significant, the only one whose character has large resonance. Brigid, the servant of Bertha and Richard, is little but an attendant figure, patient, endowed with a certain folk wisdom, but erotically passed by and therefore necessarily a minor character in a drama of this nature. But Beatrice too, though she is linked by an

5. Much, that is, as a similar opposition becomes dramatic debate in the D. H. Lawrence short novel "The Ladybird." See my article "The Continuity of Lawrence's Short Novels," *The Hudson Review,* 11, no. 2 (Summer 1958), 205.

elaborate set of Joycean devices, some of them numerological, to Dante's Beatrice, and though she has in the past had an erotic relationship with each of the men, Robert and Richard, has only relatively minor importance in the present time of the play. Her effective character is chiefly negative: she is unlike Bertha. Even the fact that she is an intellectual as Bertha is not is effectively a negative characteristic.[6]

Everything that happens to or is done by Richard and Robert, that makes up their contest and their complementary typology, occurs in reference to Bertha. She cannot be said to cause it to happen, exactly, for she is largely passive, but her passivity is accorded positive value. Beatrice's activity—even that she is instrumental in causing Richard's return to Ireland from Italy—is made vitally negative by contrast, integral to what she is not or does not possess, to the absence of that combination of beauty, power, and dignity that Bertha possesses in potent fashion. The primacy of what Bertha is or seems to be to the two men is put beyond doubt. By the play's end she has managed without apparently even intending to do so, managed passively, to take permanent possession of both their imaginations. And the play offers no opportunity to question or doubt this permanence—the situation is invulnerable presumably even to irony.

Of the two men, Richard and Robert, one is also the dominant figure, but the complementarity of the men is more complex and pressing than that of the women. The advantage lies again with the more passive figure, Richard, except that in this case it might be more accurate to say the less active figure. Richard's relative inactivity is not exactly passive. He will act in limited but critical fashion in the service of the imaginative life that he requires as his active realm. In the richly interesting notes to *Exiles,* Joyce offers this schema for the relationship between the two men: "Richard—an automystic / Robert—an automobile."[7] He also assigns Robert to the discipleship of the Marquis de Sade, Richard to that of Freiherr Sacher von Masoch. These assignments suggest not only

6. Only Bertha sees Beatrice as being superior to herself in this regard. She envies Beatrice the intellectual relationship she has or has had with Richard that she, Bertha, cannot have herself.

7. James Joyce, *Exiles* (New York: Viking Press, 1951), pp. 113 and 124. All further quotations, identified by page numbers in the text, are from this edition.

difference and complementarity but the related further possibility that each conception of character finds its source in the same divided sensibility. Such a complementarity is suggested within the play itself by associating Richard and Robert respectively with *su* and *giu* (up and down), concepts which broaden to emblematize a fall from a higher world and an emergence from a lower world.

The mystic-masochist achieves a victory over the sensualist-sadist that is too costly to celebrate, but its cost is integral to his intention and not an accidental consequence. Joyce does not allow the possibility of a complete and unwanting life, and Richard's achievement depends on his both willing and causing himself to be wounded. The action of *Exiles*—whatever it is that does or does not happen and its consequences—sounds even more contrived in summary than it seems in the play itself, where it is nonetheless sufficiently contrived to make successful staging difficult and infrequent. Robert endeavors to seduce Bertha, to whom he has long been attracted but who has for nine years been the common-law wife of Richard, his oldest and most significant friend. Richard and Bertha have been in Italy for most of these nine years, have had a son named Archie, and have just returned to Ireland when the play begins. In this time abroad their relationship has suffered not injury so much as attrition, more or less fair wear and tear rather than careless damage. But the consequent loss is nonetheless not easily borne by either Richard or Bertha, and when she tells him shortly after their return that Robert has confessed a passion for her and is pressing her for response, he instructs her to allow Robert to continue to court her and to continue to tell him, Richard, what occurs. Eventually Bertha keeps an assignation with Robert just after Richard has informed Robert that he knows what is happening. Only the ambiguous preliminaries of the meeting between Bertha and Robert take place on stage, and the next morning Richard, in a calculated reversal of their understanding, refuses to allow Bertha to tell him what has happened in the further course of that meeting. "I have wounded my soul for you," he tells her, "a deep wound of doubt which can never be healed. I can never know, never in this world. I do not wish to know or to believe. I do not care. It is not in the darkness of belief that I desire you. But in restless living wounding doubt" (p. 112). Attrition has been reversed and desire restored at the cost of a willed perpetual pain.

More astonishing still, Robert too is fated not to know what has actually happened. Having decided under suggestion from Bertha that he had dreamed that she was his, that this is the essential truth of whatever curious transaction has taken place between them, he then says: "In all my life only that dream is real. I forget the rest" (p. 106). The primacy of passive (imaginative) life over active life has been established, and so, relatedly, has the triumph of willed conditions of life over more ordinary experience. Richard's relationship to Bertha is now obsessive, unwithering, and invulnerable to irony; and the activist Robert has had his characteristic capabilities severely reduced, and his keenest life too is now also to be an obsessively imagined life. No such security though, however uncomfortable, is allowed Bertha. She is left instead with another, less contrived and more realistic Joycean possibility for permanence. When the innocent Brigid exhorts her not to cry, tells her that "good times" will come again, she replies: "No, Brigid, that time comes only once in a lifetime. The rest of life is good for nothing except to remember that time" (p. 91).

Exiles offers a version of persistent monogamy too extreme for much repetition. But despite the gross difference between *Exiles* and *Ulysses* in genre and in scale, the latter work then depends fundamentally on a variant deployment of something very like these same schematized terms. Leopold Bloom and the Stephen Dedalus of *Ulysses* are descendants of Robert Hand and Richard Rowan respectively; and Molly, though far less certainly, of Bertha. There is, however, no contest for dominance in *Ulysses,* and instead of a contrived betrayal there is an actual betrayal (though mitigated or limited in highly contrived fashion). Glory in the novel belongs *only* to memory, and the significant present life is Bloom's material existence, a life that proceeds, though imaginatively also, from what is seen, heard, smelled, tasted, and touched. Even Stephen, the less important of the two major male figures, is at his most nearly engaging when he not only struggles against his postures ("God we simply must dress the character") and his fears (of dogs and water), but struggles particularly to strengthen his hold on the material world: to see "a porter-bottle . . . stogged to its waist, in the cakey sand dough" rather than "crucified shirts" on a line.[8] This

8. James Joyce, *Ulysses* (New York: Vintage, 1961), p. 41. All further quotations, identified by page numbers in the text, are from this edition.

hold on the world's substance and simpler processes is what Bloom possesses surely, an orientation that depends on his senses first, but then on his sensual curiosity and imagination. Looking at the cat, he wonders what he looks like to her, wonders about the function of her whiskers, wonders about the roughness of her tongue. By this process of ordinary wonder, he comes to know many things.

The difference felt most immediately, I think, between *Ulysses* and Joyce's earlier work is the relative but decisive relaxation of the prose. This pervasive change is critical to the novel's amplitude, and it seems reasonable to relate both relaxation and amplitude to a greater acceptance of the given conditions of life without resort either to the sanitizing ironies of *Portrait* and *Dubliners* or to the contrived constructions that become an alternative to irony in *Exiles*. The more relaxed registration of the world—the broader criteria of what is worthy of registration—reaches an ultimate of sorts in the catechism of "Ithaca," in which anything can be of sufficient interest for inclusion:

Did the process of divestiture continue?
Sensible of a benignant persistent ache in his footsoles he extended his foot to one side and observed the creases, protuberances and salient points caused by foot pressure in the course of walking repeatedly in several different directions, then, inclined, he disnoded the laceknots, unhooked and loosened the laces, took off each of his two boots for the second time, detached the partially moistened right sock through the fore part of which the nail of his great toe had again effracted, raised his right foot and, having unhooked a purple elastic sock suspender, took off his right sock, placed his unclothed right foot on the margin of the seat of his chair, picked at and gently lacerated the protruding part of the great toenail, raised the part lacerated to his nostrils and inhaled the odour of the quick, then with satisfaction threw away the lacerated unguical fragment.   (pp. 711–712)

The irony here is very different from that of the earlier fiction, and offers no protection to the reader from the confusions of the character. It is generated by the assumption implicit in the mode of narration—an assumption in regard to which we retain, and are intended to, some stubborn skepticism—that not only is everything of interest, but that anything is of more or less equal interest to anything else. Something related to this assertion of uncontrived, nonhierarchical value occurs too when we are given a catalogue of particulars of the "ultimate ambition" in which all Bloom's "concurrent and consecutive ambitions now coalesced" (p. 712), the monstrously comfy "Bloom Cottage. Saint Leopold's. Flowerville" (p. 714). This is the conscious dream as opposed to the dreams generated by the unconscious in "Circe," but it is no less quintessentially Bloomian. Similarly, the metamorphoses of Bloom that take place in "Circe" are not necessarily to be accorded any primacy over the image he holds of himself in Bloom Cottage: "In loose allwool garments with Harris tweed cap, price 8/6, and useful garden boots with elastic gussets and wateringcan, planting aligned young firtrees, syringing, pruning, staking, sowing hayseed, trundling a weedladen wheelbarrow without excessive fatigue at sunset amid the scent of newmown hay, ameliorating the soil, multiplying wisdom, achieving longevity" (pp. 714–15).

Ulysses manages extraordinary registration of the ordinary world, both the external world and the inner world of the psyche, first by a tactical division of character comparable to that employed in *Exiles,* and then by an ironic acceptance that depends on this division. In this Joycean world though, there is little experience sufficient to human need except in memory, fantasy, or dream life, each of which is modulated by irony. There is, however, a way of reading *Ulysses* that seems intended to make as little as possible of this insufficiency. In the generous loose bag of *The Pound Era,* Hugh Kenner has a wonderful meditation on the effect of the archeological discoveries of Schliemann and others on the way in which the *Odyssey* was viewed and read in the late nineteenth and early twentieth centuries. In the light of these new finds, Kenner says, Homer "presented a world as real as Dublin's bricks." Kenner finds this influence palpable in Samuel Butler's translation of the *Odyssey,* one of the two translations supposedly known to Joyce. Butler, in the odd essay in which he claims the authorship of the *Odyssey* for Nausicaa, argues that "no artist can reach an ideal higher than his own best actual environment"—an argument, Kenner says, with which "Joyce would have explicitly concurred."[9]

Perhaps. But if Joyce was writing about "his own best actual environment" in *Ulysses,* the notion of "best" is rather limited when he writes to his aunt Mrs. William Murray for details about old

9. Hugh Kenner, *The Pound Era* (Berkeley: University of California Press, 1971), pp. 44–48.

Dublin acquaintances that he might incorporate in his novel and concludes a list of specific questions with the exhortation[10] to "get an ordinary sheet of foolscap and a pencil and scribble any God damn drivel you may remember about these people."[11] To talk about "best" need not seem wrong, but it can seem a tendentious confusion. The matrix of *Ulysses* could after a certain point apparently accommodate anything at all that was there—or anything that what was there might cause to be imagined; and whatever honor one may be moved to pay Bloom, he was for Joyce, most insistently, an ordinary person. "Is it possible," Joyce asks Mrs. Murray, "for an ordinary person to climb over the area railings of no 7 Eccles street, either from the path or the steps, lower himself from the lowest part of the railings till his feet are within 2 feet or 3 of the ground and drop unhurt?"[12] This is how Bloom will get Stephen and himself into the house after he discovers that he has left his latchkey in the "pocket of the trousers which he had worn on the day but one preceding" (p. 668), and Joyce does not wish it to appear a more than ordinary exploit.

Such fidelity to what is there, whatever its nature, inspires both confidence and a kind of moral exhilaration. It can also though, in the Joycean example, be on the edge of self-destruction. If we perceive that the attention to the actual can be accorded more or less indiscriminately to any detail of the actual, and if the expression of that attention tends to inflation or to call attention to itself as method, how does this affect the value we attach to registration? The question is, I think, necessary but not readily answerable.

In *Ulysses* extraordinary experience, experience that exceeds the limits of the diurnal actual, is chiefly but not exclusively erotic experience, and is registered as memory in "Penelope" and dream in "Circe" but never as an immediate present. Not all erotic experience in *Ulysses* is accorded this heightened or privileged status, but a significant proportion of the readers who find a positive view of life expressed in the novel attach special or even unique importance to Molly's soliloquy, a focus of attention encouraged by its position at the very end of the book as well as by Joyce's statement to Frank

10. To which Robert M. Adams has called interesting attention in *Surface and Symbol* (Oxford: Oxford University Press, 1962), p. 247.

11. Joyce, *Letters*, I, 174.

12. Joyce, *Letters*, I, 175.

Budgen, with whom he was in general more candid than he was with many other friends and admirers, that *"Penelope* is the clou of the book."[13]

There is basis though for a variant view of the value to be attached to Molly's soliloquy. The issue is not whether its effect is emetic or aphrodisiac,[14] but rather what importance is to be given to such matters as the meanness of much of Molly's thought and feeling or the situation of husband and wife head to foot (or tail) in bed, each engaged in memories and fantasies in which the other is ultimately the second principal (to this extent another version of the obsessively persistent monogamy of *Exiles*), but managing only the most minimal present exchange—what might be called a residual monogamy. My own reading of the book would go along with those critics who find more that is positive and even redemptive in Bloom's ordinary vitality than they do in Molly's sexuality.[15] I can see that this may be the substitution of one form of sentimentality for another, but I don't think it is that. Proper appreciation of Bloom, however, should recognize that the irony of *Ulysses,* unsullied by any sanitizing impulse, is as much an implicit statement of the inadequacy of life as offered as is the contrivance of *Exiles,* even though its literary generation is infinitely richer. It is a mode of acceptance of the world that is at the same time a protest, but the protest—for the record and not in the interest of change—is part of a comic perception that can be shared as the ideal life of *Exiles* is, at best, unlikely to be.

The postures and relationship of Bloom and Molly in "Penelope"—each as it were circling imaginatively about the other—could be called a form of star-polarity. The ascription would, however, be a rather waggish violation of Birkin's use of that term in *Women in Love* (a use to which Lawrence gives entire consent) to emblematize the relationship he aspires to achieve with Ursula. The aspiration is one to which Joyce would, I imagine, have granted neither reality nor desirability. Each—Lawrence in *Women in Love* and Joyce in *Ulysses*—animated a great novel with the idea of a monogamy

13. Joyce, *Letters,* I, 170.

14. The distinction made by United States District Judge John M. Woolsey on December 6, 1933, in the decision that lifted the ban on *Ulysses.* See *Ulysses,* p. xii.

15. In particular S. L. Goldberg in *The Classical Temper* (New York: Barnes and Noble, 1961).

resistant to attrition, but the domains of those conditions of monogamy are very different. The bond between husband and wife in *Ulysses* (following *Exiles*) is one of imaginative obsession with little or no room for continuing development, but what Lawrence was trying to make palpable in *Women in Love* was the struggle of a husband and wife to create a continuing relationship in the everyday material and spiritual circumstances of married life, and a relationship that was specifically freeing and not obsessive. This was to be in some ways a transcending relationship, but one that had strong analogies and partial continuities nonetheless with marriages Lawrence recollected or had heard about, that he could admire, celebrate, and entertain as strong though not complete examples because they allowed vivid and vital lives.

However much irony may be the novel's "normative mentality," there is remarkably little palpable irony in either *Sons and Lovers* or *The Rainbow,* two of the three major novels (*Women in Love* is the third) Lawrence wrote "while he still believed in the notion of marriage."[16] The effect of this absence is enormous, and so too is the contrast it affords to Joyce. For any reader able to hold in mind for implicit comparison the well-known first appearance of Leopold Bloom beginning his day making breakfast for himself and Molly, Lawrence's description of Morel making breakfast for himself and his wife in *Sons and Lovers* indicates this important difference I think so decisively that it is worth citing at considerable length:

He always made his own breakfast. Being a man who rose early and had plenty of time he did not, as some miners do, drag his wife out of bed at six o'clock. At five, sometimes earlier, he woke, got straight out of bed, and went downstairs. When she could not sleep, his wife lay waiting for this time, as for a period of peace. The only real rest seemed to be when he was out of the house.

He went downstairs in his shirt and then struggled into his pit-trousers, which were left on the hearth to warm all night. There was always a fire, because Mrs. Morel raked. And the first sound in the house was the bang, bang of the poker against the raker, as Morel smashed the remainder of the coal to make the kettle, which was filled and left on the hob, finally boil. His cup and knife and fork, all he wanted except just the food, was laid ready on

16. Marvin Mudrick, "Lawrence," *The Hudson Review,* 27, no. 3 (Autumn 1974), 427.

the table on a newspaper. Then he got his breakfast, made the tea, packed the bottom of the doors with rugs to shut out the draught, piled a big fire, and sat down to an hour of joy. He toasted his bacon on a fork and caught the drops of fat on his bread; then he put the rasher on his thick slice of bread, and cut off chunks with a clasp-knife, poured his tea into his saucer, and was happy. With his family about, meals were never so pleasant. He loathed a fork: it is a modern introduction which has still scarcely reached common people. What Morel preferred was a clasp-knife. Then, in solitude, he ate and drank, often sitting, in cold weather, on a little stool with his back to the warm chimney-piece, his food on the fender, his cup on the hearth. And then he read the last night's newspaper—what of it he could—spelling it over laboriously. He preferred to keep the blinds down and the candle lit even when it was daylight; it was the habit of the mine.

At a quarter to six he rose, cut two thick slices of bread and butter, and put them in the white calico snap-bag. He filled his tin bottle with tea. Cold tea without milk or sugar was the drink he preferred for the pit. Then he pulled off his shirt, and put on his pit-singlet, a vest of thick flannel cut low round the neck, and with short sleeves like a chemise.

Then he went upstairs to his wife with a cup of tea because she was ill, and because it occurred to him.

"I've brought thee a cup o' tea, lass," he said.

"Well, you needn't, for you know I don't like it," she replied.

"Drink it up; it'll pop thee off to sleep again."

She accepted the tea. It pleased him to see her take it and sip it.

"I'll back my life there's no sugar in," she said.

"Yi—there's one big 'un," he replied, injured.

"It's a wonder," she said, sipping again.

She had a winsome face when her hair was loose. He loved her to grumble at him in this manner. He looked at her again, and went, without any sort of leave-taking. He never took more than two slices of bread and butter to eat in the pit, so an apple or an orange was a treat to him. He always liked it when she put one out for him. He tied a scarf round his neck, put on his great, heavy boots, his coat, with the big pocket, that carried his snap-bag and his bottle of tea, and went forth into the fresh morning air, closing, without locking, the door behind him. He loved the early morning, and the walk across the fields. So he appeared at the pit-top, often with a stalk from the hedge between his teeth, which he chewed all day to keep his mouth moist, down the mine, feeling quite as happy as when he was in the field.[17]

17. D. H. Lawrence, *Sons and Lovers* (New York: Viking Press, 1958), pp. 26–28. Copyright 1913 by Thomas Seltzer, Inc. Reprinted by permission of Viking Penguin, Laurence Pollinger Ltd., and the Estate of Frieda Lawrence Ravagli.

The difference between this and the account of Bloom preparing a kidney, toast, and tea and bringing Molly her adulterous mail, a difference that is all but absolute, cannot be attributed to greater accuracy of attention in one than in the other. Joyce's attention to Bloom's activities is constantly ironic, however, and Lawrence's attention to Morel's never is. Lawrence is in fact describing Morel's activities in minute, nonironic detail in order to instruct us, and the justification for this instruction is a conviction that Morel's world at this moment in his life, whatever the disappointments it contains, is more or less commensurate with his needs. Morel is living fully. The words "happy," "joy," "loved," are used easily, convincingly, without embarrassment. Live if you can, Lawrence is telling us, as this man lives.[18] Morel's life is not without its pains, but in Lawrence's early fiction even the most painful experience is celebrated because it is vitally painful.

This confidence did not last him, however, even for his rather brief forty-five years. The two great celebratory accounts of marital trouble, *Sons and Lovers* and *The Rainbow,* are followed by *Women in Love,* which Raymond Williams has called Lawrence's "masterpiece of loss [that] enacts this loss in itself."[19] The married life Lawrence endorsed and in at least substantial part vivified in *Women in Love,* intended to preserve those aspects of marriage celebrated in the earlier two novels but to free marriage from those other characteristics of conflict and strain that made it "more of a duel than a duet,"[20] is as extreme a contrivance in its own way as is the married life of Richard and Bertha at the end of *Exiles.* In *Exiles,* however, the condition of the continuing marriage is a perfect, presumably permanent imaginative obsession created and imposed by Richard; whereas in *Women in Love,* it is an admittedly imperfect but jointly achieved condition of conscious daily life, the fragility and cost of which are palpable to both principals. Similarly or relatedly, though the registration of the actual in each of these works about marriage is highly purposeful and, consequently, comparatively narrow, the two actualities are decisively different, and

18. This is apparent, I think, even if in the struggle between Morel and his wife the weight of the novel seems most often to be on the side of the wife. Lawrence is reported, perhaps apocryphally, to have said late in his life that had he had *Sons and Lovers* to write again, he would have made Morel the hero of the book.

19. Raymond Williams, *The English Novel from Dickens to Lawrence* (Oxford: Oxford University Press, 1970), p. 182.

20. D. H. Lawrence, *The White Peacock* (London: Heinemann, 1955), p. 298.

the comparative narrowness must be measured in relation to the work that followed *Exiles* but that preceded *Women in Love*.

The strategic locations of these works of contrivance in their authors' respective careers, that is, are as different as possible. The tactical division of characters in *Exiles,* a sport in Joyce's canon and the most constrained of his works, was probably critical to the new expansiveness of *Ulysses*. In Lawrence's career, however, *Women in Love* signals and demonstrates the closing down of an earlier fullness.

Irony certainly occupies a more palpable place in *Women in Love* than it does in either *Sons and Lovers* or *The Rainbow*. The almost tyrannically controlled conversation about marriage that opens the novel is a sustained sequence of ironies.

Ursula and Gudrun Brangwen sat one morning in the window-bay of their father's house in Beldover, working and talking. Ursula was stitching a piece of brightly-coloured embroidery, and Gudrun was drawing upon a board which she held on her knee. They were mostly silent, talking as their houghts strayed through their minds.

"Ursula," said Gudrun, "don't you *really want* to get married?" Ursula laid her embroidery on her lap and looked up. Her face was calm and considerate.

"I don't know," she replied. "It depends how you mean."

Gudrun was slightly taken aback. She watched her sister for some moments.

"Well," she said, ironically, "it usually means one thing! But don't you think, anyhow, you'd be—" she darkened slightly—"in a better position than you are in now."

A shadow came over Ursula's face.

"I might," she said. "But I'm not sure."

Again Gudrun paused, slightly irritated. She wanted to be quite definite.

"You don't think one needs the *experience* of having been married?" she asked.

"Do you think it need *be* an experience?" replied Ursula.

"Bound to be, in some way or other," said Gudrun, coolly. "Possibly undesirable, but bound to be an experience of some sort."

"Not really," said Ursula. "More likely to be the end of experience."

Gudrun sat very still, to attend to this.

"Of course," she said, "There's *that* to consider." This brought the conversation to a close. Gudrun, almost angrily, took up her rubber and began to rub out part of her drawing. Ursula stitched absorbedly.[21]

21. D. H. Lawrence, *Women in Love* (New York: Viking Press, 1960), p. 1.

Though we are told that Gudrun speaks ironically, it is possible or even probable that the fuller and more interesting ironies of the exchange can be no more than suspected on a first reading and must wait instead for a second reading in which what follows is already known.

Even at its fullest though, even in *Women in Love,* the place Lawrence allows to irony is distinctly limited compared to its place in, say, *Ulysses.* Yet this limited presence is sufficient to illustrate how profoundly different Lawrentian and Joycean irony are, not just in character but also in function. What had by the time of *Ulysses* become for Joyce an expansive mode was for Lawrence always a mode of closure. In any of its multiple modes and forms, however, irony is likely to be a way to reveal fixity even under the guise of apparent change. The serial ironies of *Portrait,* for example, reveal that the changes and triumphs that Stephen heralds with exhilaration at the end of each of the first four chapters are little more than illusion. The relative absence of irony in Lawrence's best fiction, therefore, should be related to his refusal to allow that we live as we do by necessity,[22] his conviction that there was—had been and had to be again—a life that was endorsable. The only possible equivalent for Joyce to these married lives attributed by Lawrence not only to Morel but to many other denizens of the midlands in the early fiction—lives that could be endorsed without irony—was the ideal life of Richard Rowan in *Exiles.* If the prescribed life of Birkin and Ursula in *Women in Love* also has something of the character of ideal rather than substantial existence, that is another indication of how much this prescription was Lawrence's last desperate resort or contrivance to keep alive his belief in monogamy.[23]

22. This is a significant part of the dislike Lawrence felt for so many of his English contemporaries. For example: "I hate Bennett's resignation. Tragedy ought really to be a great kick at misery. But *Anna of the Five Towns* seems like an acceptance—so does all the modern stuff since Flaubert. I hate it" (Lawrence, *Letters,* I, 150). Or: "Conrad . . . makes me furious—and the stories are *so* good. But why this giving in before you start, that pervades Conrad and all such folks—the Writers among the Ruins. I can't forgive Conrad for being so sad and for giving in" (Lawrence, *Letters,* I, 152).

23. Jay Cantor, John Kelleher, and Frank Kermode have read earlier versions of this essay, which now profits from their suggestions. These good friends, however, are not to be charged with any persistent stupidities by which it may still be disfigured.

THOMAS MALLON

The Great War and Sassoon's Memory

The stage nerves Siegfried Sassoon may have experienced before addressing the Poetry Club at the Harvard Union in the spring of 1920 were mitigated by the formidable assurances of Miss Amy Lowell, who had recently written to tell him that he "was the one man whom the Harvard undergraduates wanted to hear."[1] Such assurances were more necessary than might be supposed; Sassoon had discovered upon arriving in New York in January that, little more than a year after the Armistice, more than enough British authors were touring America to fill the already slackening desire to hear from and about the soldier-poets. In fact, the war was sufficiently receding in people's minds that Sassoon had to rely on himself, rather than the Pond Lyceum Bureau, to scare up most of his engagements. But at Harvard Sassoon did find a receptive audience for the last of his pleas against militarism, and he finished his tour feeling that his "diminutive attempt to make known to Americans an interpretation of the war as seen by the fighting men" had been "not altogether ineffective" (*SJ*, p. 305).

In some respects the Harvard appearance was the end of a phase in Sassoon's life that began in 1917 with the appearance of *The Old Huntsman* and his public statement against the war, climaxed with

1. Siegfried Sassoon, *Siegfried's Journey* (New York: Viking, 1946), p. 304. Hereafter cited as *SJ;* further quotations are identified by page numbers in the text.

81

the publication of *Counter-Attack* on June 27, 1918, and had its denouement in his post-Armistice lecture tour. In less than four years he went from being a sometime versifier to something of an international literary celebrity, the man who more than any other had brought about the post-Somme poetic rebellion in diction, subject matter, and outlook. Without question these were the most public years of his life, and although he would live for nearly another half century, nothing in his later works would so impress itself on readers' minds and literary history as the angry ironies of "Base Details," "The General," "To Any Dead Officer," and "Suicide in the Trenches."

He would continue publishing poetry into the 1960's, including some extremely beautiful and neglected religious verse in the last decades of his life, but after *Counter-Attack* he is best known as a memoirist who twice wrote three volumes about his early years. The "fictional" memoirs, with the non-poet George Sherston as Sassoon's reductive stand-in (*Memoirs of a Fox-Hunting Man,* 1928; *Memoirs of an Infantry Officer,* 1930; *Sherston's Progress,* 1936) were followed by the "real" autobiographies (*The Old Century and Seven More Years,* 1938; *The Weald of Youth,* 1942; and *Siegfried's Journey,* 1945). The Sherston books run from George's childhood until a few months before the Armistice; the autobiographies (as the "real" memoirs will be called hereafter) show Sassoon two years beyond that. The lines marking the refraction and reflection of actual experience are not always clearly drawn in either set. In the Sherston books, for example, the actual Dr. W. H. R. Rivers (who treated Sassoon in Craiglockhart War Hospital, site of conversations between Sassoon and Wilfred Owen) makes more than one appearance, like a "real" character in *Ulysses* or a present-day novel by, say, E. L. Doctorow or Truman Capote. Conversely, Sassoon sometimes admits to a slight bending of material in the autobiographies toward a particular logical or aesthetic effect. Finally, and most important in the case of Sassoon's ordeal on the Western Front, he will occasionally tell the reader of the autobiographies to look to the Sherston memoirs, where the fictional treatment of actual experience is close enough to the way events really happened to make any further discussion in the autobiographies more or less redundant.

In this essay some attention will be drawn to such congruities and discrepancies, but my main purpose is to isolate the—to use a word familiar to soldiers of the Great War—salient features of mind and memory possessed by Sassoon himself, the man who lived between 1886 and 1967, and to determine the extent to which the war did or did not change him.

"Pre-lapsarian" is one of those drearily overused academic adjectives, but is it ever less avoidable than in discussions of the doomed patterns of English country life in the last years before 1914? That those patterns would be extinguished by conflicts originating on the remote continent of Europe was unthinkable to most of the young men who had grown up slowly and securely in English villages. Sassoon's Sherston says that before the war "Europe was nothing but a name to me. I couldn't even bring myself to read about it in the daily paper."[2] Fox hunts and horse races provide the only notable conflicts in Sherston's prewar world: thus the only *agon* he participates in are manufactured and ceremonial ones.

Sassoon's own childhood was spent amidst the considerable comforts assured by an unusual pedigree. Descended from the commercial, but exotic and remotely Oriental, Sassoons and the native Thornycrofts (who included shipbuilders and artists), Siegfried matured in a large Kentish house, was educated mostly by tutors at home, played with by older brothers, cast (once as Mustard Seed) in his mother's *tableaux vivants,* and exposed to such venerable villagers as Miss Horrocks, whom King George IV once kissed. An impractical boy, regarded as delicate, he was often dreamy, and quite unsingleminded about anything. He would later recall the way he was at age eleven: "My undistracted imagination had been decently nourished on poetry, fairy-tales, and fanciful illustrations, and my ideas of how people behaved in real life were mainly derived from *Punch, The Boy's Own Paper,* and F. Anstey's *Voces Populi.*"[3] Sherston is depicted in the same sort of unchallenged and

2. Siegfried Sassoon, *The Complete Memoirs of George Sherston* (London and Boston: Faber and Faber, 1972), p. 176. Reprinted by permission of Faber and Faber Ltd. and K. S. Giniger Co. Inc. Hereafter cited as *MGS;* further quotations are identified by page numbers in the text.

3. Siegfried Sassoon, *The Old Century and Seven More Years* (New York: Viking, 1939), pp. 137–138. Reprinted by permission of Viking Penguin Inc. Hereafter cited as *OC;* further quotations are identified by page numbers in the text.

undemanding security as he approaches adolescence. Life seems so
calmly and reasonably hospitable as to encourage a natural passivity, even a sort of empirical solipsism: "In this brightly visualized world of simplicities and misapprehensions and mispro-
nounced names everything was accepted without question . . . The
quince tree which grew beside the little pond was the only quince
tree in the world" (*MGS*, pp. 22–23).

Fox hunting and poetry became the chief imaginative excitements
of Sassoon's youth, but if economics gently curbed his pursuit of the
first, an admittedly intermittent attraction limited his engagement
with the second. Poetry touched in him "a blurred and uncontrolled
chord of ecstasy" (*OC*, p. 51) and became associated with "an
undefined heart-ache" (*OC*, p. 83). This uncertainty of response (as
well as spotty and haphazard reading) caused his own first efforts at
composition to be touched by "a fine frenzy of aureate unreality"[4]
that he would admit he could still lapse into years later, even after
he had achieved the disciplined fury of his antiwar productions (*SJ*,
p. 26). When he at last went away to school, at Marlborough, the
verse he entered in a competition came from a "poetic impulse" that
he admits had lain "dormant for three years" (*OC*, p. 200). He
collected books as much for the feels and smells of their bindings as
the revelations within: "I cannot say that the insides of my anti-
quated acquisitions made much impression on my mind" (*OC*, p.
207). The experience of Cambridge remains almost completely
unchronicled in the Sherston memoirs and is only hastily recounted
in the autobiography. Sassoon says that he left the university convinced of his desire to be a poet, but the enervating split between his
comfortable "reynardism" and casual versifying would be part of
his life for several more years, until the Great War arrived. In both
the early memoirs and the first volumes of autobiography, the announcement that the subject has reached his majority provides the
reader with one of the few starts he receives from the tranquilly
beautiful narratives.[5] Sherston and Sassoon both seem, at twenty-

4. Siegfried Sassoon, *The Weald of Youth* (New York: Viking, 1942), p. 29.
Reprinted by permission of Viking Penguin Inc. Hereafter cited as *WY*; further
quotations are identified by page numbers in the text.
5. It is useful to keep in mind how much older Sassoon was than many of the most
famous "post-Somme" poets. He was born in 1886; Owen in 1893; Graves in 1895;
Blunden in 1896.

one, not only far away from adulthood, but even uninterested in it. Sherston recalls: "The word maturity had no meaning for me. I did not anticipate that I should become *different;* I should only become *older*. I cannot pretend that I aspired to growing wiser. I merely *lived*, and in that condition I drifted from day to day" (*MGS*, p. 72). Already more predisposed to remember than anticipate, Sassoon and Sherston impress themselves on the reader as static and ambered; the effect is beautiful in the way that innocence can be, but troubling, too, like a plane that cannot gain altitude.

One experience that imposes narrative movement on the account of any adolescence is sexual exploration. In both the Sherston memoirs and the autobiographies—all three volumes of each, which take both persona and author past the age of thirty—it is almost eerily absent. Allowing for any standard of reticence, literary or social, its want is conspicuous. Sherston and Sassoon are protected from the emotional ravages of love, but their worlds seem deoxygenated, like toys under glass. When women appear they are generally aunts. Men may be models of grace and bearing—like the memoirs' foxhunter Stephen Colwood, or Mr. Hamilton, the cricketing tutor from Cambridge, or, most important, Denis Milden, Master of the hunt—but their erotic force of attraction is carefully circumscribed. The figure who is Milden in the memoirs and Norman Loder in the autobiographies provides one of the key differences between the two sets of books. The real Loder is considerably endowed with virtues, but of a rather unglamorous kind: "He was kind, decent, and thorough, never aiming at anything beyond plain common-sense and practical ability" (*WY*, p. 150). Milden, however, even as he behaves with similar strength and simplicity, has a more romantic allure. Sherston meets him when they are both boys: "Already I was weaving Master Milden into my day dreams, and soon he had become my inseparable companion in all my imagined adventures . . . It was the first time that I experienced a feeling of wistfulness for someone I wanted to be with" (*MGS*, p. 37). Years later an invitation from Milden is cause for rapture in Sherston, and the dependable simplicities of the hunt-master's routine are observed with something like awe: "Thought . . . how surprised Stephen [Colwood] would be when I told him all about my visit. Meditated on the difference between Denis hunting the hounds (unapproachable and with 'a face like a boot') and Denis indoors—

homely and kind and easy to get on with; would he really want me to come and stay with him again, I wondered" (*MGS*, p. 192). These are the familiar thrills and worries of schoolboy crushes; but Sherston is twenty-five.[6]

If Sassoon gives no indication that romance suddenly galvanized his character, neither does he show London achieving such a result. As an uncertain young poet in the city just before the war, he is encouraged and aided by such professional encouragers as Edmund Gosse and Edward Marsh. But his vocation is not overpowering; he continues to move confusedly between the field and the desk: "I may have wondered why it was so impossible to amalgamate my contrasted worlds of Literature and Sport. Why must I always be adapting my manners—and even my style of speaking—to different sets of people?" (*WY*, p. 200). His métier was no more defined than his personality. This adaptability, which is after all only a sort of active passivity, is something Sassoon repeatedly admits in himself and ascribes to Sherston. In *The Old Century* he tells us that he has always been "self-adapting to people's estimation of [himself]" (p. 219); Sherston, in the memoirs, says he has "always been inclined to accept life in the form in which it has imposed itself upon [him]" (p. 34), admitting that "on the whole [he] was psychologically passive" (p. 520), a man whose "terrestrial activities have been either accidental in origin or else part of the 'inevitable sequence of events'" (p. 563). In his diary from 1922, Sassoon refers to his "mental coma." Of the diary itself he says: "From this jungle of misinterpretations of my ever-changing and never-steadfast selves, some future fool may, perhaps, derive instruction and amusement."[7]

In the summer of 1914, having moved to Gray's Inn at the suggestion of Edward Marsh, Sassoon had a feeling of being "on the

6. Sassoon's recently published *Diaries, 1920–1922* (ed. Rupert Hart-Davis, Faber and Faber, 1981) show his involvement in two homosexual affairs. He writes on August 13, 1922: "I must remember all the years of sexual frustration and failure, and be thankful. I must not ask too much of P. who has limitations which at present are charming to me" (p. 214). But "this cursed complication of sex" (p. 81)—made worse, one feels, by what he admits was his "prolonged youthfulness" (p. 85)—remains a frequently unhappy and confused theme. Annotating these diaries in 1939, Sassoon wrote: "Homosexuality has become a bore; the intelligentsia have captured it" (p. 53).

7. *Diaries*, pp. 108, 104.

verge of some experience which might liberate [him] from [his] blind alley of excessive sport and self-imposed artistic solitude" (*WY*, p. 202). The war was to make him not only a poet, but one with a mission: all that is certain. But despite Sherston's claim that the war "re-made" him (*MGS*, p. 607), there is much more evidence that the personality of Sassoon himself (as well as that of his fictional iso-tope) emerged from the war with most of the protean tentativeness with which it embarked for the Front. His splendid military per-formance and his brave subsequent protest against the fighting were no more disparate actions that eventually synthesized into a solid character than fox hunting and poetry had been. The evidence of both the memoirs and autobiographies is that far from being remade by the war, Sassoon had his constitutional capacity to shift and adapt made even more habitual. Wilfred Owen approached him as novice to mentor while they were both in Craiglockhart War Hospi-tal, but in *Siegfried's Journey* Sassoon would admit: "When con-trasting the two of us, I find that—highly strung and emotional though he was—his whole personality was far more compact and coherent than mine" (p. 91). The war transformed Owen with al-most molecular thoroughness; it seems to have left Sassoon's most fundamental dimensions unpenetrated.[8]

Any clear separation of Sassoon and Sherston will remain forever impossible to achieve. Even when Sassoon attempted it himself, it was with a whimsy that soon became avoidance. In *The Weald of Youth* he decides that to assert Sherston "was 'only me with a lot left out' sounds off-hand and uncivil" (p. 66); after Sherston has made an awkward appearance in the autobiographies, Sassoon must gently dispatch him, apologizing for "a collision between fictionized reality and essayized autobiography" (*WY*, pp. 68–69). Never-theless, for purposes of looking at the war, which we now come to,

8. Paul Fussell, in his splendid book *The Great War and Modern Memory* (Oxford: Oxford University Press, 1975), offers a view of both Sassoon and the construction of the Sherston memoirs that is very different from the one put forth in this essay. He sees a great change between "prewar and postwar Sassoon," whereas I would emphasize similarity, and finds the Sherston trilogy "elaborately structured," whereas I see it as loosely and episodically presented. Readers of this essay will want to contrast its argument to that found on pp. 90–105 of Fussell's book. In addition, an extended and workmanlike discussion of both the Sherston memoirs and the autobiographies can be found in Michael Thorpe's *Siegfried Sassoon: A Critical Study* (Leiden: Universitaire Pers Leiden, 1966).

Sherston can indeed be taken as Sassoon with a lot—namely, the poetry—left out: the autobiographies and the memoirs contain essentially the same features of personality that were exposed to killing and inspired to protest.

Both Sassoon and Sherston volunteer for the army with the sort of dutiful inertia that led many of the educated soldier-poets to the Front. Irony and bitterness set in a good deal thereafter. Sherston listens uneasily to the same "Spirit of the Bayonet" lecture that Sassoon did. Echoing Prince Hal's remark about Hotspur and the Scots, Sherston reflects: "Man, it seemed, had been created to jab the life out of Germans. To hear the Major talk, one might have thought that he did it himself every day before breakfast" (*MGS*, pp. 289–290). But a raid can still be as important to the ego as a point-to-point race (*MGS*, p. 296), and after protesting the war, being hospitalized (instead of court-martialed), and being pronounced fit to return to the Front, he can still have war dreams in which he is "vaguely gratified at 'adding to [his] war experience' " (*MGS*, p. 555). (Indeed, there is good reason to believe that Sassoon himself conceived the famous lines of "The Kiss"—inspired by the bayonet lecture—in a pre-Somme spirit of romance, and only later invited them to be read as satire.)[9] Even after Sherston has learned to be bitter towards the "happy warrior attitudes" (*MGS*, p. 427) imagined back home and recommended by superiors, he can still—a year after the Somme—assume a heroic stance as a kind of prophylactic against danger and death: "I had always found it difficult·to believe that these young men had really felt happy with death staring them in the face, and I resented any sentimentalizing of infantry attacks. But here I was, working myself up into a similar mental condition, as though going over the top were a species of religious experience. Was it some suicidal self-deceiving escape from the limitless malevolence of the Front Line?" (*MGS*, p. 420).

It was not so much suicidal as psychologically self-preserving. To act from a sense of purpose, with whatever suspension of disbelief that may involve, is to reduce the possibilities of panic and despair that follow upon a sense of absurdity. So Sherston would "play at being a hero in shining armour" (*MGS*, p. 421) even after he knew

9. Thorpe, *Siegfried Sassoon*, pp. 17–18.

better. It was the same with Sassoon himself. On rereading his
actual war diary from the end of 1916, he notes in *Siegfried's
Journey:* "Some of its entries suggest that I was keeping my courage
up by resorting to elevated feelings. My mental behaviour was still
unconnected with any self-knowledge, and it was only when I was
writing verse that I tried to concentrate and express my somewhat
loose ideas" (p. 61–62).

When Sherston is convalescing from a "blighty" he makes a
comic list of the chameleonlike poses he adopts depending on his
visitor of the moment: to a hunting friend he is "deprecatory about
sufferings endured at the front"; to the sister of a fellow officer he
is "jocular, talkative, debonair, and diffidently heroic" (*MGS*, p.
451). When alone except for other patients, he is "mainly disposed
toward self-pitying estrangement from everyone except the troops
in the Front Line" (*MGS*, p. 452). The reflexes of response here are
more psychological than social; they are part of Sherston's (and
were of Sassoon's) instinct, in the face of an unusual absence of
fixed character, to improvise selves as they are needed.

Although *Siegfried's Journey* gives reasons to form an impression
that Sassoon was not quite so dependent on Bertrand Russell and H.
W. Massingham as Sherston was on their fictive refractions—
"Tyrrell" and "Markington"—the autobiography serves to reinforce many of the features of the memoirs' account of Sassoon's
famous written protest against the war in 1917. Both Sherston's and
Sassoon's protests are characterized by ambivalence and motives
that are at least as personal as political. Just as so many English
poets of the 1930's, from Auden to Julian Bell, would have difficulty casting their lot with politics that would, if successfully carried through, do away with the privileged milieux in which they had
learned so many humane values, so Sherston, at home on leave,
wonders whether his indictment is too inclusive:

Walking round the garden after tea—Aunt Evelyn drawing [Captain Hux-
table's] attention to her delphiniums and he waggishly affirming their inferiority to his own—I wondered whether I had exaggerated the "callous complacency" of those at home. What could elderly people do except try and
make the best of their inability to sit in a trench and be bombarded? How
could they be blamed for refusing to recognize any ignoble elements in the
War except those which they attributed to our enemies? (*MGS*, p. 499)

He concedes that his protest "was an emotional idea based on [his] war experience and stimulated by the acquisition of points of view which [he] accepted uncritically" (*MGS*, p. 521); he admits that he was as interested in becoming a good golfer in this period as he was in becoming an intellectual.

The real Sassoon, in *Siegfried's Journey*, correspondingly confesses that his protest "developed into a fomentation of confused and inflamed ideas" (p. 32) and that his "disillusionment was combined with determination to employ [his] discontents as a medium for literary expression" (p. 60). The suggestion by the portrait painter Glyn Philpot that the protest is a Byronic gesture helps "to sustain [his] belief that [he is] about to do something spectacular and heroic" (*SJ*, p. 77). He soon realizes that "army life had persistently interfered with my ruminative and quiet-loving mentality. I may even have been aware that most of my satiric verses were to some extent prompted by internal exasperation" (*SJ*, p. 111).

The protest was, like so much else about both Sherston and Sassoon, somewhat impromptu. As its consequences were felt, there were too few certainties of intellect and character on which they could fall back. The protest crumbled; Sassoon accepted a diagnosis of "shell shock" instead of being court-martialed, and after his stay at Craiglockhart he ended up back at the Front—still as inchoate as he was gallant.

The anger Sassoon felt toward the war had an almost boyish sense of right and wrong as its propellant. He endowed Sherston with it, too. Shortly after Dick Tiltwood, another ideal friend—"a young Galahad" (*MGS*, p. 258)—is killed at the Front, Sherston says: "I was angry with the War" (*MGS*, p. 276)—the simplicity of the declaration having an emotional genuineness beyond the usual literary force of the understatement that was employed so often, and with such calculated effect, by First World War poets and memoirists. After observing an unforgivably severe doctor during his convalescence, Sherston says: "I hope that someone gave him a black eye" (*MGS*, p. 460); in real life Sassoon had an altercation with a photographer who upset the dignity of the grave site of T. E. Lawrence—whose *Seven Pillars of Wisdom*, incidentally, exhibits, like Sassoon's books, heroic behavior proceeding from a personality that remains curiously ad hoc and incipient.[10] Very late in the

10. See D. Felicitas Corrigan's *Siegfried Sassoon: Poet's Pilgrimage* (London: Gollancz, 1973), p. 238.

war, Sherston is at Company H. Q. in a château behind the lines at Habarcq. In his diary he locates himself in "this quiet room where I spend my evenings ruminating and trying to tell myself the truth— this room where I become my real self, and feel omnipotent while reading Tolstoy and Walt Whitman" (*MGS*, p. 628). But how can our real selves reside in the fantasies insurgent from our reading? Here again Sherston seems younger than his age. It is a year since his protest, and he records: " 'I want to go up to the Line and really do something!' I had boasted thus in a moment of vin rouge elation, catching my mood from those lads who look to me as their leader. How should they know the shallowness of my words? They see me in the daylight of my activities, when I must acquiesce in the evil that is war. But in the darkness where I am alone my soul rebels against what we are doing" (*MGS*, p. 628). He is still "catching" his mood from circumstance instead of imposing his will on it. Surely the horror of his circumstances would make any such imposition heroic, but Sherston's confusion and impotence remain notable.

The memoirs end with Sherston once again in hospital, almost thirty-two and despairingly baffled as to whatever meaning the war may have had for him. Rivers, the mind's physician, appears as a deus ex machina. His smile is a "benediction," and Sherston understands that this is what he has "been waiting for" (*MGS*, p. 655): "He did not tell me that I had done my best to justify his belief in me. He merely made me feel that he took all that for granted, and now we must go on to something better still. And this was the beginning of the new life toward which he had shown me the way" (*MGS*, p. 656). In this biblical language, Sherston delivers his will into Rivers' hands. The final words of the trilogy are these: "It is only from the inmost silences of the heart that we know the world for what it is, and ourselves for what the world has made us" (*MGS*, p. 656). The implication of this line, recognizable from evidence throughout the memoirs and the autobiographies, seems to be that somehow we carry such knowledge in us, but that it remains unspoken to our conscious minds.

The Sherston memoirs, it has already been noted, do not follow Sassoon's fictive self beyond the Armistice, but the autobiographies give evidence that their author reacted to the first circumstances of peacetime with many of the same traits, and much of the same uncertainty, that he displayed in London before the war. Sassoon turned fitfully to reviewing (for the *Daily Herald*) and to Labour Party politics as he made the acquaintance of many of the important writers of the day. *Siegfried's Journey* shows Sassoon in encounters with Hardy, Masefield, Bridges, T. E. Lawrence, Galsworthy, Firbank, Blunt, and Belloc. In most cases he is accompanied or propelled thither by someone like Osbert Sitwell or the indefatigable Ottoline Morrell. His literary celebrity seems as much managed by others as, several years before, his obscurity was by Marsh. He still exhibits the same compelling blankness with which Virginia Woolf endowed Jacob Flanders, destined to move from party to party and house to house and be appreciated for his freshness and potential—but to remain somehow ungraspable, leaving, one suspects, more of an afterglow than an impression. Aware of his still diaphanous personality, Sassoon recalls:

I am sure that if, for example, my Gosse, Galsworthy, Marsh, and Arnold Bennett selves could have been interchanged, some perplexity would have been present in their acutely observant minds. I resembled the character in a Pirandello play who was told, "Your reality is a mere transitory and fleeting illusion, taking this form today and that tomorrow, according to the conditions, according to your will, your sentiments, which in turn are controlled by an intellect that shows them to you today in one manner and tomorrow . . . who knows how?" (*SJ*, p. 157)

This adaptability would soon serve him well on his American lecture tour; and it would continue to provide temporary bridges between his fox-hunting and poetry-writing worlds. But it also left him with a persistent lack of identity. (Sassoon's diaries from the early twenties show a persisting split between the worlds of the Morrells' Garsington and "Loder-land," with sometimes literature and sometimes sport gaining sway over his ambitions and routine.)[11]

The literary moment was actually receding from Sassoon even as he was attempting to find his place in it. As his wartime subject matter vanished, the poet's boldly colloquial diction and "knockout" (*SJ*, p. 43) last-line ironies had fewer poems to go into. He was left with his more placid prewar pastoralism and his regular Edwardian metrics. He traveled on a very fast sound wave from being *le dernier cri* to being a respected echo. But the autobiographies show a distinct pride in his place in literary history. Of his prewar

11. *Diaries*, p. 114.

encounter with Rupert Brooke, he writes in *The Weald of Youth:* "There is no need to explain that our one brief meeting had a quite unpredictable significance. Nor need I underline the latent irony of the situation" (p. 217). But as the above list of arranged literary pilgrimages shows, Sassoon was really more attuned to the writers of an earlier generation, one soon to be the literary past, than he was to those who would create the great modernist poetry and fiction of the twenties.

His premature eclipse by the literary future complemented Sassoon's constitutional attraction to the past. In *The Weald of Youth* he imagines that "the present is only waiting to become the past and be laid up in lavender for commemorative renewal" (p. 44). During his childhood his Grandmother Thornycroft's senility appeals to his imagination as a kind of magic carpet to the past; when his nurse, Mrs. Mitchell, quits the household, he cannot understand why she doesn't feel the same nostalgia as he does for the past that they shared (*OC*, p. 39). Sherston, too, frequently draws attention to his naturally retrospective habits. Inclined "to loiter . . . as long as possible" (*MGS*, p. 11) among the details of the past, he makes fun of himself as a "professional ruminator" (*MGS*, p. 563) and displays an amused awareness of the conventions of memoir writing.

The rovingly retrospective mind that makes the writing of memoirs a generally less intellectual and shape-making task than the practice of autobiography is nevertheless the same mind that gives rise to the "real" books I have been calling autobiographies throughout this essay. Sassoon may refer in *Siegfried's Journey* to his "comparisons between the crude experience and its perspectived proportions as they emerge in matured remembering" (p. 310), but even in the autobiographies the past seems more often conjured than interpreted. This would be so in a man who can recall experiencing "the first instance . . . of a detached sense of proportion about [his] doings in relation to life as a whole" at the age of twenty-seven (*WY*, p. 139). The autobiographies make frequent use of the present tense ("I see him, chalking the dates of famous battles on the blackboard" [*OC*, p. 54]), calling the dead and the past to life in the same sort of séance manner Sassoon used in a number of poems about the dead.[12] He romantically describes his way of recollecting

12. See my essay "All Souls' Nights: Yeats, Sassoon and the Dead," in *Irish Studies I*, ed. P. J. Drudy (Cambridge: Cambridge University Press, 1980), pp. 85–99.

in *The Weald of Youth:* "Forgetful of the pen between his fingers, forehead on hand, middle-age looks back across the years, while the clock ticks unheeded on the shelf, and the purring flames of the fire consume the crumbling log" (p. 146). The memoirist Sherston's frequent assertion that the past is apprehended more vividly than it was when it was merely the present would not be contradicted by Sassoon as autobiographer.

The autobiographer's sense that "when you get close up to life, little things are just as important as big ones" (*WY*, pp. 53–54), and Sherston's apology that "it is [his] own story that [he is] trying to tell, and as such it must be received; those who expect a universalization of the Great War must look for it elsewhere" (*MGS*, p. 291), display some rare affinities between Sassoon's mind and the modernist sensibility that produced *Ulysses* and *Mrs. Dalloway*—a sensibility that sought, with the logic of paradox, to achieve universality by exploring the particular with more particularity than ever before. But a gentle fastidiousness prevents the reader from seeing almost all of the earthy or unpleasant minutiae of Sassoon's days; indeed, even in the autobiographies the author confesses to enough distortions to make shaky any claim that those books are much more focused into reality than the memoirs: "I prefer to remember my own gladness and good luck, and to forget, whenever I can, those moods and minor events which made me low-spirited and unresponsive. Be at your best, vision enchanting, I cry" (*OC*, p. 214). One need not recall one's school days with Dotheboys horror, or, to move to the opposite boundary, the detachment of Orwell's "Such, Such Were the Joys," yet all but the most naive reader is likely to be left more quizzical than charmed by the way Sassoon clearly romances schooltime unpleasantness into the picturesque. Nor does Sassoon choose to subject parent-child relations to the realistic but forgiving probings of a Gosse. Conflicts with his mother are only hastily alluded to in the autobiographies; in the Sherston memoirs the deserted and, one suspects, complicated Mrs. Sassoon is woollied and neutered into "Aunt Evelyn." John Lehmann correctly points out the "curious fact that when Sassoon came to write *Memoirs of an Infantry Officer* in 1930 . . . several of the episodes which form the stark subjects of his poems of the time suffer a modification, or rather mollification of effect."[13] In both sets of war

13. John Lehmann, *The English Poets of the First World War* (New York: Thames and Hudson, 1982), p. 50.

recollections the sharp sarcasm of a Graves is avoided in favor of the understatement of an Edmund Blunden, and a periphrasis that is both humorous and self-protecting: "This was a mistake which ought to have put an end to my terrestrial adventures, for no sooner had I popped my silly head out of the sap than I felt a stupendous blow in the back between my shoulders" (*MGS*, pp. 444–445).

Sassoon admits that the "unrevealed processes of memory are mysterious" (*WY*, p. 97), and he wisely refrains from probing them too strenuously. Throughout the first two volumes of the auto-biography he draws attention to the unsystematic nature of his mind, the traits that make it more given to intense apparitions than chains of thought. He says his brain takes in facts one at a time and has trouble relating them to each other (*OC*, p. 129), that information best reaches him slowly and visually (*OC*, p. 212), that "abstract ideas are uncongenial" to him (*WY*, p. 105), and that the study of history made sense to him only in terms of drama or chronology (*OC*, p. 237). Chronology is the basic organizing principle of the memoirs and the autobiographies. The continually tentative and experimenting nature of both Sherston's and Sassoon's person-alities makes an episodic structure inevitable. The progression of titles in the autobiographies (*The Old Century, The Weald of Youth, Siegfried's Journey*) seems to suggest a steady movement toward personal definition: set beside each other the book spines show first the name of a time, then the name of a phase, finally the name of the person. But this is misleading, because Sassoon's character really hardens very little; the autobiographer's retrospection must still rely more on the movement of time, rather than on particular traits or any ruling passion, for its narrative trellis. In *The Weald of Youth* Sassoon compares the movement of one of his chapters to the meanderings of the river Teise (p. 46), and although he remarks elsewhere on his "perspectived" and "matured" rememberings, it is also in that second volume of autobiography that he admits "it seems reasonable to ask how a mind which understood so little of itself at the time can be analysed and explained by its owner thirty years afterwards!" (p. 27).

The episodic recollections of all six volumes are often extremely beautiful. To read of the lonely young Londoner's accidental encounter, at the Regent's Park zoo, with his old, defensive friend Wirgie, or of Sherston sitting in a dugout, "tired and wakeful, and soaked and muddy from [his] patrol, while one candle made unsteady brown shadows in the gloom" (*MGS*, p. 639) is to experience moments of great and quiet power. The opacity of the central figure's personality in each set of recollections is as appealing as it is frustrating. The presentation, like the personality, tantalizes; both excite, entice, and somehow defeat the reader. T. S. Eliot's remark that Henry James "had a mind so fine that no idea could violate it" sounds like a clever dismissal, but it was offered as a kind of awed compliment. One could say the same words, and in something of the same spirit, about all of Sassoon's books of memory.

On his American tour, Sassoon stood and talked with Carl Sandburg on the roof of a large building in Chicago during a sunset. Years later in *Siegfried's Journey* he took exception to Sandburg's definition of poetry as "a series of explanations of life, fading off into horizons too swift for explanations," raising the following Frost-like objections: "I mistrust random improvisings, even when performed by the pioneering genius and bright vocabulary of a Sandburg. 'Explanations of life' should be evolved and stated once and for all, not incontinently ejaculated in blissful immunity from the restrictions of versecraft. For this 'poetry of the immediate present,' invented, of course, by Whitman, is a medium which has deliberately abrogated finality of form" (pp. 297–298). The metrical and logical regularity of Sassoon's poetry is striking to the point of anachronism if it is considered against the production of modernists of the same generation as himself. But his prose recollections certainly exhibit the "deliberately abrogated finality of form" he criticizes above. That they do will impress the reader of all six volumes not simply as a matter of aesthetic decision, but as a case of psychological inevitability as well.

The *Imperator* (a ship once confiscated from the Germans by the allied governments and then allocated to the Cunard Company) brought Sassoon home from New York to Southampton in the summer of 1920. At this point, Sassoon admits, he was remarkably unchanged from the man who, in London at twenty-eight, could be irresolutely "reduced to boarding an omnibus just to see what sort of places it went to" (*WY*, p. 197). It is unsettling and wondrous that gunfire, celebrity, and the simple accrual of years made so little difference to the uncertain spirit within, but Sassoon shows himself to be by 1920 nearly as baffled and improvisational as he was in

1914 or 1904. There remains something startlingly unformed about the thirty-four-year-old man set before the reader's eyes for one last look. The man in his late fifties who sets him there says that he may, even in these "real" memoirs, be rendering him "stupider than he actually was" in an attempt "at unity of effect" (*SJ*, p. 337), but at the least he assumes his readers are convinced of the great difference between the pliant youth and the matured autobiographer. But was there such a difference? Let us briefly think about the man who wrote and published the autobiographies during his sixth decade.

Sassoon says that the self which stood in a sunny Trafalgar Square one day after his arrival from America "realized that he had come to the end of the journey on which he had set out when he enlisted in the army six years before. And, though he wasn't clearly conscious of it, time has since proved that there was nothing for him to do but begin all over again" (*SJ*, p. 338). But if he did begin again, it was mostly to explore his "impercipient past" (*SJ*, p. 337), first in the Sherston books which were, he admits, in some ways a substitute for the long poem Gosse urged him to write, and then in the actual autobiographies. Certainly nothing to equal the literary impact of *Counter-Attack* was again to come from his pen. He was eventually to become Heytesbury's hermit. In a sense he went home from that Saturday afternoon in Trafalgar Square more to recall life than to live it; his uncertain efforts toward existence were over and a sort of afterlife had begun.

In the final pages of *Siegfried's Journey,* Sassoon speculates:

Once in his lifetime, perhaps, a man may be the instrument through which something constructive emerges, whether it be genius giving birth to an original idea or the anonymous mortal who makes the most of an opportunity which will never recur. It is for the anonymous ones that I have my special feeling. I like to think of them remembering the one time when they were involved in something unusual or important—when, probably without knowing it at the time, they, as it were, wrote their single masterpiece, never to perform anything comparable again. Then they were fully alive, living above themselves, and discovering powers they hadn't been aware of. For a moment they stood in the transfiguring light of dramatic experience. And nothing ever happened to them afterwards. They were submerged by human uneventfulness. It is only since I got into my late fifties that I have realized these great tracts of insignificance in people's lives. My younger self scornfully rejected the phrase "getting through life" as reprehensible. That I now

accept it with an equanimity which amounts almost to affection is my way
of indicating the contrast between our states of mind. The idea of oblivion
attracts me; I want, after life's fitful fever, to sleep well.   (pp. 333–334)

Surely the remarks on "anonymous ones" apply to no one more than
himself, however much shielding is given by the third person and
the plural; and even the distance between the older and younger
selves he contrasts is not as great as he imagines it to be. Sassoon
says that the younger one "scornfully rejected the phrase 'getting
through life' "; yet the essential passivity of that self is more to be
remarked on than anything else. The older autobiographer is just
giving final intellectual acceptance to what, for all its fitful
rebellions and genuine heroism, was the essential temper and practice of his youth. The later perspective is neither so long, nor the
sensibility so different, as the older Sassoon thinks. The narrative
lacunae, present-tense reveries, and watercolored judgments found
in the autobiographies all spring from the mental and emotional
habits of his younger days. Not only is the child father to the man,
in this case; the sporadic boy-poet is father to the autobiographer.

Sassoon writes that he is "inclined to compare the living present
to a jig-saw puzzle loose in its box. Not until afterwards can we fit
the pieces together and make a coherent picture of them. While
writing this book I have often been conscious of this process" (*SJ*,
p. 336). But that process does not go very far toward coherence. Just
when Sassoon wonders if it can be "that the immediacy of our
existence amounts to little more than animality, and that our ordered
understanding of it is only assembled through afterthought and
retrospection," he stops short: "But I am overstraining my limited
intelligence and must extricate myself from these abstrusities" (*SJ*,
p. 337).

Although both sets of recollections are full of amused
self-depreciation, this last line comes not from coyness or false
modesty. Sassoon's interpretive intelligence was and remained limited. It could not be otherwise. The dreaming and tentative boy was
not meant to become a thinker at thirty-four or even fifty-nine. To
say that this is a limitation in his character is to say very little,
because it is also the key to that character's unusual beauty. There
was something permanently inviolate about it, even in the most
exciting and dangerous circumstances. And much of it survived the

"old century" well into the miseries of the mid-twentieth. Sassoon remained in large part unreachable to life.

It took a higher power to break the spell. God came to him late, but succeeded in transporting him fully and finally. Religion brought his last volumes of verse new life, and he awaited the next world with far more sustained ambition and interest than he ever really displayed toward this one. But this is another, and better, story.

Neither Worthy nor Capable:
The War Memoirs of Graves,
Blunden, and Sassoon

Those of the modernist generations who experienced at first hand the apocalypse of the Western Front faced unusual difficulty in achieving that "impersonality" variously prescribed by Eliot and by Stephen Dedalus. By those who had lived through 1914–1918 at some greater distance from Ypres and the Somme, the war could be used as the substance or material of great, if harsh, art—the no-man's-landscape of *The Waste Land,* for instance, or the history that Virginia Woolf borrows for Septimus Smith. One can trace in the war poets an attempt to find or to make a form and language that could control the immediate and shocking experience of the trenches, an effort all too often cut short by death. The survivors of the war did not necessarily prosper as a result of their apparent good fortune; for it fell to them to devise a way to recall the war both fairly and usefully. To many it seemed, as Erich Maria Remarque insisted in his dedication of *All Quiet on the Western Front,* that even those who had survived physically were nevertheless destroyed by the war.

In an essay written to commemorate the fortieth anniversary of the Armistice, Robert Graves poses what must have been, for those who found themselves still alive after 1918, the supreme question: "Death lurked around every traverse, killing our best friends with monotonous spite. We had been spared, but why? Certainly not

101

because of our virtues."[1] The question is both unanswerable and inescapable. Beneath the question of physical survival there lies another problem, as is made clear by Edmund Blunden's poem "The Welcome," which describes the first moments in the Line of a man just back from leave. No sooner does he sit down in the headquarters pillbox than it is struck by a shell which reduces six men to "a black muck heap." The newcomer, the sole survivor, finds himself "alive and sane"; and the poem, which has up to that point been couched in the plain language of reportage, suddenly rises into near-Scripture: "it shall be spoken / While any of those who were there have tongues."[2] It is not just life, but sanity as well, that is miraculous.

The problem of psychological survival has been extensively studied with reference to survivors of concentration camps and of the Hiroshima bombing,[3] but not, I think, with reference to the veterans of World War I. One need not necessarily equate the experiences of Auschwitz and Ypres to see parallels. R. J. Lifton, writing of the *hibakusha*, the survivors of Hiroshima, mentions, as what he calls "an indirect manifestation of guilt," the *hibakusha's* "stress upon the 'accidents of survival' ";[4] and it is exactly this element of accident which recurs not only in the Blunden poem, but throughout the memoirs of the First World War.

What I propose to do is to look at three memoirs—those of Robert Graves, Edmund Blunden, and Siegfried Sassoon—and to consider some of the mechanisms of psychological survival which they describe. As artists, these writers faced the problem of lending at least the appearance of coherence to a situation that was, by all accounts, utterly inchoate. They all write, in apparent contradiction to the norm of modernism, about themselves; but only in a curiously abstract way. We will be true to the intention of each work if we see

1. Robert Graves, "What Was That War Like, Sir?" in *The Crane Bag and Other Disputed Subjects* (London: 1969), p. 59.

2. All quotations from Blunden are taken from *Undertones of War* (New York: Harcourt, Brace and World, 1965). The poem "The Welcome" is on page 235 of that volume. Further quotations will be identified by page numbers in the text.

3. The two books I have especially in mind are R. J. Lifton, *Death in Life: Survivors of Hiroshima* (New York: Random House, 1967) and Terence Des Pres, *The Survivor: An Anatomy of Life in the Death Camps* (New York: Pocket Books, 1977).

4. Lifton, *Death in Life*, p. 53.

it less as confession or "personality" than as an attempt to generalize from the muddle of the war a description of the peculiar kinds
of "heroism" that were effective in the trenches. While description
could not provide explanation, it was, at least, a way of at once
accepting and deflecting the shame of having lived when so many
had died; and such description might allow each writer to rise far
enough above the emotions of the war to endeavor to make of those
emotions the stuff of art.

I emphasize the psychological rather than the physical aspect of
survival, since all three writers agree that the latter was purely a
matter of luck. In each book the protagonist, early on, sees graphic
representation of exactly how widespread and arbitrary death at the
Front is. Blunden, for example, fills the first chapter of his book
with reminders that the war is inescapable: ". . . the knowledge that
the war had released them [he is referring to the convalescent soldiers he had been in charge of] only for a few moments, that the war
would reclaim them, that the war was a jealous war and a long
lasting" (p. 21). And that people in its grip are essentially powerless
and doomed: "I never saw them [a troop headed from Etaples to the
Front] again; they were hurried once more, fast as corks on a mill-
stream, without complaint into the bond service of destruction" (p.
23). He provides a chilling instance of the omnipresence of death—
and of the fact, as he says, that "experience was nothing but a casual
protection" (p. 47). The grenade instructor, having just announced,
"I've been down here since 1914, and never had an accident,"
promptly manages to blow up himself and his students (p. 23).[5]

One could multiply examples almost indefinitely—the cricket
game in *Goodbye to All That* which must be abandoned because of
a literal and deadly rain of bullets is an especially striking instance
(p. 116). In contrast to these intrusions of death stand the "lucky"
moments when a character who by any kind of logic or reason
should be killed, survives. So, for instance, Blunden, about to leave
the Front for good, through "ill-luck and stupidity" flashes a signaling lamp at the German lines and, by a "lucky jump," escapes the
ensuing hail of machine-gun bullets (p. 207).

The irony—the word seems unavoidable—which is at the heart of

5. Much the same episode can be found in Robert Graves, *Goodbye to All That*
(New York: Doubleday, 1957), p. 191. All references to Graves's memoir are from
this edition and are identified by page numbers in the text.

all three books is the persistence, to borrow a phrase from Terence
Des Pres, of life in death:[6] human beings manage to play cricket,
write poetry, form and maintain friendships, joke, enjoy jam from
Selfridges, in the midst of a world that seems absolutely devoted to
death. As Blunden puts it, "There was a grace that war never
overcast" (p. 35), even though war, like some great beast, was
characterized by a "long talon reaching for its victim at its pleasure" (p. 27).

It is of course the pressure of this irony that, psychologically, was
one of the greatest obstacles to keeping one's sanity. Graves's
admission in *Goodbye to All That* that it took ten years for his blood
to recover (p. 172) points to the immensity of the task, and the
limited success these memoirists had. The war, like more recent
holocausts, was not something to be gotten over.

GRAVES: IRONY, CONDITIONING, CARICATURE

At the most obvious level, the means of psychological survival in
Goodbye to All That is what we have since become used to as battle
humor. Graves claims it was common—he says, in what he describes as a letter written from the Front, that "the men are much
afraid, yet always joking" (p. 112). This sense of humor operates
at two levels. In the first place, it is the ability to see the ironies
inherent in battle. So, for example, Graves takes note that, on the
eve of battle, the regiment invariably received "the usual inap-
propriate message" from headquarters: "Division could always be
trusted to send a warning about verdigris on vermorel-sprayers, or
the keeping of pets in trenches, or being polite to allies, or some
other triviality, exactly when an attack was in progress" (p. 217).
War does not, then, make one ironic; the war is itself ironic, and one
need only watch and record.

But that is only half the story; for ironic humor is a defense as
well. Every time Graves's regiment is ordered to attack, the officers
end their summary of the plan with the same bitter joke: "Person-
ally, I don't give a damn either way. We'll get killed whatever
happens" (p. 145; cf. pp. 216–217). The irony is double; it is both
a hardening of the mind to meet death and (especially in such battles
as the Somme) very nearly an accurate calculation of the chances.

6. Des Pres, *The Survivor*, chapter 5.

The problem with this ironic humor is that at times—and those the most crucial times—it fails to work. So Graves encounters a man wounded in the head: "One can joke with a badly-wounded man and congratulate him on being out of it. One can disregard a dead man. But even a miner can't make a joke that sounds like a joke over a man who takes three hours to die, after the top of his head has been taken off by a bullet fired at twenty yards' range" (p. 115). This comes, Graves says, from a letter written in 1915. We can see the reflex of irony making its small gesture even as its efficacy is denied; Graves cannot resist a jibe at the miners.

This attitude of ironic humor has become almost a commonplace in war literature; indeed, Paul Fussell argues that *Goodbye to All That* is in some sense the founder of the line that extends to *Catch-22* and *Gravity's Rainbow*.[7] A more fundamental and perhaps less obvious psychological device is portrayed in Graves's memoir, a device that links the war sections of the book with the chapters on his life before and after the war. Graves would, I think, deny that his upbringing and education in any way "prepared" him for the war—indeed one of the elements which that war has in common with later holocausts is the way in which it could not have been prepared for. But I would argue that some elements of Graves's "education"—both formal (at Charterhouse) and informal (in rock climbing)—were in fact preparations, in an important sense, for survival at the Front.

Consider his explanation of the reason for his nightly patrols: "I had cannily worked it out like this. My best way of lasting through to the end of the War would be to get wounded. The best time to get wounded would be at night and in the open, with rifle-fire more or less unaimed and my whole body exposed. Best, also, to get wounded when there was no rush on the dressing-station services, and while the back areas were not being heavily shelled. Best to get wounded, therefore, on a night patrol in a quiet sector" (p. 131). One thing that cannot be overlooked in this is the way it prescribes, in a clear and calculated fashion, actions which seem, in normal circumstances, utterly illogical and even mad. What he decides on is a kind of controlled self-*destruction* (a wound) as a means of self-*preservation*. Instinct and peacetime logic would suggest that

7. Paul Fussell, *The Great War and Modern Memory* (New York: Oxford University Press, 1975), p. 220.

the best course would be to stay as far away from the enemy and as well concealed as possible; Graves decides to move forward—without being ordered to—and to expose his whole body.

In a way this is another irony of war, which (being at its core mad and illogical) demands a kind of inverted sanity from its participants—a premonition, we might say, of *Catch-22,* where sanity and insanity are hopelessly confused. But this is, after all, something Graves says he has worked out, not merely something he has observed. The war demands, he reasons, a kind of repression or conversion of instinct. The result can be a stereotype of British unflappability, as in the case of Dunn, an officer Graves much admires, who greets the news of a gas attack with a request for more marmalade (p. 105). If irony is a psychological preservative which demands awareness of the absurdity and totality of the situation, there is another means of self-protection which insists that one absolutely refuse to acknowledge circumstances. This reserve, this denial of emotion or instinct, has a great appeal to Graves, although he usually approaches it only by (to use his word) caricature. It explains, at least in part, his affection for the trivia of regimental history and discipline at the same time that he ridicules it. He knows how absurd it is to demand good tailoring as a standard of judgment of an officer (pp. 72–74), but he defends at least the motivation of officers' immense concern for the fine points of discipline and dress (p. 136). Spit and polish and the regalia of historical battles are a kind of ritualized repression of the individual, the emotional, the instinctive.

In terms of this protective repression of instinct, Graves's upbringing was really not so bad a preparation. It taught him, for example, to turn mental anguish into action, and apparently unrelated action, as when he learns, during his near-breakdown at Charterhouse, that boxing is a better solution than honest expression of anxiety (chapter 7). His education and heritage allow him to "masquerade as a gentlemen," as later he will have to masquerade as an officer.

The most significant element of his education was, in a way, not Charterhouse but rock climbing; and it is a case in point of overcoming instinct. As he admits, he was afraid of heights: "Having a bad head for heights myself, I trained myself deliberately and painfully to overcome it. We used to go climbing in the turrets and towers of Harlech Castle. I have worked hard on myself in defining and dispersing my terrors. The simple fear of heights was the first to be overcome" (pp. 34–35). One would not want to push the point too far; as I have already said, no education could adequately prepare one for the Ypres Salient; still the young Graves fighting with his fear of heights would seem to represent an important step toward the older Graves, who could so carefully calculate the best chance of surviving without mention of the fear of darkness or wire or mines or even bullets.

The same element of self-mastery may help explain the presence in the book of Mallory and T. E. Lawrence, who are placed so as to bracket Graves's war experiences. Of course one should not overlook the fame of the two men;[8] Mallory's disappearance on Everest in 1924 was still much in the popular mind when Graves's book came out, and Graves said he wanted to write a popular book. But the two men have in common this element of overcoming their own nature. Graves mentions in passing that Mallory "originally took to climbing . . . as a corrective to his weak heart" (p. 62); and as if to emphasize the point, Graves uses the word "corrective" about a page later, in talking of another of his climbing companions, Conor O'Brien, who "climbed, he told us, principally as a corrective to bad nerves" (p. 63). Lawrence is an even clearer case. *The Seven Pillars of Wisdom,* which had not yet been published but which Graves had read in preparing his book on Lawrence in 1927,[9] is full of conscious and extreme mortifications of flesh and instinct, and of a consistent contempt for the "animal" and the emotional.

Of course, Mallory and Lawrence share a contempt for the conventional as well, a contempt that suits Graves's title and purpose. Graves recalls a small example of that streak in Lawrence which made him march around Versailles in full Arab dress: Lawrence rings a captured Turkish station bell out his window at Oxford, because the place "needs waking up" (p. 302). And Mallory,

8. I have slighted Hardy, who takes up much of the chapter in which Lawrence appears, largely because he does not fit my argument at this point. He had, when the book appeared, just died, and so he fits with the idea of including "famous contemporaries I have known." A case could be made, too, for his presence as an opponent of convention; but that title, however well it fits the Hardy of *Tess* and *Jude,* seems a bit harsh for the rather avuncular Grand Old Man whom Graves met.

9. Robert Graves, *Lawrence and the Arabian Adventure* (Garden City, N.Y.: Doubeday, Doran: 1928), Preface.

Graves says, was in constant trouble with the authorities at Charterhouse and had, at the time of his death, grown "tired of trying to
teach gentlemen to be gentlemen" (p. 62). This fits perfectly with
what Graves says he was able to accomplish by 1928: "If condemned to relive those lost years I would probably behave again in
very much the same way; a conditioning in the Protestant morality
of the English governing classes, though qualified by mixed blood,
a rebellious nature, and an over-riding poetic obsession, is not easily
outgrown" (p. 347). Indeed, one can wonder how completely
Graves did outgrow it. His apparent devotion to the Royal Welch
(his son joined the regiment in World War II; one suspects not over
any objection from his father) and his blithe contempt for foreigners
at the Front and for his Egyptian students both fit a more conventional figure than the title of the work might suggest. Neither
subject is treated with any of the corrective irony which Graves
elsewhere uses to show how he has gotten beyond his "conditioning."

So too with the caricature scenes—it is not at all clear to what
degree and in what sense they are caricatures. The first—Graves's
attendance at a dressing-down of the battalion officers by a colonel
outraged at an enlisted man's addressing a corporal by his Christian
name—is reasonably unambiguous: "Myself in faultless khaki with
highly polished buttons and belt, revolver at hip, whistle on cord,
delicate moustache on upper lip, and stern endeavour a-glint in
either eye, pretending to be a Regular Army captain; but crushed
into that inky desk-bench like an overgrown schoolboy" (p. 180).
The caricature cuts two ways, and Graves the character, it would
appear, is aware of both—the pretense of being an officer, and the
presence of an officer in a schoolboy's desk. In later caricatures the
element of masquerade seems to be mostly in the eye of the older
Graves, although the exact perspective is not clear—as at his wedding (p. 272) or in his shop (p. 308) or on the parish council (p.
317). In any case the scenes—which occur more and more frequently as the book progresses, ending with a catalogue of instances
(p. 341)—represent a dismissal of the possible roles Graves might,
by class or training or circumstance, have taken up; and so a preparation for saying "goodbye to all that." As well they represent
Graves's later recognition of the limitation of the protective mas-
querades his conditioning led him to attempt. But to read some of

Graves's essays is to realize how much of the tone and manner of "the Protestant morality of the English governing classes" he never quite relinquished.[10] In a sense, Graves, to survive, had to take on the trappings of the gentleman officer, even while he saw the ironies of that role; and as he admits, such trappings, no matter why they are taken on, are not easily gotten rid of.

BLUNDEN: LITERATE IGNORANCE

Edmund Blunden begins *Undertones of War* with what would appear to be a sane, if understated, assertion: "I was not anxious to go" (p. 21). Only two pages later (and just after the grenade accident) he has changed his mind: "This particular shock, together with the general dreariness of the great camp [Etaples], produced in me (in spite of the fear with which I had come into France) a wish to be sent quickly to the line" (p. 23). The juxtaposition of the two thoughts points up the essential naiveté of the character Blunden creates for himself; his fear of France is more than anything else a case of anxiety about the unknown, not based on any real knowledge. That Etaples, no matter how unpleasant it was, could drive him toward, and not away from, the Front, is a sign of how little he knew about the trenches. Indeed, the most he can say about the front lines is this: "There was something about France in those days which looked to me, despite all journalistic enchanters, to be dangerous" (p. 21). If we ran across that sentence in *Goodbye to All That*, it would carry a heavy freight of irony. But in Blunden's memoir it must be taken much more at face value, although Blunden is not without irony. Still, it is essential to the nature of Blunden's book that we realize from the beginning how innocent, indeed how ignorant "Bunny" Blunden the character is; and that the naive young officer is not the subject of "caricature" as he is in Graves.

Blunden himself suggests the term "ignorant"; as he remarks when his unit hears rumors of an attack: "With some, unbelief, and with me, ignorance, made a shelter 'against eating cares' for the time being, and at all events some busy weeks must pass before the attack was made" (p. 55). Again and again he emphasizes his lack of knowledge; even after his first trench experiences he observes,

10. See especially "Five Score and Six Years Ago," in *The Crane Bag*. pp. 141–152.

"As yet my notion of modern war was infinitesimal" (p. 34). In the "slaughter-yard" at Cuinchy, Blunden again takes on a protective layer of ignorance: "My ignorance carried me through it with less ado than I can now understand" (p. 46). Much later, not long before Third Ypres, Blunden is yet again protected from news of an impending attack: "Ignorant of the secret news, I went round with Harrison, and was startled by his merciless arrest of a sentry, who, contrary to orders, was wearing a knitted comforter to keep his ears from freezing" (pp. 137–138). The punch line in this case is that Blunden is the intelligence officer of the unit, and he should know the "secret news" if anyone does.

The point is not just that Blunden is naive—the same case could be made about most newly arrived officers—but that ignorance and naiveté are virtues in *Undertones of War;* they allow Blunden to keep his sanity, to "carry through." To be sure, this protective ignorance cannot last. After Third Ypres Blunden allows himself a moment of real despair: "The uselessness of the offensive, the contrast in the quality of ourselves with the quality of the year before, the conviction that the civilian population realized nothing of our state, the rarity of thought, the growing intensity and sweep of destructive forces—these views brought on a mood of selfishness. We should all die, presumably, round Ypres" (p. 181). The content of this passage could easily be paralleled in other memoirs, and it represents a great change from the naiveté of the opening chapters. But the tone is odd; the "I" has disappeared (as often happens in Blunden when any kind of battle or catastrophe hits), and in its place is a "we" that partakes of the tone of regimental histories. Notice too the lack of an object to which one can attach that "mood of selfishness." Blunden uses the same device earlier— "Cambrin was beginning to terrify" (p. 63). But terrify *whom,* exactly?

In any case, at the end of the book, after the horror of Ypres, Blunden's personal knowledge is still limited: "I might have known the war by this time, but I was still too young to know its depth of ironic cruelty" (p. 209). The manner of speaking is characteristically tentative—"I might have known." What is not altogether clear is whether this is another instance of unreliable memory—"I suppose I knew, but I can't quite recall for certain"—or a statement that Blunden has somehow (and intentionally?) avoided knowledge—"It was altogether possible for me to have known, but I did not."

Part of the problem is the distance between Blunden the character and Blunden the memoirist; for it is only the former who is naive. Of course Graves and Sassoon stand in a somewhat similar relation to their characters; but they never try to make their characters quite so naive. The young Graves and George Sherston share with their creators a sense of irony and of their own shortcomings; the young Blunden does not seem to have this. Blunden the memoirist, despite his frequent use of the present tense, constantly reminds us that all that he describes is past and that, no matter how bad things were, they got worse. Blunden the character observes, "It was as though war forgot some corners of Flanders"—and Blunden the memoirist immediately adds a parenthesis: "Next year, war remembered that corner with a vengeance" (p. 196). And at the end of the book the writer comments directly on the limited vision of the character, who had, as he rode through a small town on his way home from the front, "no conjecture that, in a few weeks, Buire-sur-Ancre would appear much the same as the cataclysmal railway cutting by Hill 60" (p. 209).

The point is that, just as Graves saw the limitations of irony as a psychological defense (there were times when it simply did not work), Blunden sees the limitations of naiveté. No matter how persistent and resilient it may be, it cannot last—but it may allow one to survive the immediate experience of war.

This naiveté is not merely a psychological device; it is as well a literary device, a part of Blunden's effort to "place" the war in a literary tradition. The literariness of World War I writings is one of their most distinguishing features, especially to an American reader more familiar with World War II, Korea, and Vietnam; it is hard, in an immensely less literary culture and time, to imagine a world in which an enlisted man was constantly reminded of *Henry V,* as David Jones says he was.[11] The attempt to use literature, or rather to find a literary tradition that might adequately fit the war, is more than an odd quirk of mind or a legacy of Edwardian education. In the first place, literature was one of the few forms of relief in the trenches, as Blunden mentions: "During this period my indebt-

11. David Jones, *In Parenthesis* (London: Faber and Faber paperback, 1975), p. 196 (Note 24).

edness to an eighteenth-century poet became enormous. At every spare moment I read in Young's *Night Thoughts on Life, Death, and Immortality* . . . The mere amusement of discovering lines applicable to our crisis kept me from despair" (p. 187). Literature is a pastime and, as well, a means of keeping one's sanity; the same is true of the *making* of literature out of the war.

The effort to make literature is a means of organizing and comprehending an experience which seems otherwise utterly foreign, chaotic, and incomprehensible. The persistent note in all these memoirs—that the war is somehow indescribable[12]—is more than a writer's complaint about the intractability of his material; it is a statement of the fundamental nature of the experience of the war. Insofar as that experience could be made to stand in some literary tradition, insofar as some traditional form or language could successfully be applied to life in the trenches, the experience of the Front could be made sensible and coherent.

But of course the great difficulty is that the war does not seem to have fit any tradition of form or language very well at all; so the integration of the experience in literary terms was inevitably difficult and ambiguous. This can be demonstrated in terms of Blunden's use of the pastoral. We have already seen the pastoral innocence or naiveté of his protagonist. Some elements of the form seem forced—asides like "turn, Amaryllis, turn" (p. 94) are hard to stomach. But we should not lose sight of the complex use Blunden makes of the pastoral scene.

The pastoral is a kind of escape, as the rural world of the fox-hunt is for Sassoon. The difference is that Blunden sees the pastoral during the war, not merely in some Golden Age before 1914. Indeed, Blunden says almost nothing about his past. The pastoral is present and very real. After his first tour in the Line, Blunden is immensely refreshed by rural France:

The joyful path away from the Line, on that glittering summer morning, was full of pictures for my infant war-mind . . . The empty farm houses were not yet effigies of agony or mounds of punished, atomized material; they

12. The point that the experience of war generally is not only indescribable but, despite the vast literature on the subject, *undescribed,* has been powerfully argued by the historian John Keegan in his fine book *The Face of Battle: A Study of Agincourt, Waterloo and the Somme* (New York: Viking, 1976); see especially his first chapter.

could still shelter, and they did . . . Acres of self-sown wheat glistened and sighed as we wound our way between, where rough scattered pits recorded a hurried firing-line of long ago. Life, life abundant sang here and smiled; the lizard ran warless in the warm dust; and the ditches were trembling quick with odd tiny fish, in worlds as remote as Saturn.   (pp. 38–39)

The passage is only one example; there are any number of others that parallel it almost exactly. Nature is alive, abundant, regenerative, restorative—at least to the naive Blunden. What is just as important as the sense of joy and relief is the note of ominous threat. Blunden the writer will not let us forget that he knows more than his character did; so the small phrase "not yet" serves to show the limitations of the "infant war-mind." The result is a picture of Eden under siege, and perhaps doomed.

But the natural, the pastoral, the orderly is not only endangered by war, it is implicated in it; at times Nature is not an alternative but an active partner: "A deluge of heavy shells was rushing into the ground all round, baffling any choice of movement, and the blackness rocked with blasts of crashing sound and flame. Rain (for Nature came to join the dance) glistened in the shocks of dizzy light" (p. 45). What is most characteristic of the pastoral scenes in the book is not a contrast between the idyllic and the warlike, but the immixture of the two. So the headquarters at Potijze Chateau "enjoyed a kind of Arcadian environment" (p. 136), which Blunden goes on to describe in a long paragraph—only to end with this: "In the ground floor of this white chateau, which still had a conservatory door, was a dressing-station; outside lay a dump of steel rails, concertina wire, planks and pit-props, now mostly frozen into the ground; opposite was a low farm building, Lancer Farm, in which was the bomb store" (p. 137). The war has literally settled itself in the heart of the pastoral; the question is whether the pastoral can possibly endure, or whether it will be utterly effaced by the physical reality of the war: "A line of slender trees, and a strip of grass, gave us a hint of pastoral as we looked out, but what one was most aware of was the interminable clump, clump, clump of boots on trench boards" (p. 149).

In any case, the issue will not easily be decided; and the mind that seeks out the pastoral as a means of establishing some sort of sanity is left with a tense alternation of the pastoral and the horrible:

"Auchonvilliers at that time was a good example of the miscellaneous, picturesque, pitiable, pleasing, appalling, intensely intimate village ruin close to the line" (p. 93).

SASSOON: THE ACCIDENTAL HERO

Siegfried Sassoon's three-volume "memoir" of George Sherston seems to me to be not only the longest but the richest and most complex of the three memoirs, in part at least because it combines the irony and "caricature" of *Goodbye to All That* with elements of pastoral and protective ignorance such as we find in *Undertones of War*.

The texture of the book is apparently so straightforward that it is easy to ignore how carefully arranged it is. For example, Sassoon uses the early pages of the first volume to establish some fundamental paradigms, especially a pattern of what we might call "accidental heroism." Part 2 of the *Memoirs of a Fox-Hunting Man* ("The Flower Show Match") is a convenient case in point.[13] The atmosphere of remembrance and rural simplicity is characteristic, as is the gently deflating humor, much of it directed at Sherston himself. What is not so apparent at first reading is the way the narrative shape of the incident parallels many of Sherston's later experiences.

The incident is quite simple: George is involved in the match unexpectedly and by someone else. His initial reaction is disbelief, although he manages a brave front for his Aunt Evelyn; but he seriously doubts his own ability. The match involves Sherston rather little. George spends much of the day watching, not the match but the flower show; and the underlying question of whether he will bat and if so, how well he will do, is present only as a kind of counterpoint. In the end, he does bat; and, almost accidentally, he wins the match: "There was the enormous auctioneer with the ball in his hand. And there I, calmly resolved to look lively and defeat his destructive aim. The ball hit my bat and trickled slowly up the pitch. 'Come on!' I shouted, and Peter came gallantly on. Crump

13. All references to Sassoon's Sherston trilogy are to the following editions: *Memoirs of a Fox-Hunting Man*, identified in the text as *Fox-Hunting* (New York: Coward-McCann, 1929); *Memoirs of an Infantry Officer*, identified in the text as *Infantry* (New York: Coward-McCann, 1930); *Sherston's Progress*, identified in the text as *Progress* (Garden City, N.Y.: Doubleday, Doran, 1936). "The Flower Show Match" is on pages 52–81 of *Fox-Hunting*.

was so taken by surprise that we were safe home before he'd picked up the ball. And that was the end of the Flower Show Match" (*Fox-Hunting*, p. 81).

The pattern of unwitting involvement, self-doubt, waiting, and abrupt and ironically "heroic" (to everyone but Sherston) activity is repeated almost exactly later in the race for the Colonel's Cup (*Fox-Hunting*, part 6, pp. 187–227). And it fits rather well many of his experiences in the war, most especially Sherston's part in the Battle of the Somme (*Infantry*, pp. 58–115). Indeed, it could stand as a kind of outline of the war itself, which was full of orders from above, anxiety and doubt (especially when apparently superior men are killed), long periods of waiting, and sudden and often apparently pointless (to the participants) activity which is quickly (on the Home Front) converted to great deeds and heroic victory.

Even when the entire pattern does not recur, elements of it do. Consider how many figures nearly take over Sherston's life, as Tom Dixon the groom does in the early chapters: Denis Milden later in Sherston's hunting career, Cromlech/Robert Graves and Tyrel/Bertrand Russell during the antiwar crisis, and finally the psychologist Rivers. The power of each of these men over Sherston is based on Sherston's sense of inadequacy and his fear of shame. Sherston, like Graves, feels himself much involved in masquerade; and, even more than Graves, he is morally uncertain about that masquerade. The morning of the flower show match, his great worry is that his pads will not be appropriately white; that is, that he will not look the part (*Fox-Hunting*, pp. 56–57). And of course at the crucial point, quoted above, he wants to "*look* lively." Later Sherston again and again will feel himself to be a fraud or imposter.[14] His skills as an actor reach a high point of sorts when, having been seriously wounded, he receives visitors in hospital and carefully tailors his behavior to suit the taste of each (*Infantry*, pp. 236–237). Running all through his gesture against the war is a persistent note of play-acting; as if Sherston (and Sassoon) can never quite be sure of his own motivation.

Part of that doubt is Sherston's sense of his own lack of knowledge. Waiting to confront the authorities with his statement on the war, Sherston goes home to Butley "resolved to read for dear

14. See, for example, *Fox-Hunting*, pp. 301 and 358; *Infantry*, p. 76.

life—circumstances having made it imperative that I should accu-
mulate as much solid information as I could. But sedulous study
only served to open up the limitless prairies of my ignorance"
(*Infantry,* p. 288). Sherston reads, it would appear from this, only
under the pressure of circumstance; earlier, he spends most of his
time perusing the hunting news and Surtees novels. Sherston feels
his ignorance, but not necessarily as a bad thing or an accident. In
the present circumstance it chafes a bit, to be sure; but earlier he has
made it clear that his parochialism is a matter of choice. For example, he consciously and intentionally ignores lawyer Pennett's advice to go back to Cambridge, even though he admits that "everything [Pennett's] letter said was so true" (*Fox-Hunting,* p. 86).

Sherston, then, seems able to combine the play-acting which is so
important to Graves with something like the protective ignorance of
Blunden; but with a crucial element of self-consciousness added to
the latter, an element which Blunden (the character) totally lacks.
As a result, Sherston's moments of heroism, however real they may
be, seem to him to be based on fraud and stupidity. This is one
reason he can so easily accept the Medical Board as a way out of his
antiwar dilemma; he has throughout the affair been rather doubtful
about the whole business. He seems (by his description) to have
stumbled into the decision almost by accident of circumstance. A
wound, a convalescence, a period in the country, an impulsive letter
and lunch with an antiwar editor—all add to the possibility of the
ultimate decision, but none seems to have been more than accident
or impulse. Finally Sherston makes his decision: "I was conscious
of the stream of life going on its way, happy and untroubled, while
I had just blurted out something which alienated me from its acceptance of a fine day in the third June of the Great War . . . I saw myself
'attired with sudden brightness, like a man inspired,' and while
Markington continued his counsels of prudence my resolve
strengthened toward its ultimate obstinacy" (*Infantry,* p. 271). The
language is of great importance: "blurted" and "obstinacy" combined with the self-important literary tag line allow Sassoon to
deflate what might otherwise have appeared to the reader to be a
moment of heroism; and Sassoon implies that this deflation is not
the act of the older man thinking back, but an essential part of
Sherston's mind at the time. Linguistically, it is the same as the way
in which, at the climax of the flower show match, he deprives young

George of any real credit for his game-winning blow by arranging the syntax so that the ball hits the bat, and not vice versa.

But the language here fits another side of Sherston's character as well. Aside from his moments of rather detached "accidental heroism," Sherston is from time to time seized by fits of irrational or (as Sassoon calls them) "suicidal" activity. Here the motive force is not suggestion but news of a death which strikes Sherston with unusual force—the death of Dick Tiltwood, or of Lance Corporal Kendle during the Somme, or, as a kind of variation on a theme, his own wound: "I began to feel rabidly heroical again, but in a slightly different style, since I was now a wounded hero, with my arm in a superfluous sling . . . I felt that I must make one more onslaught before I turned my back on the War . . . My over-strained nerves had wrought me up to such a pitch of excitement that I was ready for any suicidal exploit" (*Infantry*, pp. 228–229). Again the language is the key—"rabidly" and "suicidal" are the important words. This is, in a sense, what Sherston has in place of the apparent calculation and logic of Graves; but Sherston at least knows precisely how mad it is, while Graves, explicitly at least, would deny any madness whatever.

In the third volume of the memoir all these characteristics come into play to get Sherston through his last tour in the trenches. His sense of masquerade and fraud underlies his mood as he returns to the Battalion: "In what, for the sake of exposition, I will call my soul (Grand Soul Theatre; performances nightly;) protagonistic performances were keeping the drama alive" (*Progress*, p. 77). But now the masquerade is not something to feel guilty about, despite the irony of the description; it is a vital part of continuing to live, psychologically: "For my soul had rebelled against the War, and not even Rivers could cure it of that. To feel in some sort of way heroic—that was the only means I could devise for 'carrying on' " (*Progress*, p. 77).

The previous two volumes make it clear what an immense task it was for Sherston "to feel in some sort of way heroic." He must now intensify his mental limitations into a kind of willed stupidity (he calls it being "as brainless as I could," *Progress*, p. 78), and he must learn to play-act without discomfort, to allow "myself to become what they expected me to be" (*Progress*, p. 86). His sense of irony—which depends on a kind of detachment—must become something greater; he must, as he puts it, get completely outside what is going on, not physically (he has in fact immersed himself intentionally in the war) but psychologically: "Since last year I seem to be getting outside of things a bit better" (*Progress*, p. 155).

But this detachment founders. Sherston feels a loyalty to the men which at times verges on the Messianic, but which at least provides a purpose for his life and for his presence in the trenches. And his old impulsiveness crops up again: "I was lapsing into my rather feckless 1916 self" (*Progress*, p. 221). In the end what allows him to survive, really, is luck—the good fortune that makes the shell landing right next to him a dud (*Progress*, p. 225)—and, in the real crisis, his humor. Lying wounded he thinks, "I had been young and exuberant, and now I was just a dying animal, on the verge of oblivion. And then a queer thing happened. My sense of humour stirred in me, and—emerging from that limbo of desolate defeat—I thought, 'I suppose I ought to say something special—last words of a dying soldier' " (*Progress*, p. 233).

"Emerging from that limbo of desolate defeat"—expanded a bit beyond its immediate context, the phrase can stand rather well as a motto for the survivors. *How* to emerge is the problem; and more, how to emerge *sane*. To Sassoon, it is only possible by means of a complex of devices, such as he recreates in the mind of Sherston.

FORMULATIONS AND MEMOIRS

These three men did survive, physically and (at least to some degree) psychologically; but all of them find it difficult to decide precisely how this came to be. Each writer sees the limitations of the psychological devices he proposes; which points to the greater problem. Granted that they survived at the time; could they survive the remembering?

To put it another way, each of these men had to face the problem of guilt, the sense that their survival was undeserved—the feeling that is the common inheritance of all survivors of twentieth-century holocausts. R. J. Lifton emphasizes the crucial importance of "formulation," the "process by which the [survivor] re-creates himself" as a means of dealing with this guilt:

Formulation includes efforts to re-establish three essential elements of psychic function: the *sense of connection*, or organic relationship to the people as well as non-human elements in one's life space, whether immediate or distant and imagined; the *sense of symbolic integrity*, of the cohesion and significance of one's life . . . and the *sense of movement*, of development and change, in the continous struggle between fixed identity and individuation.[15]

These war memoirs represent, I think, a polished and literary form of "formulation," a way of making psychological order out of the experience of the First World War.

But as a literary form, the memoir adds a difficult dimension to this process of formulation. Formulation as Lifton defines it is personal and need have no necessary correspondence to reality. It need not, in other words, be factually correct, because (if for no other reason) few people except its creator will ever hear of it. A memoir, on the other hand, pretends to be a kind of history, however impressionistic; and these memoirists were all aware of their audience. That audience would inevitably test the memoir against its own war experience; these men wrote, quite consciously, to their fellow survivors, and even to those who did not survive. The memoirists could find some protection in an acknowledgment of the distortions of memory, as Blunden does: "I know that memory has her little ways, and by now she has concealed precisely that look, that word, that coincidence of nature without and nature within which I long to remember" (p. 11). And they could indulge, to a degree, in an artistic rearrangement to heighten the consistency of their experience. So Blunden says nothing about his own wounds or gassing, maintaining the picture of the oddly protected "Bunny"; Sassoon, to draw more fully perhaps on the tradition of the dim-witted country gentleman, says nothing of the literary career that was well under way while Sherston was still single-mindedly fox-hunting; and Graves, as Fussell shows,[16] changes the chronology of his own near-fatal wounding for dramatic effect.

But neither the "little ways" of memory nor the usually allowable distortions of fiction would justify straying too far from the nature of the war experience, as these three men had known it and as their fellow-soldiers, like the mysterious Stetson in *The Waste Land*, had also known it. But then, of course, they were brought face to face again with the commonly agreed upon fact that the war was, in

---

15. Lifton, *Death in Life*, p. 367.
16. Fussell, *The Great War and Modern Memory*, p. 215.

almost all important ways, indescribable, even unimaginable. Both
segments of their audience—those who had been in the war and
those who had not—were potential critics, the one because what
was said did not match their own knowledge, the other because the
description seemed unreal. The idea that the experience cannot be
communicated—"you had to have been there"—is precisely the
note that one finds in the accounts of survivors of other holocausts.
Here, for example, is Blunden: "I know that the experience to be
sketched is very local, limited, incoherent; that it is almost useless,
in the sense that no one will read it who is not already aware of all
the intimations and discoveries in it, and many more, by reason of
having gone the same Journey. No one? Some, I am sure; but not
many. *Neither will they understand*—that will not be all my fault"
(p. 11; italics Blunden's). And here is Elie Wiesel, talking about a
recent television recreation of the later and always capitalized Holocaust: "The witness feels here dutybound to declare: What you have
seen on the screen is not what happened *there*. You may think
you know now how the victims lived and died, but you do not.
Auschwitz cannot be explained nor can it be visualized . . . The dead
are in possession of a secret that we, the living, are neither worthy
of nor capable of recovering."[17]

But alongside that sense of the impossibility of the task goes what
Terence Des Pres calls "the will to bear witness."[18] Blunden states
it as a matter of necessity: "I must go over the ground again" (p.
12). His poem "II Peter ii, 22" amplifies that statement (p. 239); it
is the sense that knowledge of the war is somehow fading away, that
people will not remember, that drives him to write.

Although the war in the trenches seems to an outsider neither as
catastrophic nor as unimaginable as the death-camps or Hiroshima,
in one way at least the psychological problem may have been worse
for these memoirists than for later survivors. Instead of being mere
victims, these men were volunteers and agents. They enlisted freely
and they were officers; and therefore they were inescapably responsible for what happened to themselves and to those around
them. Graves, in a typically pseudo-scientific way—Sassoon says

17. Elie Wiesel, "The Trivializing of the Holocaust," *New York Times*, Sunday,
16 April 1978, sec. 2, p. 29.

18. Des Pres, *The Survivor*, Chapter II.

"he was always fond of a formula" (*Infantry*, p. 157)—explains the peculiar difficulties of the officer:

> After a year or fifteen months [in the trenches] he was often worse than useless. Dr. W. H. R. Rivers told me later that the action of one of the ductless glands—I think the thyroid—caused this slow general decline in military usefulness, by failing at a certain point to pump its stimulating chemical into the blood. Without its continued assistance the man went about his tasks in an apathetic and doped condition, cheated into further endurance . . . Officers had a less laborious but a more nervous time than the men. (pp. 171–172)

Of course, as Sassoon realized, even for an officer there was nothing much to be done about the war; and for him, at least, his own agency, his ability to make things a little easier for his men, was a vital part of his ability to carry on. But the burden of that responsibility and guilt was something that Blunden and Sassoon at least seem never quite to have overcome (Graves may have been a bit tougher and therefore more able to go on). In any case the difficulty of psychologically surviving the war and the scars it left on its survivors may be a partial explanation of the fact that the greatest art of that generation was made either by those not involved in the war at all, or by those involved only rather peripherally. The participants could neither escape nor completely accomplish the difficult task of personal, psychological self-preservation.

It is important to remind ourselves that modernist detachment is more than an aesthetic rebellion against the "personality" of Romanticism; it is as well a response to what modernists felt was an increasingly unlivable present: paralyzed Dublin, Mauberly's culturally vapid London, Eliot's yellow fogs and gas works, the monstrous forces of Conversion personified by Woolf's sinister Dr. Bradshaw, Chatterley's sterility—the list is nearly endless. Graves, Blunden, and Sassoon, as memoirists, are modernist in their effort to work out this response under conditions of unusual pain. As works of art their books are unlikely to challenge *Ulysses* or *Mrs. Dalloway,* but they stand, at the very least, at the head of that tragically rich vein of twentieth-century writing which has its roots both in modernism and in atrocity: the literature of survival.

PHYLLIS ROSE

Modernism: The Case of Willa Cather

In the 1950's David Daiches cannily predicted that literary historians would have difficulty placing Willa Cather.[1] He did not foresee that Cather's work would be underrated because it was hard to place, but such may have been the case. It could be said that Cather has been ignored because she was a woman, but that would not explain why her rediscovery has taken ten years longer than Virginia Woolf's. Generally perceived as a traditionalist, Cather has been patronized. Many people read her for pleasure, but for the past twenty years few have taught her works or written about them. The novels seem curiously self-evident. They are defiantly smooth and elegant, lacking the rough edges that so often provide convenient starting points for literary analysis. To a critical tradition that has valued complexity, ambiguity, even obscurity, the hard-won simplicities of Cather's art seem merely simple. Her lucidity can be read as shallowness; her massive, abstract forms can be—and have been—viewed as naively traditional, the appropriate vehicle for an art essentially nostalgic and elegaic.

Although I am deeply distrustful of the way in which, for twentieth-century writers, the term "modernist" is not merely an honorific but the precondition of attention from literary critics and

1. David Daiches, *Willa Cather: A Critical Introduction* (Ithaca, New York: Cornell University Press, 1951), p. 189.

scholars, I will nonetheless try to show ways in which Willa Cather's work is allied to modernism. I do this by way of redressing a balance. Her public stance was so belligerently reactionary (perhaps in order to mask the radically unacceptable nature of her private life) that she herself encouraged the flattening of her work into a glorification of the past, a lament for the shabbiness of the present, which has persisted for decades. The writer who titled a collection of essays *Not Under Forty* would have been the last person to feel congratulated at being called a modernist. But it is time to risk her wrath. In part because of her defensive self-presentation, in part because her fiction so perfectly embodies certain aesthetic ideals of modernism—monumentality, functionalism, anonymity—we have overlooked its innovative nature. To see its modernist elements is to readjust and enrich our response to her work—and also to widen our notions of modernism. If Cather is a modernist, she is a tempered, transitional modernist closer to Hardy than to Pound. Nonetheless, her work is moved in important ways by a modernist urge to simplify and to suggest the eternal through the particular. Because we have paid more attention to other aspects of literary modernism—the overtly experimental, the representation of subjectivity, the literary analogues of cubist collage—we react to Cather's novels as though we have stumbled across some giant work of nature, a boulder, something so massive that it seems inhuman, uncrafted. But I would suggest that what we have stumbled upon in fact is something like the literary equivalent of an Arp, a Brancusi, a Moore.

I would point first of all to her scale. I do not mean, of course, the size of her books, for they are conspicuously slender, little masterpieces of economy; I mean the size of the subjects to which her imagination responds. In her strongest work, the land is as much a presence as the human characters, and the landscapes that move her imagination are large and unbroken ones, the plains and fields of the American Midwest, the canyonlands and deserts of the Southwest. Reading *O Pioneers!*, *My Ántonia*, or *Death Comes for the Archbishop*, we experience the exhilarating potential of clear blank spaces.[2] Few novels I can think of are less cluttered than these; they

---

2. I borrow the phrase from Robert Pinsky, whose tribute to Cather forms an important part of his epic poem, *An Explanation of America* (Princeton, N.J.: Princeton University Press, 1979).

offer the breathing space of all outdoors, and one feels that Cather may be describing herself when she says of Alexandra Bergson, the Swedish immigrant farmer who is her first great female protagonist, that she was uncertain in her indoor tastes and expressed herself best in her fields, that properly speaking her house was the out-of-doors.[3]

The vast Nebraska prairie, which Cather saw for the first time when she was ten, transplanted from the hill-enclosed perspectives of Virginia, determined—or answered to—her sense of scale. Whether it happened when she was ten, or, as seems more likely to me, when as a grown woman, a harried and successful magazine editor in New York, she turned her inner eye back to the landscape of her childhood, the landscape of her dreams, the impact of the prairie on her sense of self was probably such as her narrative stand-in, Jim Burden, describes in *My Ántonia:*

There seemed to be nothing to see; no fences, creeks, or trees, no hills or fields. If there was a road, I could not make it out in the faint starlight. There was nothing but land: not a country at all, but the material out of which countries are made . . . I had the feeling that the world was left behind, that we had got over the edge of it, and were outside men's jurisdiction. I had never before looked up at the sky when there was not a familiar mountain ridge against it. But this was the complete dome of heaven, all there was of it . . . I don't think I was homesick. If we never arrived anywhere, it did not matter. Between that earth and that sky I felt erased, blotted out.[4]

To feel "erased, blotted out" is not, from Cather's perspective, such a bad thing. The scale of the landscape erases trivialities of personality, and in one of the most beautiful passages in American literature Cather presents Jim at his happiest, most fully alive, when he has become a mere creature on the earth, sitting in his grandmother's garden, resting his back against a sun-warmed pumpkin, his individuality transcended. "I kept as still as I could. Nothing happened. I did not expect anything to happen. I was something that lay under the sun and felt it, like the pumpkins, and I did not want to be anything more. I was entirely happy. Perhaps we feel like that when we die and become part of something entire, whether it is sun

---

3. Willa Cather, *O Pioneers!* (Boston: Houghton Mifflin, n.d.), p. 84. Further citations of this work, identified by page numbers in the text, refer to this edition.

4. Willa Cather, *My Ántonia* (Boston: Houghton Mifflin, n.d.), pp. 15–16. Further citations of this work, identified by page numbers in the text, refer to this edition.

and air, or goodness and knowledge. At any rate, that is happiness; to be dissolved into something complete and great" (p. 18).

Against the background of the plains, only the biggest stories stand out, only stories based on the largest, strongest, most elemental emotions. "There are only two or three human stories," Cather wrote in *O Pioneers!*, "and they go on repeating themselves as fiercely as if they had never happened before; like the larks in this country, that have been singing the same five notes over for thousands of years" (p. 119). If you approach *O Pioneers!* as a naturalistic account of the conquest of new land, four-fifths of the book is anticlimactic, even irrelevant, and you must wonder why the story of the adulterous love of Emil Bergson and Marie Shabata and their murder by her jealous husband is taking up so much space in a book about pioneers. In fact, the love of Emil and Marie, growing as inevitably as Frank's murderous jealousy, is the focus of the story, along with the autumnal attachment of Alexandra Bergson and Carl Lindstrum, Alexandra's ambition, and her fatigue. The rhythms of the seasons are matched by the natural growth of human emotions. Typically, Cather uses a metaphor of seed-corn to compare Emil's guilty passion for Marie with the happy love of his friend, Amédée: "From two ears that had grown up side by side, the grains of one shot joyfully into the light, projecting themselves into the future, and the grains from the other lay still in the earth and rotted; and nobody knew why" (p. 164). As in ballads, motivation is played down; motives in such oft-enacted human stories are assumed to speak for themselves. Amédée dies in the prime of life of a ruptured appendix; Emil dies from the gunshot blast of a man who is so enraged he hardly knows what he is doing and who is presented as acting with no conscious volition. In a curious way, both deaths seem equally natural in this novel which presents the life of man and the life of earth as concurrent, equivalent.

In the American Southwest, which Cather visited for the first time in 1912, she found not only another monumental landscape but the temporal equivalent for the vast spaces of the Midwest. For these were not, like the plains, uninhabited spaces whose history was just beginning. Here and there, tucked in the great half-dome caverns on the cliff-sides of canyons, were the remains of an ancient, civilized people. The cliff-dwelling Indians had lived, cultivated the land, and, in their weavings and pottery, produced art, long before Europeans had landed on American soil. The effect of Anasazi art and architecture on Cather's aesthetic was profound, but for the moment I want to concentrate merely on the imaginative impact of a long-inhabited, long-abandoned monumental landscape. It lengthened the past. If you included the Indians, American history, which had seemed so small and cramped a thing, suddenly became vast. When Thea Kronborg in *The Song of the Lark* and Tom Outland of *The Professor's House* encounter the canyonlands, the effect on their senses of themselves is like the effect of the prairie on Jim Burden: it obliterates the trivial and raises them, spiritually, to its own scale, uniting them to something larger than themselves.

Cather's imagination craved and fed on large scale, both in time and space, and her books repeatedly struggle to break outside the confines of town or city life and make their way, quite against the grain of the narrative, back to the wilderness. *The Song of the Lark* gets to Panther Canyon by way of the unlikely premise that Thea Kronborg, studying music in Chicago, needs the experience of exactly that locale to change her from a good artist into a great one. The relationship between Tom Outland's story of the discovery of the cliff-dweller ruins on the Blue Mesa (a version of the true story of the discovery of Mesa Verde by Richard Wetherill) bears an even more tenuous plot connection to the rest of *The Professor's House,* which concerns a transitional crisis in the life of a midwestern university professor. Thematic justification for the interpolated story may of course be found, but I find it more interesting to note how it does *not* fit into the rest of the novel. In the sudden, eccentric switch to the southwestern locale, we witness a Catherian compulsion. Explaining it, however, as an experiment in form (a tactic that would have been more persuasive had she not done something so similar in *The Song of the Lark*), Cather said she wanted to reproduce the effect of a square window opening onto a distant prospect set into a Dutch genre painting of a warmly furnished interior. She said she wanted the reader first to stifle amidst the trappings of American bourgeois domesticity, then to feel the clean air blowing in from the mesa.[5] This suggests that the contrast between inside and outside worlds is essential to the power of both. But the effect of the massive dislocation within *The Professor's House* is less like the

5. Willa Cather, "On *The Professor's House,* " in *Willa Cather on Writing* (New York: Knopf, 1949), p. 31.

effect of Dutch genre painting, which carefully subordinates one scale to the other, than it is like the effect of surrealism, with its willful changes of scale and its reminders, within a canvas, of the artificiality of the canvas—Magritte's painting of a view out the window blocked by a painting of a view out the window, or Charles Sheeler's ironic *The Artist Looks at Nature* which depicts Sheeler out-of-doors, painting a kitchen interior. It is Cather herself who stifles in the house-bound, small-town scenes, craves open air, and inserts the outdoors into the indoors as willfully as Sheeler's self-portrait does the reverse, justifying the change however she can. (The novel's epigraph, a quotation from itself, also seems a justification of the form: "A turquoise set in silver, wasn't it? . . . Yes, a turquoise set in dull silver.") The first part of the novel seems to me strained—overly didactic, underlining all points, the dialogue forced—but when we move to the mesa, the writing achieves that effortless symbolic quality which is Cather's distinctive note and best achievement, in which everything seems radiant and significant, but in a way no one could precisely explain.

The pattern in *The Song of the Lark* and *The Professor's House* is repeated in her work as a whole. She alternates between two modes—a more conventional realism, which is evoked when she sets herself the task of describing people in groups, living in houses, and a more abstract and lyrical mode, evoked by people against a landscape. Writing about indoor people—Thea Kronborg, Bartley Alexander, Godfrey St. Peter—she writes in small strokes, with more circumstantial detail, with more accounts of what people think and say. Her first novel, *Alexander's Bridge,* was in this mode and has always reminded readers of the work of Henry James and Edith Wharton. Later, Cather preferred to think of *O Pioneers!* as her first novel, because it was the one in which she discovered the lyrical mode that she considered her authentic style. It is the mode in which her best books—*My Ántonia,* and *Death Comes for the Archbishop* as well as *O Pioneers!*—are written.[6] Deeply associated with it, perhaps necessary to generate it, is the quality I have been calling scale.

I have already touched on the way in which scale determines an approach to character, but I would like to go into it more fully. The

6. See Cather, "My First Novels [There Were Two]," in *Willa Cather on Writing,* pp. 91–97.

illusion of grandeur in her protagonists is another feature of Cather's most exhilarating work, and this illusion, I suggest, depends on simplification.

We are first introduced to Alexandra Bergson, for example, through the eyes of a traveling salesman who is never named, whose role is never developed, whose sole function is to provide a perspective on the heroine. And what does he think of her? That she is "a fine human creature" who makes him wish he was more of a man. That is, she makes an impact without individuation. Although Alexandra has a good deal of character—she is placid, firm, in some ways a visionary (about the future of the Divide), yet wholly unimaginative about other people's emotions—Cather's presentation of her consists of broad strokes. Alexandra is not clever in the manner of city-bred and well-educated people, such as the characters Cather had written about in *Alexander's Bridge;* and that absence of cleverness allowed—perhaps forced—Cather to treat character in a new way in *O Pioneers!.* Alexandra cannot be an interesting "center of consciousness" in a Jamesian sense, because her consciousness is insufficiently complex. Nor is it the most important part of her. "Her personal life, her own realization of herself, was almost a subconscious existence; like an underground river that came to the surface only here and there, at intervals months apart, and then sank again to flow under her fields" (p. 203). Her conscious mind is a "white book, with clear writing about weather and beasts and growing things. Not many people would have cared to read it" (p. 205). So we do not explore her consciousness. We see her resolutely from the outside, and this, along with Cather's persistent contrast of her in terms of size to those around her (" 'What a hopeless position you are in, Alexandra!' [Carl] exclaimed feverishly. 'It is your fate to be always surrounded by little men,' " p. 181), creates the illusion of grandeur which is a distinguishing trait of Cather's heroines, although they may be as different in background and personality as Ántonia Shimerda and Marian Forrester.

For Jamesian centers of consciousness, Cather substitutes objects of admiration. Her favorite narrator is the adoring young person, usually a man, creating out of some woman a creature with mythic resonance: Jim Burden and Ántonia, Niel Herbert and Marian Forrester in *A Lost Lady,* also Nellie Birdseye and Myra Henshawe in *My Mortal Enemy.* Ántonia provides the best example, for she is not so much characterized as mythicized from the opening—"This girl seemed to mean to us the country, the conditions, the whole adventure of our childhood"—to the conclusion: "She lent herself to immemorial attitudes which we recognize by instinct as universal and true . . . She had only to stand in the orchard, to put her hand on a little crab tree and look up at the apples, to make you feel the goodness of planting and tending and harvesting at last . . . She was a rich mine of life, like the founders of early races" (p. 353). Ántonia lingers in the mind more as a goddess of fertility than as an individuated woman; to Jim, certainly, she is archetypal woman, her face "the closest, realest face, under all the shadows of women's faces" (p. 322).

Cather shared the impatience with individuated character that she saw reflected in the way southwestern Indians spoke English or Spanish, dropping the definite articles: not "the mountain" but "mountain"; not "the woman" but "woman."[7] She often presents her characters as conduits for a divine spirit, raised above human powers by some force above or below consciousness, approaching the condition of gods, goddesses, or saints. In her portrait of Archbishop Latour, who could so easily have been made to seem a cathedral-building, executive, and managerial paragon, Cather goes out of her way to deemphasize willed activity. We see him first when he is lost in the desert, able to forget his own thirst through meditation on and identification with Christ's agony on the cross, and from then on, his "story" is largely a record of his finding or losing the spirit of God. Cather repeatedly chooses artists as subjects because she has an archaic sense of the way, in performing or creating, they are possessed by divine inspiration, a sacred breath that blows away consciousness of the petty circumstances of their lives, so that Thea Kronborg, for example, can look harried and fatigued in the afternoon, but that night, performing at the Met, she is the essence of youthful idealism.

Cather's art is peculiarly keen at registering surges of energy and at noting the presence or absence of spirit—in an innocent girl like Lucy Gayheart or in an amoral woman like Marian Forrester, who resembles Lucy only in that she puts her whole heart into everything

7. See Cather, *Death Comes for the Archbishop* (New York: Vintage Books, 1971), p. 91. Further citations of this work, identified by page numbers in the text, refer to this edition.

she does. Indeed, most of Cather's heroines—Lucy, Marian, Antonia, and Alexandra—have the capacity, sometimes harmful to themselves, to live so intensely that they seem like powers more than people, and one sometimes feels that Cather has set herself the task of portraying pure spirit divorced from circumstance, that background and circumstance are merely accidents, and that in the earth-mother Ántonia as in the bitchy, bitter Myra Henshawe, what is essential is the vital breath. Although she would have been appalled by the terms "blood knowledge" and "head knowledge," Cather resembles Lawrence in her desire to bypass the conscious and intellectual elements in her characters in quest of the instinctual and unconscious. These elements she found most accessible in simple people like the farmers of the Divide, in the devout, like the Old World Catholics of her later books, or, in their ideal imagined form, Indians. (When Mabel Dodge married Tony Luhan, a Taos Indian, and many of her friends asked how she could do it, Willa Cather reportedly said, "How could she not?")

But if Cather and Lawrence were in some sense after the same thing in their characters, they went about it in very different ways, and she attacks him as a mere cataloguer of physical sensations and emotions in her most important critical statement, "The Novel Démeublé." Most of this essay is a rather predictable attack on the novel of physical realism which she calls "over-furnished," overly devoted to description and observation. Balzac serves as her example of misguided labor, as Bennett, Wells, and Galsworthy served in Virginia Woolf's comparable manifestos, "Modern Fiction" and "Mr. Bennett and Mrs. Brown." Balzac, says Cather, wanted to put the city of Paris on paper, with all its houses, upholstery, games of chance and pleasure, even its foods. This was a mistake, she believes. "The things by which he still lives, the types of greed and avarice and ambition and vanity and lost innocence of heart which he created—are as vital today as they were then. But their material surroundings, upon which he expended such labor and pains . . . the eye glides over them."[8] At this point Cather moves away from Woolf, who rejected physical realism in favor of psychological realism, outer for inner, including Lawrence in her camp, and moves instead toward an aesthetic of the archetypal, toward Jung

8. *Willa Cather on Writing*, pp. 38–39.

rather than Freud. In a brilliant maneuver, she asserts that it is possible to be a materialistic enumerator about the inner life as well as the outer and offers Lawrence as her example. Cataloguing sensations, he robs the great stories of their intrinsic grandeur. "Can one imagine anything more terrible than the story of *Romeo and Juliet* rewritten in prose by D. H. Lawrence?"[9] The minds of one's characters can be overfurnished, too, and in detailing the crockery and footstools of their interior life we can lose track of the distinctive forms of their humanity.

In her insistence on presenting her characters from the outside, in her refusal to explore their subjectivity, Cather seems to fly most conspicuously in the face of modernism, but that is because we have overidentified modernism in the novel with the techniques of interior monologue and stream of consciousness. Interior monologue and Cather's resolutely external treatment are equally reactions against traditional characterization. If we posit a traditional method of characterization in which the inner expresses itself in the outer— both action and physical surroundings—in which character is compassable, knowable, and if we think of this as a middle-distance shot, then interior monologue may be thought of as a close-up, emphasizing uniqueness and individuality to the point of unknowability, and Cather's method of characterization as a kind of long shot, emphasizing the archetypal and eternally human, acknowledging individuality, perhaps, but not exploring it. Joyce tried to incorporate both the close-up and the long shot in his presentation of Leopold Bloom by suggesting that this highly individuated man was an avatar of Odysseus; Virginia Woolf seems to want to present eternal types in *The Waves* and to some extent in *Between the Acts;* and Lawrence likes to show his characters in the grip of cosmic forces, wrenched away from the personal. By abandoning the attempt to represent interior consciousness, by her resolute externality, Cather in her own way participated in the attempt to render the generally human as opposed to the individual. This is what I mean by the urge to abstraction in her handling of character (although "abstraction" is inevitably an imprecise and somewhat irritating word as applied to literature): her downplaying of individuality, her lack of interest in "personality" as opposed to essential force.

9. Ibid., p. 42.

Heroic simplification is the essence of Cather's approach to character, and I will offer a visual analogy of this which Cather herself provides. In *My Ántonia,* Jim Burden and the Bohemian girls picnic on the banks of the river, and, as the sun begins to set, they notice a curious and striking phenomenon:

Just as the lower edge of the red disk rested on the high fields against the horizon, a great black figure suddenly appeared on the face of the sun. We sprang to our feet, straining our eyes toward it. In a moment we realized what it was. On some upland farm, a plough had been left standing in the field. The sun was sinking just behind it. Magnified across the distance by the horizontal light, it stood out against the sun, was exactly contained within the circle of the disk; the handles, the tongue, the share—black against the molten red. There it was, heroic in size, a picture writing against the sun.   (p. 245)

When the sun goes down further, the plough sinks back into its own littleness somewhere on the prairie, but it is the moment of heroic magnification that intrigues Willa Cather.

Naive readers responding to *O Pioneers!* or *My Ántonia* or *Death Comes for the Archbishop* have trouble seeing these works as novels. They appear to be collections of vignettes or sketches, and the connection between the parts is not always evident. This response is useful, reminding us how unconventional Cather's approach to form really is. Except in *The Song of the Lark,* her most traditional novel, Cather pays no more attention to plot than Woolf does in *To the Lighthouse* and looks for unity to mood. "It is hard now to realize how revolutionary in form *My Ántonia* was at that time in America," wrote Edith Lewis, Cather's companion. "It seemed to many people to have no form."[10]

In the first part of *My Ántonia,* for example, one comes suddenly upon a story so powerful that it threatens to throw the novel off track: the story of Pavel and Peter, who, back in Russia, had been carrying a bride and groom home from their wedding in a sled over snow by moonlight, when the entire party was set upon by wolves. To lighten their load and make it to safety, Pavel and Peter throw the bride out of the sled to be devoured by the wolves. At first this

10. Edith Lewis, *Willa Cather Living* (New York: Knopf, 1953), p. 107.

violent, horrific story seems separate from the novel as a whole, but with time one's mind weaves it into the fabric. It serves as a prologue to the grim winter in which Mr. Shimerda, unable to endure longer the hostility of nature, shoots himself. And in the sacrifice of the bride so that Pavel and Peter may reach the safety of town, the story states, with the starkness of folktale, the theme of sexuality sacrificed to advancement which is the heart of the book. But the real power of the story, it seems to me, comes from our awareness that Pavel and Peter are ordinary men whose lives had once been suddenly shifted into the realm of elemental forces, then dropped back down again into the ordinary, men metaphorically struck by lightning who go back the next day—or the next month—to milking cows. Their detachment from their horrendous experience is what is so moving, precisely their failure to incorporate it into the texture of their lives. The narrative exemplifies the way in which Cather's fiction moves between the quotidian and the elemental, not forcing the former to render up its potential for transcendence, nor demanding that the latter be everywhere manifest, but acknowledging the abrupt transformations of the ordinary into the ghastly or elemental or transcendent.

Other writers, hardly modernists, have used inset stories— Cervantes and Dickens, for example. But in Cather the folktale material is not framed by the rest of the narrative; it penetrates it, bringing what might be read merely as naturalistic narrative into the realm of the mythic, so that, later in the novel, we are aesthetically prepared, though still surprised and shocked, when a tramp wanders in from the prairie, climbs onto a threshing machine, waves his hand gaily, and jumps head first into the blades. Why should a tramp be immune to despair? Heroic emotions are not just for heroes. Cather routinely works with mythic incident (Jim's killing of the giant rattlesnake, a dragon-slaying episode that proves his manhood, although the rattlesnake is definitely a rattlesnake at the same time as it is, psychically, a dragon), with folk material, and with dreams. Naturalism coexists with symbolism. Lena Lingard may be an upwardly mobile, sexy, independent dressmaker in Lincoln, Nebraska, when Jim is a student there, but she is at the same time what she appears to him in a dream: a woman in a wheat field with a scythe, both a symbol of harvest and a figure threatening death, the pleasant death of his will and ambition by surrender to her compelling sensuality. Lena, the Danish laundry girls, and the three Bohemian Marys are to Jim—and Cather—joyous, evocative figures out of Virgilian rural life ("If there were no girls like them in the world, there would be no poetry"), and Jim, the student, is simultaneously Virgil ("For I shall be the first if I live to bring the Muse into my country," p. 264).

With such an emphasis on the timeless, with the way in which human beings embody recurrent impulses and attitudes, with Swedish immigrant girls in Nebraska as avatars of Virgilian rustics, no wonder *My Ántonia* defies the traditional temporal organization of plot. Dorothy Van Ghent has noted how, out of homely American detail, Cather composes in *My Ántonia* "certain frieze-like entablatures that have the character of ancient ritual and sculpture."[11] "The suffering of change, the sense of irreparable loss in time, is one polarity of the work; the other polarity is the timelessness of those images associated with Ántonia, with the grave of the suicide at the crossroads, with the mute fortitude of the hired men and the pastoral poetry of the hired girls, and most of all with the earth itself."[12] In appreciating Cather's instinct for the timeless, Van Ghent begins to see the implications in formal terms of that instinct, the "frieze-like entablatures," the sculptural and abstract forms throughout Cather's work. "The boldest and most beautiful of Willa Cather's fictions are characterized by a sense of the past not as an irrecoverable quality of events, wasted in history, but as persistent human truths—salvaged, redeemed—by virtue of memory and art."[13]

Most critics have noticed only the nostalgia, the "sense of irreparable loss in time" in Cather's work, a thematic emphasis that leads them to misperceive her art as traditional. This is like confounding

11. Dorothy Van Ghent, *Willa Cather*, University of Minnesota Pamphlets on American Writers, no. 36 (Minneapolis: University of Minnesota Press, 1964), p. 23. Like just about everything Van Ghent wrote, this is an inspired piece of literary criticism and the best short appreciation of Cather that exists. The closest thing to a standard biography of Cather is E. K. Brown, *Willa Cather: A Critical Biography* (New York: Knopf, 1953), completed by Leon Edel after Brown's death. Also useful is James Woodress, *Willa Cather: Her Life and Art* (New York: Pegasus, 1970), and Dorothy Tuck McFarland's brief treatment of all the novels, *Willa Cather* (New York: Frederick Ungar, 1972).

12. Van Ghent, *Willa Cather*, pp. 24–25.

13. Ibid., p. 5.

Georgia O'Keeffe's skulls, crosses, and flowers with Landseer's
dogs. Leon Edel, for example, demanding a representational three-
dimensionality foreign to Cather's art, can only be dissatisfied with
The Professor's House for offering, as he says repeatedly in his
"psychoanalytic" reading of that novel, no explanation for the professor's depression.[14] Forced to invent a narrative wholly outside
the text, Edel offers an explanation, essentially that Cather herself
was regressive, infantile, and so depressed when she was deprived
of Isabelle McClung's maternal attention by her marriage to Jan
Hambourg that she wrote her depression into Godfrey St. Peter
without enough distinction between herself and her character to
provide him with motivation. But Cather has her own notion of
personal development, which is very well articulated in *The Professor's House:* she imagines childhood as a stage of pure being,
divorced from accomplishment; in the middle years, from adolescence on, fueled by sexual energy, one asserts one's identity both
through one's work and family life; old age is a return to a stage of
pure being, a sadder or a richer childhood. The professor is at the
end of the second stage of his life, his identity played out, his
daughters grown and his work accomplished; his depression marks
his transition to the third stage. In *Death Comes for the Archbishop*
Cather would present her protagonist as having successfully per-

14. In Leon Edel, *Literary Biography* (New York: Doubleday, 1959), pp.
99–122. Edel's brief overview of Cather's career, a lecture printed as a pamphlet and
called "The Paradox of Success," is equally punitive, arguing that Cather projects
her personal experience onto American history—life is good and interesting to her
when she is struggling for success, but once she achieves it everything goes flat, and
she becomes nostalgic for the past and its struggles. Consequently, Edel sees
Cather's career in three stages: the great early period (*O Pioneers!*, *The Song of the
Lark*, *My Ántonia*), the middle years of disillusionment (*One of Ours*, *A Lost Lady*,
The Professor's House, *My Mortal Enemy*), and the final period of nostalgia (*Death
Comes for the Archbishop*, *Shadows on the Rock*, *Lucy Gayheart*). This means that
her "early period" lasted about five years (1913–1918), her middle period seven
(1919–1926), while her late period extended over the last twenty years of her life.
I prefer to see the period of Cather's greatest creativity as running from 1913, with
the publication of *O Pioneers!*, right through to 1927, the year in which *Death Comes
for the Archbishop* was published. That was also the year Cather had to leave the Bank
Street apartment in which she and Edith Lewis had lived very comfortably from
1912. Lewis says their enforced departure from Bank Street marked an epoch in
Cather's life, and without meaning to imply that her creativity was tied to that
apartment, I will say that to regard the years from 1912 to 1927 as a single "period"
makes more sense than Edel's three-stage paradigm.

formed the transition that was so difficult and painful for Professor St. Peter. The Archbishop "was soon to have done with calendared time, and it had already ceased to count for him. He sat in the middle of his own consciousness; none of his former states of mind were lost or outgrown. They were all within reach of his hand, and all comprehensible" (p. 290). Van Ghent, with her interest in primitive religion and myth, can understand what Cather is trying to do in her representation of old age. Edel, with his interest in Freudian analysis of a crude sort, insisting on the individual etiology of every "symptom," cannot even begin to understand. For him, *Death Comes for the Archbishop,* one of Cather's masterpieces, is an exercise in nostalgia, signaling Cather's final retreat into the past. That, indeed, is the way most critics of the forties and fifties—all dominated by a moralistic response to Cather, all disposed to condemn her for retreating into the past, all viewing her as a traditionalist—saw that book.[15]

In fact, from a formal point of view, *Death Comes for the Archbishop,* that extraordinary compilation of vivid scenes and great

15. Maxwell Geismar is typical, reproving Cather for "this movement *back* in terms of time and place, this movement *away* from the real areas of human feeling," in *The Last of the Provincials: The American Novel, 1915–1925* (Boston: Houghton Mifflin, 1947), p. 196, but Kazin, Trilling, and Daiches are equally agreed that Cather is concerned only with the past and are equally censorious. See Alfred Kazin, "Elegy and Satire: Willa Cather and Ellen Glasgow," in *On Native Grounds* (New York: Harcourt Brace, 1942), pp. 247–264; Lionel Trilling, "Willa Cather," in *After the Genteel Tradition,* ed. Malcolm Cowley (New York: Norton, 1937), pp. 52–63; and David Daiches, *Willa Cather: A Critical Introduction,* cited above. James Schroeter, in *Willa Cather and Her Critics* (Ithaca: Cornell University Press, 1967), suggests it was Cather's status in the thirties as a literary darling of right-wing critics that generated the attack from the left, of which he offers as an example Granville Hicks's "The Case against Willa Cather" (1933). Left and right, however, differed little in what they saw in Cather's work; they differed only in whether or not they approved of it.

Nina Baym has argued that critics of American literature have always been more interested in defining the American "character" and American cultural essence than in literary questions, and she shows how this preoccupation has led to the exclusion of women writers from the canon of American literature. See "Melodramas of Beset Manhood: How Theories of American Fiction Exclude Women Authors," *American Quarterly,* 33, no. 2 (Summer 1981), 123–139. In Cather's case, the persistent approach to her work in terms of content (the search for "cultural essence") has led to a misunderstanding of the novels' form, which further distorts readers' perceptions of their content.

stories which ignores chronological time, is the most daring and innovative of Cather's works. It perfectly embodies the anti-illusionist aesthetic which many of her early books strove for. I will quote Cather's own excellent description of what she was trying to accomplish and, I believe, did accomplish:

I had all my life wanted to do something in the style of legend, which is absolutely the reverse of dramatic treatment. Since I first saw the Puvis de Chavannes frescoes of the life of St. Genevieve in my student days, I have wished that I could try something a little like that in prose; something without accent, with none of the artificial elements of composition. In the Golden Legend the martyrdoms of the saints are no more dwelt upon than are the trivial incidents of their lives; it is as though all human experiences, measured against one supreme spiritual experience, were of about the same importance. The essence of such writing is not to hold the note, not to use an incident for all there is in it—but to touch and pass on. I felt that such writing would be a discipline in these days when the "situation" is made to count for so much in writing, when the general tendency is to force things up. In this kind of writing the mood is the thing—all the little figures and stories are mere improvisations that come out of it.[16]

Cather had begun her writing career imitating the "dramatic treatment" of Henry James. But what she had always been moving toward was what she calls here "legend." The distinctive note of modernism appears in her aspiration to do "something without accent," in her impatience with "artificial elements of composition," with traditional climaxes and resolutions ("not a single button sewn on as the Bond Street tailors would have it," said Virginia Woolf).[17] Musically speaking, this lifelong lover of opera repudiates the operatic ("holding the note") as a model for fiction and turns instead—rather astonishingly—to jazz, with its emphasis on mood-generating "improvisations."

The attempt to write "something in the style of legend" involved

16. *Willa Cather on Writing*, pp. 9–10.
17. Virginia Woolf, "Modern Fiction," in *Collected Essays*, 4 vols. (New York: Harcourt, Brace and World, 1967), II, 106. "The accent falls differently from of old; the moment of importance came not here but there; so that, if a writer were a free man and not a slave, if he could write what he chose, not what he must, if he could base his work on his own feeling and not upon convention, there would be no plot, no comedy, no tragedy, no love interest or catastrophe in the accepted style, and perhaps not a single button sewn on as the Bond Street tailors would have it."

the pursuit of another aesthetic quality: anonymity. This was hard for Cather to achieve. She had been a high school teacher; more important, she had suffered in her youth from the disapproval of her community, who regarded her nonconformity with distaste. She could never quite stop telling them off for it, and the theme of opposition between philistine materialism and artistic dedication too often evokes a marring didacticism in her work. The way she overcame the urge to preach was by complete submission to her material, which she said she learned from the example of Sarah Orne Jewett. And when she suppressed herself, she did it more completely than any writer I can think of.

The clarity and simplicity—the sheer absence of eccentricity—of Cather's prose style contributes to the effect of anonymity. She adheres to the traditional structure of the English sentence—subject, verb, object—as the surest way of suppressing individuality. Rarely does one find any complicated syntax. There are passages in Cather's writing that stop the heart with their beauty, but they are never purple passages in the usual sense. They tend, as in this passage, to depict moments of quiet, and they are signaled, if at all, by a toning down of the prose rather than a keying up:

In stopping to take a breath, I happened to glance up at the canyon wall. I wish I could tell you what I saw there, just *as* I saw it, on that first morning, through a veil of lightly falling snow. Far up above me, a thousand feet or so, set in a great cavern in the face of the cliff, I saw a little city of stone, asleep. It was as still as sculpture—and something like that. It all hung together, seemed to have a kind of composition: pale little houses of stone nestling close to one another, perched on top of each other, with flat roofs, narrow windows, straight walls, and in the middle of the group, a round tower . . . It was red in colour, even on that grey day. In sunlight it was the colour of winter oak-leaves. A fringe of cedars grew along the edge of the cavern, like a garden. They were the only living things. Such silence and stillness and respose—immortal repose. That village sat looking down into the canyon with the calmness of eternity.[18]

Although the moment Cather describes here is characteristic—the small and particular raised to the monumental, the once-busy seen in eternal repose—the force of this passage resides as much in its

18. Willa Cather, *The Professor's House* (New York: Vintage Books, 1973), p. 201.

style, in the calm, methodical notation of colors and shapes, the note of awe suggested with no overtones of hysteria, as in its content. It insists on the sculptural qualities of its subject, as Cather tends to in her descriptions of prairie and sky as well. The prose is by no means flowery, but neither is it as stark as it might be, as Hemingway's is, for example, There is a softness about it which comes from Cather's willingness to offer neutral elaboration. "In the sunlight it was the colour of winter oak-leaves"—this is a nice detail but not hypercharged, as it might appear in Hemingway, where the excessively stripped-down quality of the prose makes everything seem almost too significant. Cather's range is more comfortable, and the effect is to reduce, symbolically, the glare. Georgia O'Keeffe comes to mind again, as opposed to Dali or Magritte.

O'Keeffe, Sheeler, and other visual artists allied, however loosely, with Precisionism in America offer a good example of aesthetic urges similar to Cather's, generated from analogous but different sources and worked out quite independently. The aim of the Precisionists was simplification of form, and this joined an impulse toward monumentalizing ordinary objects—Sheeler's "Totems in Steel," for example, a rendering of steel girders on a building project, or his eerie stairwells or imperious ladder-back chairs, or O'Keeffe's resonant adobe houses. Cather particularly recalls O'Keeffe in her response to the Southwest, in her homage to the scale of the American landscape, in her ability to monumentalize the ordinary, and in her gift for generating a sense of mystery out of simplified forms.[19] Cather's sources of inspiration

19. See Jules David Prown and Barbara Rose, *American Painting* (New York: Rizzoli, 1977), p. 144. On Sheeler, see Martin Friedman, *Charles Sheeler* (New York: Watson-Guptill Publications, 1975). The thrill of the native discovery of abstraction is recorded—so ecstatically as to verge on the comic—in the Daybooks of Edward Weston, particularly in those sections dealing with his 1930 photographs of peppers: "Twenty years of effort . . . have gone into the making of this pepper, which I consider a peak of achievement. It is classic, completely satisfying—a pepper—but more than a pepper: abstract, in that it is completely outside subject matter. It has no psychological attributes, no human emotions are aroused: this new pepper takes one beyond the world we know in the conscious mind. To be sure much of my work has this quality,—many of my last year's peppers, but this one, and in fact all the new ones, take one into an inner reality—the absolute—with a clear understanding, a mystic revealment." *Edward Weston: The Flame of Recognition,* ed. Nancy Newhall (Millerton, N.Y.: Aperture Monograph, 1975), p. 34.

invite comparison with Sheeler's. Sheeler's formalism fed on a deeply native tradition which was not in itself modernist: he was a student of Shaker furniture and Shaker barns. Similarly, Cather took strength from what she saw as a native example of functionalism, the stories of Sarah Orne Jewett. In describing Jewett's work, Cather distinguished between two kinds of beauty: the beauty of the Chinese junk, which comes from ornamentation and embellishment, and the beauty of the racing yacht, in which every line is subsumed to purpose.[20] The beauty of Jewett's prose, to Cather, was the sleek, functional, pared-down beauty of the yacht, and although it is possible to imagine a stripping down and functionalism that goes well beyond Cather's—Hemingway, again—that is certainly the beauty she aspired to herself.

Every great writer is an innovator, forging his or her own style in the face of the seductive force of the conventional. We must mean more than that when we use the term "modernist." Critics of the sixties tended to identify modernism in the novel with subjectivity, but newer accounts of modernism tend to emphasize art's awareness of its own artificial status.[21] The modernists themselves, however, did not unanimously recognize that what they were producing was semiotically precocious fiction; nor were all of them effective theorists of their own positions. Joyce talked about the artist refined out of existence. Eliot talked about art as an escape from personality. Flaubert aspired to write a novel about nothing. Woolf talked about capturing the luminous halo of life. In this company, Cather, with her talk of the "novel *démeublé*," seems the least critically sophisticated, yet it is certainly in this company that she belongs. In modernist critical writings, including Cather's, certain themes recur: an urge to shake loose of clutter, a refusal to accept the mimetic function of art as previously defined, a feeling that a certain "spirit" was escaping the older forms, an urge toward anonymity. The vessel is emphasized rather than the content; art is imagined as a fragile container for the ineffable substance of life. Thea Kronborg

20. See Willa Cather, "Preface to *The Best Short Stories of Sarah Orne Jewett*," in *Willa Cather on Writing*, pp. 57–58. She takes the image from Gilbert Murray, who used it to define the beauty of ancient Greek literature.
21. See David Lodge, *Modernism, Antimodernism, and Postmodernism* (Birmingham, England: University of Birmingham Press, 1977).

speaks for Cather: "What was any art but an attempt to make a sheath, a mould in which to imprison for a moment the shining, elusive element which is life itself,—life hurrying past us and running away, too strong to stop, too sweet to lose? The Indian women had held it in their jars."[22] The modernists were aware of art as created artifact, not as a mirror reflecting reality or a camera eye absorbing and imprinting it. Nothing could be further from the modernist temper than Dreiser's boast about *Sister Carrie* that it was not intended as a piece of literary craftsmanship but as a picture of conditions. The modernists often, like Cather, looked to Flaubert as their Ur-aesthetician, with his emphasis on style, surface, disciplined craft; but the wittiest theorist of modernism was Oscar Wilde, whose assertion that life imitates art may be seen as the key to the modernist spirit.

If we describe the modernists as self-conscious artificers who rejected mimesis as their chief business, we risk overemphasizing the intellectual, game-playing, Nabokovian element in modernism. Not all experiment took place for the sake of experiment, but out of a conviction that the old forms did not capture something important in life, a "spirit," a force, a religious or spiritual dimension existing somewhere below or above consciousness but beyond the purviews of traditional fiction. Hence modernism's impatience with describing the here-and-now and its persistent urge to see the here-and-now in the light of, united to, all of human history: Eliot in *The Waste Land,* Pound in the *Cantos,* Joyce in *Ulysses,* and, I would suggest, Cather, in her continuing effort to tie contemporary life to a past that stretched back, in America, to the cliff dwellers and to see all human life in relation to the enduring earth.

An interest in the past and particularly in primitive cultures characterized the early twentieth century and was not just a piece of isolated nostalgia or conservatism on the part of Willa Cather. Gauguin had been impressed by Aztec sculpture at the Paris Exposition as early as 1889. Vlaminck began collecting African sculpture around 1903 and was followed in his enthusiasm for primitive art by Derain, Matisse, Modigliani, Brancusi, Moore, and Picasso, who, in 1907, incorporated renderings of African sculptures into *Les*

22. Willa Cather, *The Song of the Lark* (Lincoln: University of Nebraska Press, 1978), p. 304.

Demoiselles d'Avignon. [23] Picasso had visited Altamira in 1902 to see the neolithic cave paintings. Lawrence left the Old World for the New in search of civilizations more ancient than the former could offer. The same impulse drove Cather to Walnut Canyon, Arizona, and later to Mesa Verde, where she found in the buildings and pottery of the Anasazi an objective correlative for aesthetic impulses she had felt in herself. Form in these cliff-dwellings followed function; the buildings blended with the landscape; towns were set inside natural caverns with the cliffs themselves providing protection from the elements. The pottery was elegantly functional, embellished only with abstract designs. No more in these designs than in Indian pictographs, no more than in the cave paintings of Altamira or in certain Greek vase painting, was there an attempt to imitate three-dimensionality on a flat surface. It is no surprise that a woman so moved by this art should also have responded strongly to the frescoes of Puvis de Chavannes, whose flat, almost friezelike figures emphasize the picture plane and refuse to create the illusion of receding space. Although Puvis de Chavannes was not himself a modernist figure, he influenced Seurat, Gauguin, Matisse, and Picasso. Most modern painting has stemmed from a refusal like his to create the illusion of three-dimensional space, often encouraged by the example of primitive, non-Western, or pre-Renaissance art. Cather's antinaturalistic *Death Comes for the Archbishop,* a series of stories so arranged as to blur the distinction between the past and the present, the miraculous and the mundane, is, I would argue, a true even if somewhat surprising example in literature of the modernist aesthetic in art, and much of her early work should be seen as moving in that direction. [24]

23. Stieglitz channeled the European interest in primitivism into America, organizing a show of African sculpture at his gallery in New York in 1914. For an excellent summary of modern artists' interest in primitive art (a term the author would dislike), see Douglas Newton, "The Art of Africa, the Pacific Islands, and the Americas," *The Metropolitan Museum of Art Bulletin,* 39, no. 2 (Fall 1981), especially pp. 7–10.

24. For Puvis de Chavannes' influence on modernist painting, see Robert Hughes, *The Shock of the New* (New York: Knopf, 1981), p. 116. For my sense of how the modernist novel is engaged in "transmuting the time world of history into the timeless world of myth" and of how the reaction against temporal sequence is the key to its form, and for much else, including analogies between modernist

Visual analogues for Cather's modernism are many. The deter-
mining factor, as in so much modernist painting which exploded out
of the confines of easel-sized canvases, is scale. One thinks of the
wall-sized works of Picasso and Matisse, such as *Guernica* and *The
Dance of Life;* one thinks of the giant canvases of Jackson Pollock
and the vast areas, made to seem even vaster by their minimalist
treatment, of works by Rothko, Frankenthaler, Barnett Newman;
one thinks of the murals of Orozsco and Thomas Hart Benton. To
work on that scale involves simplification. The reduction to essential forms, which began in the visual arts with Cézanne, finds a literary analogue in Cather's insistence on there being only a few human
stories which are told over and over. Her refusal to follow the twists
and turns of her characters' individual thoughts, her insistence on
seeing them as "human creatures," subject to an endlessly recurring
cycle of emotions, recalls Cézanne's insistence that the cone, the
circle, and the square are at the basis of everything we see. If her
novels seem consequently simple, their simplicity has the same aim
as Klee's figures, Matisse's late abstract cutouts, or Picasso's consciously childlike drawings. It is a simplicity that aims to capture the
elemental and enduring and that requires the greatest art to produce.
    However fragmented their initial impact, both *The Waste Land* in
its relation to *The Golden Bough* and *Ulysses* in its relation to the
Odyssey attempt to transcend the complexity of modern life by
annexing the structural simplicities of myth. Embracing multiplicity
but animated by an urge to abstraction, they attempt to search
through the historical and accidental to the fundamental. The appropriate stance for the artist in the face of such mythic and archetypal
material is anonymity. The appropriate style is no style. Joyce in
Ulysses sought to approximate "no style" by parodying all styles.
Gertrude Stein and Hemingway sought to produce an anonymous
surface by means of prose styles of the utmost plainness, stripped
of all ornament and connotation. But the lucid prose of Willa Cather
makes even Hemingway's sentences look mannered. And as for
Gertrude Stein, it is one of the many ironies of modernism that the

literature and the visual arts and an account of how naturalistic and nonnaturalistic
styles have tended to alternate through history, I am indebted to Joseph Frank's
"Spatial Form in Modern Literature," in *The Widening Gyre: Crisis and Mastery in
Modern Literature* (Bloomington, Ind. and London: Indiana University Press, 1963),
pp. 3–62.

pursuit of simplicity and anonymity produced works of such futile complexity and obtrusive personality. Like many other modernist artists, Cather sought to bypass consciousness and the circumstantial details with which it concerns itself and to produce an art that appealed to the most elemental layers of our minds. Her enduring popularity with readers shows that she succeeded, and critics ought now to take account of her success.[25]

25. I would like to express my gratitude to Paul Alpers and to Alex Zwerdling for discussions of the material in this essay and critiques of the manuscript and to the students in my course on Willa Cather in the spring quarter of 1982 at the University of California, Berkeley, for specific insights and general enthusiasm.

Jacob's Room and *Roger Fry:*
Two Studies in Still Life

Near the beginning and again toward the end of her career, Virginia Woolf created literary portraits, each inspired by a man she had loved and associated with Bloomsbury and with crucial moments in her life. Though one book is a novel and the other a biography, the works invite comparison on several grounds: they are the only two books by Woolf in which a male is the central figure; both repeatedly assert the impossibility of representing character accurately in words and thereby undermine their apparent reason for being; both reveal an interest in modern painting, evident in all Woolf's work but in these cases more than usually intense and self-conscious; and from both narratives the protagonist has somehow escaped. Jacob Flanders and Roger Fry are not there. The easel is ready, the room has been prepared, but the model's chair is empty. Instead of a fleshed-out portrait, what we find more nearly resembles a still life, a painstakingly careful arrangement of objects within a frame. As the arrangement differs in each book, so necessarily does the nature and effect of the absence of the assumed central figure. Jacob and Roger are "not there" in fascinatingly different ways.

The parallels between Jacob Flanders and Thoby Stephen are as obvious as the fact that *Jacob's Room* is a work of fiction, not a biography. The Cambridge education, love of literature, visit to Greece, intention to study law, even the awkward good looks and the tendency to be tongue-tied they have in common. Woolf once referred to her brother as "a charming great inarticulate creature,"[1] in very much the same words that are applied in the novel to Jacob. But as Woolf knew, these traits and experiences did little to distinguish her brother or the protagonist of her first experimental novel from hundreds of other young Englishmen of their generation.

Many years after Thoby's death, Woolf wondered how he would have turned out, whether he might have been "Mr. Justice Stephen . . . with several books to his credit."[2] For a biographer, the speculation seems idle; for a sister and an artist not at all. Woolf felt that there was much she had not known or understood about her brother. At first she appealed to his Cambridge friends for help. But information was not really what she wanted; as she was to say later, facts did not have the power to convey life or to allay the feeling that "the best in us had gone."[3]

Left with the memory of an important but unclear presence and the anguish caused by absence, Woolf experienced a grief of a peculiarly frustrating kind. Her sense of loss was powerful, yet the more time went by and the more she reflected on it, though the feelings did not vanish, the object to which they referred seemed to lose whatever shape and solidity it had possessed. For the artistic sensibility, it must have seemed an almost too familiar Romantic dilemma: to be overcome by emotions without having ready at hand a clearly defined object to which they can be attached or a satisfactory verbal formula through which they can be expressed.

Two attempts at resolving this problem favored by Romantic writers were the mythic reconstruction of character into an immortal being of absolute worth and dispersal of emotion into a landscape transformed by an atmosphere of nostalgia and melancholy. Woolf had a tendency—one might say a genius—for the latter.

Jacob's Room shows her first prolonged experiment with another way to give form to the emotions and, in doing so, to hint at the life that had inspired them. It is also at this stage that her years of observing Vanessa and her painter friends at work and her exposure

1. *The Letters of Virginia Woolf,* ed. Nigel Nicolson and Joanne Trantmann (New York: Harcourt, Brace Jovanovich, 1975), I, 74.

2. Quentin Bell, *Virginia Woolf: A Biography* (New York: Harcourt, Brace Jovanovich, 1972), I, 112.

3. *Letters,* I, 374.

to the post-Impressionists through the influence of Roger Fry converged to give her a concrete analogue to the writer's craft that helped her to break away from certain literary preconceptions.

In an essay entitled "Life and the Novelist," Woolf observed that for the writer too there is a studio, a solitary room where life is "curbed," even "killed." As the painter's perceptions and memories are broken into components of color and shading, so the writer's are "mixed with this, stiffened with that, brought into contrast with something else."[4] What emerges may be "stark" and "formidable" but it can be "enduring," "the bone and substance upon which our rush of indiscriminating emotions was founded." Woolf's artistic economy has much to do with Cézanne and little to do with Gaudier-Brzska and the Vorticists. Hers is a salvage operation, not an act of hostility. Her literary counterpart of *nature morte* begins in negation, not of life or the value of art, but of certain assumptions about the relation between the two. In dealing with her unfocused emotion, she suspends belief in the suspension of disbelief, pares down her materials, dismisses illusion. From her earliest references to *Jacob's Room,* she comments on what is lacking: "The theme is a blank to me; but I see immense possibilities in the form."[5] And later, "Beauty . . . is only got by the failure to get it . . . by facing what must be humiliation—the things one can't do."[6] When Lytton Strachey wrote to her praising the novel, she responded in a characteristic way, pointing to an achievement while acknowledging an apparent shortcoming: "Of course you put your infallible finger upon the spot—romanticism. How do I catch it? Not from my father. I think it must have been my Great Aunts. But some of it, I think, comes from the effort of breaking with complete representation. One flies into the air. Next time I mean to stick closer to facts."[7]

By admitting at the outset that in planning *Jacob's Room* she had no theme in mind, that the work makes no claim to beauty or completeness of representation, Woolf does more than disarm her critics. She reveals a state of mind. Upon retiring to her solitary

---

4. Virginia Woolf, *Granite and Rainbow* (London: The Hogarth Press, 1960), p. 41.
5. Virginia Woolf, *A Writer's Diary* (New York: Harcourt, Brace, 1954), p. 22.
6. *Letters,* II, 599.
7. *Letters,* II, 568–569.

room to compose *Jacob's Room,* like the painter of a still life, she chose a subject—the education of a young man—familiar to the point of being a cliché; furthermore, like the painter whose subject is fruit or flowers, emblems of perishable beauty, she exposes the tension created by imposing an appearance of permanence on that which cannot be preserved; finally, and perhaps most importantly, she takes advantage of being able to compose twice. In contrast to the illusion created by much landscape and portrait painting, it is apparent to a viewer of a still life that the painter has "set up" what he has painted and then painted it. There are two clearly visible arrangements. In a certain sense, all writers of fiction do this. But that Woolf was particularly conscious of doing it may well have set her on course not only for *Jacob's Room* but for the greater works to follow, in which the preoccupation with composition does not obscure the subject but becomes the subject while allowing a great deal else—beauty, for example, emotion, and even a theme or two—to slip between the crevices.

In allowing Jacob to be featureless or a blurred composite of the ways in which different people see him, Woolf may have confounded many of her first readers, but she seems to have discovered simultaneously her method and her subject. From the first scene on the beach when Mrs. Flanders gets up and prepares to leave, thereby spoiling the composition of Charles Steele's painting, the reader's attention is drawn to the experience, certainly not peculiar to artists, of trying to capture and frame that which keeps moving out of view. Like his mother and his friend Fanny, whose flashes of beauty cannot be caught by the painter Bramham, Jacob seems to defy the art of portrait painting. Mrs. Norman, his fellow traveler on the train to Cambridge, studies his features but only concludes that he appeared "out of place" (p. 30).[8] Later, as he takes leave of the Durrants, another guest regrets his escape: " 'Not to sit for me,' said Miss Eliot, planting her tripod upon the lawn" (p. 63). Even Jacob's quiet reverie at the Acropolis is interrupted when he notices Madame Lucien Gravé trying to take a photograph of him: "Damn these women . . . How they spoil things" (p. 151). And once again he jumps out of the picture.

8. Quotations, identified by page numbers in the text, are from Virginia Woolf, *Jacob's Room* (New York: Harcourt, Brace and World, 1959), published in a single volume with *The Waves.*

Those who had tried to capture Mrs. Flanders and Fanny were male painters, while it was more often women who wished to photograph, draw, or summarize Jacob; this difference not only suggests elements of sexual attraction, curiosity, and possessiveness in the artistic impulse but serves to remind us in Jacob's case, at least, that the refusal to be pinned down, which is his most consistent trait, is not a weakness in his character nor in Woolf's method, but an essential expression of his youth. Though Woolf recognized no theme as she planned *Jacob's Room*, it becomes apparent that her preoccupation with form and her refusal to aim for a "complete representation" coincided with a fascination with youth and its effects on the lives around it. Woolf's novel is not a portrait of an artist or barrister as a young man because, though law and marriage could have been in Jacob's future, serious considerations of his future are among the many elements the artist eliminates for her canvas.

What is most attractive, puzzling, infuriating, and fundamental about Jacob and the fluid, almost casual fashion in which Woolf lets him escape categorization is just that: the refusal to settle down and take responsibility. Jacob has no character not necessarily because he is weak, stupid, spoiled, or selfish (though at times he seems to be all of these), but because he does not survive. In this he is like Rachel Vinrace in *The Voyage Out*. Yet his story, for all its underlying sadness, is unlike hers in its many moments of joy. Jacob's exits, his leaps to freedom, out of the train compartment, away from Professor Plumer's lunch party—"oh God, oh God, oh God!" (p. 35)—away from late-night philosophical discussions, out of bed with Florinda, out of London, out of Paris, out of Athens—all have about them the incomparable gusto and exhilarating sense of freedom possessed by the very young who do not yet have to choose.

The oppressiveness of *The Voyage Out* stems in part from the protagonist's sex, which prevents her, within the social conventions of the time, from exercising the temporary and illusory freedom so briefly but vigorously enjoyed by Jacob. Rachel's movement is not, like Jacob's, a series of leaps, one step ahead of those friends, relatives, or artists who are waiting nearby with a trap. She is trapped from the beginning. She moves from shelter to shelter without abandon and without apparent alternative. Jacob's death is one final surprising exit, one last abrupt departure accomplished with something midway between clumsiness and perfect style. Rachel's death is slow and lingering, a "drowning," a going under, a submission.

Like the fresh flower or fruit of a still life, the young Jacob is set up for admiration by the artist in full consciousness of the paradox of endowing his condition with an appearance of permanence. The death's head in the shape of a sheep's skull or the memory of a young father who had also quit the scene abruptly are never far from view. But for the most part Jacob seems to be miraculously unaware of and untouched by these reminders of decay, so obvious to the reader and to his middle-aged mother. Indeed, the various *memento mori* strewn about the beach and throughout the text, which endow the book with pathos, also highlight the fragile and almost unbelievable innocence of the protagonist. Jacob basks in unawareness. To have made him knowing would have been to give him a character and a maturity of which Woolf seemed deliberately to wish to deprive him. It would also have provided a direct link with the reader that she seems not to have wished to forge. Like Cézanne's apples, Jacob is familiar, commonplace, undistinguished; and by virtue of his unconsciousness of time, he inhabits a realm the reader can imagine but not reach. In contemplating him, we contemplate a figure at once familiar and unfathomably strange.

Though a certain portion of Jacob's unconsciousness might be attributed to flaws in his character—insensitivity, egotism, absentmindedness—Woolf provides the reader with a number of messages about time's devastation structured in such a way that Jacob could not possibly have access to them. These messages are not embedded in sheep's skulls or gravestones, which any imaginative youth might interpret, but in brief collapsed biographical asides to the reader in which various minor characters' lives are foretold. For example, Mr. Floyd, the clergyman who proposed to Mrs. Flanders, went off to "Sheffield, where he met Miss Wimbush, who was on a visit to her uncle, then to Hackney—then to Maresfield House, of which he became the principal, and finally, becoming editor of a well-known series of Ecclesiastical Biographies, he retired to Hampstead with his wife and daughter, and is often to be seen feeding the ducks on Leg of Mutton Pond" (p. 22).

Similar brief biographical sketches are given of Sopwith, Professor and Mrs. Plumer, Erasmus Cowan, Miss Umphelby, Mrs.

Pascoe, Florinda, Jinny Carslake, Cruttendon, and innumerable
other characters in the novel. To list their names is to be surprised
at how many there are and at how much trouble Woolf has taken
over seemingly trivial details in the lives of these people, most of
whom have relatively little to do with Jacob. It begins to be clear
that the function of these fortune-teller's vignettes is not their direct
relation to Jacob, but precisely that they contain information that
Jacob cannot possess and will not live to learn or imitate. They
provide illustrations, plainly visible to the reader, all but invisible
to Jacob, of the way time confines and diminishes life. In painter's
terms, they compose a background, a well-defined darkness,
against which the vague outlines and ambiguous lights of the fore-
ground are intriguing and increasingly beautiful.

The radicalness of Woolf's experiment seems all the more impressive when we remember that biography, even fictional
biography, is nearly always linear, causal, and explanatory. The
most common reason for writing biography is to explain how X
became prime minister or Y a violinist. Both the information offered and the manner of its organization is determined, to a large
extent, by the achievement (or interesting failure) that justifies the
story in the first place. Since Jacob, like Thoby, did not live long
enough to succeed or fail at anything important, the recorder of his
life is free to arrange her materials in whatever manner she sees fit.
Furthermore, since the whole idea of culmination is antithetical to
her purpose, she does not assemble things so that they will point
away from themselves, but, on the contrary, toward themselves and
even toward the fact that their arrangement is arbitrary.

Like the painter of still life, Woolf makes no effort to conceal the
fact that she is no neutral observer merely copying down what she
sees and hears, but a highly active and intrusive organizer. All
writers of fiction arrange twice: they establish an order, a sequence
of events, a juxtaposition of moments; then they translate that order
into language, give it a voice. What is so interesting about *Jacob's
Room* is the care Woolf takes in making certain that the artificiality,
the deliberateness of the process is noticed. She has no wish to cover
her tracks, to naturalize. When, for example, she introduces Mrs.
Flanders, before offering the usual biographical information, she
shows an empty room: "Mrs. Flanders had left her sewing on the
table. There were her large reels of white cotton and her steel

spectacles; her needle-case; her brown wool wound round an old postcard. There were the bulrushes and the *Strand* magazines; and the linoleum sandy from the boys' boots" (p. 12).

There are a number of ways in which this material can be interpreted. One might go on about the solitude of the empty room, the signs of domestic activity, the economies and tastes of a family that is not rich, and so forth. Woolf undoubtedly expects this. But the repeated use of such descriptions—static, framed, complete in themselves, observed only by the narrator and reader—invites another kind of attention, one that does not yield meanings so much as recognitions. They stop us in our tracks and call our attention to the discipline of discerning the inadvertent designs of particular lives.

Obviously, the designs and the images that constitute them are not independent of each other, yet the fact that their relationship is not simple, not indisputably significant, endows them with a special energy. Woolf's arrangement of Mrs. Flanders' belongings is neither pure abstraction nor complete meaning. It is enough of a set piece to call attention to itself as such, and yet its components lend themselves readily to being interpreted with reference to other elements in the book. The reader's freedom consists not in ignoring form or substance but in assessing them and their interconnection without epistemological intimidation. By being permitted to see the imposition of design so clearly, we feel free to imagine both the life it delimits and the life that escapes it.

Woolf's descriptions of Jacob's rooms are the major set pieces of the novel and the ones that best illustrate the artistry of confinement and release. Jacob's room at Trinity is first seen after he has settled in at Cambridge, but at the moment of the description, he, of course, is not at home: "Jacob's room had a round table and two low chairs. There were yellow flags in a jar on the mantlepiece; a photograph of his mother; cards from societies . . . notes and pipes. There follows a seemingly random list of some of Jacob's books— Dickens, Spenser, all the Elizabethans, Jane Austen "in deference, perhaps, to someone else's standard." The paragraph concludes: "Listless is the air in an empty room, just swelling the curtain; the flowers in the jar shift. One fiber in the wicker arm-chair creaks, though no one sits there" (p. 39).

Like the items on Mrs. Flanders' table, the objects in Jacob's
room lend themselves easily to interpretations about the character of
the young man who inhabits the space—his youth, masculinity,
class, intellectual promise, literary taste. The final two sentences,
however, with their emphasis on silence and emptiness, have an
unusual and important effect. On one hand, they create a dramatic
need, the need for an entrance, a gesture or voice to fill the void. On
the other, they create a need for a key that might help to decode the
signs that are so neatly but insignificantly placed about the room.
For though youth, masculinity, and the rest are all apparent, the
particular individual life that would give direction and specificity of
meaning to these objects is missing. Once again, design and meaning are but loosely linked. As long as Jacob might come in, speak,
strike a pose, the reader may be full of anticipation, but meanwhile
he learns to make do with what is given.

The sudden elimination of that anticipation and the real force of
"making do with what is given" constitute Woolf's presentation of
Jacob's death. The final short chapter of the novel is full of exact
repetitions of words and phrases from earlier sections. Though
Bonamy remarks "Nothing arranged" on seeing letters strewn
about, the chapter is the most carefully arranged in the book. The
ram's skull, the high ceilings, the voice crying, "Jacob! Jacob!" the
mother trying to make order out of confusion—all call attention to
a formal symmetry even while delivering messages of grief. The
most elaborate refrain echoes exactly the last two sentences originally used to describe Jacob's room at Trinity: "Listless is the air in
an empty room, just swelling the curtain; the flowers in the jar shift.
One fiber in the wicker arm-chair creaks, though no one sits there"
(p. 176).

This time, of course, the design really is all there is. Jacob will
not come in to pick up his letters and his life, to bring focus and
meaning to the various traces of himself he has left behind. For the
last time, the biographical, data-laden, knowable, summarizable
Jacob has escaped. But is this escape, this absence, a failure in
Woolf's art? On the contrary, it is her first important success. We
know that Mrs. Flanders had "merchant of this city" inscribed on
the gravestone of her husband, though that label had almost no
bearing on his life or its meaning to her. One wonders what she

might have come up with for Jacob; possibly, *pro patria mori*. Without ridiculing such branding, indeed filled with the ironic sense of its necessity for artists as well as for grieving survivors, Woolf calls our attention to the realities that make it inadequate. In a sense, not necessarily lugubrious, all efforts at capturing a life in words are like writing an epitaph or creating a literary *nature morte*. The achievement of *Jacob's Room* is that in conceding to Jacob's absence, in collaborating so ingeniously in his various vanishing acts, Woolf lets the individual go and, in the process, preserves and illuminates images of a wider common life.

In turning to the biography of *Roger Fry,* we turn to another genre and a later stage in Woolf's career. The writing of this book seemed arduous in a new way to Woolf. In a reversal of what had been the case with *Jacob's Room,* the conventionality of the form seemed to fit ill with the relative unconventionality of the life of her subject. The entire task represented a more public gesture than *Jacob's Room* did. There was the question of Fry's reputation to consider, as well as the feelings of his children and Helen Anrep. Like Mrs. Flanders choosing an inscription for her husband's monument, Woolf had to—or thought she had to—subordinate her own feelings to the demands of propriety and the obligations of friendship.

The absence of Roger Fry—that is, of an impression of a vital, distinctive, memorable character—from most of the pages of the biography differs from the more tantalizing absence of Jacob from *Jacob's Room* partly because there is no controlled or distinctive narrative voice. *Jacob's Room* is not narrated by a single character or an intrusive authorial persona, but from the first view of the bay "quivering" through Mrs. Flanders' tear-filled eyes, an intimate, elegiac, restrained mood is established that gives its own kind of definition to a remembered presence, a felt emptiness.

In her biography of Fry, Woolf changes tone and viewpoint repeatedly. There are passages in which she appears to adopt the posture of the detached Victorian biographer—businesslike, impersonal, slightly bored—taking an un-Romantic leaf from her father's books, perhaps. She could not have been happy about this approach, since she had once observed disapprovingly that Victorian biographies "have a depressing similarity" and that the "eminent men" whose lives are recorded in them appear "strangely formal and remote. "[9] But her efforts at a friendlier, more informal mode provide an oddly weak alternative, because though the conversational tone promises interesting gossip, the speculative anecdote—at which Woolf could be so brilliant—is almost invariably withheld: "Whether the fault lay with Roger . . ."; "Whatever Roger's latent revolt may have been . . ."; "To fall in love in Venice must have been exciting . . ." All of these provocative clauses drift into vagueness, a polite refusal to probe or, more surprising, a modest denial of inspiration that often sounds like lack of curiosity.

One of Woolf's most peculiar approaches to her subject appears at the beginning of chapter 7 when she describes her own first meeting with Fry: "To a stranger meeting him then for the first time [1910] he looked much older than his age" (p. 149).[10] Of course, before people meet they are strangers. But given the earlier waverings between formal detachment and informal vagueness, the use of the word "stranger" to describe herself and the tone of the rest of the paragraph introduce a new level of remoteness at precisely that moment when their lives intersected. Near the end of the book, in praising Fry's study of Cézanne, Woolf remarks on its value to the "common reader." Like the word "stranger," the phrase has its obvious significance and emotional content to those friends (and students) who already know Woolf's story as well as Fry's. But the choice remains an oddity, a half-hearted effort to break out of her self-imposed anonymity. Woolf was able, with professional competence, to assemble the facts, but not her own attitude toward them. Her solution, whether intended or not, was to keep herself— the details of her own life, and more importantly, her personal voice—out of the book. In doing so, except for a few unguarded moments, she eliminates Fry as well.

In an essay of the art of "New Biography," as practiced by Lytton Strachey and Harold Nicholson, Woolf anticipates the problem. She agrees that the aim of biography is "the truthful transmission of personality" but does not find the difficulty resolved by a simple statement of objective. "If we think of truth as something of granite-like solidity and of personality as something of rainbow-

9. Virginia Woolf, *Contemporary Writers* (London: The Hogarth Press, 1965), p. 29.

10. Quotations, identified by page numbers in the text, are from Virginia Woolf, *Roger Fry: A Biography* (New York: Harcourt, Brace Jovanovich, 1968).

like intangibility and reflect that the aim of biography is to weld
these two into one seamless whole, we shall admit that the problem
is a stiff one."[11] The difference between *Roger Fry* and *Jacob's
Room* is not that one is a book of facts and the other of fiction, but
that in one the author and her subject are nearly overwhelmed by
granite and in the other she counteracts the threat with a well-shaped
contemplation of the rainbow.

Facts were a threat to Woolf's artistry in more than one way.
There was what she considered to be the tedium of listing dates,
places, and the minute concrete details of dress, physiognomy, or
conversation. It was clearly not the concreteness or the coloration of
detail that bothered her, but rather the sheer number of items of
minutiae competing for attention. For her, attempts at completeness
of representation nearly always produced the opposite of their intended result. But facts meant something else to Woolf, as they do
to all who imagine stringing together the events of a lifetime. There
are invariably the "hard facts of life"—illness, instability, failure,
passion, death. These do not intimidate the artist through dull
weight. They are harrowing. And to deal with them requires more
than selectivity. Three facts in this sense of the word, interrelated
and of crucial importance to Fry's life, presented unusual problems
for Woolf: his energetic sexuality, the madness of his wife, Helen
Coombe, and the suicide of a French woman with whom he was in
love in the 1920's. Fry's numerous love affairs, including one with
Vanessa Bell, are touched on only in brief and indirect ways. "What
Roger Fry could not say . . . must be left unsaid by another." And
when Helen Coombe's madness forced Fry to commit her to an
asylum, Woolf writes with painful economy, "The agony . . .
cannot be described" (p. 103).

Woolf's perplexity about sexuality is partly resolved in *Jacob's
Room* by her adopting the viewpoint of Betty Flanders, as if she had
been sitting outside the bedroom where Jacob and Florinda are
making love: "[as] if the pale blue envelope lying by the biscuit-box
had the feelings of a mother" (p. 92). But the sexual facts of life
represent to Woolf a threat not entirely explained by a mother's
protectiveness or jealousy. "Behind the door was the obscene thing,
the alarming presence, and terror would come over her as at death,

11. *Granite and Rainbow*, p. 149.

or the birth of a child" (p. 92). Without the same need to respect the feelings of next of kin, as was the case in writing of Roger Fry, Woolf comes closer in *Jacob's Room* to touching on her own feelings about sexual passion. Though the scene is set up—with the image of gullible youth, disingenuous girl, and disapproving mother—for comic satire or moralizing, Woolf speaks not of judgment but of "terror" and "alarm." Like birth or death or mental or physical illness, sexual passion is treated as a fact of nature— unreasonable, unavoidable, disorienting. That Jacob emerges from his first sexual encounter "like a baby after an airing" suggests once again his impenetrable male innocence, not the baselessness of Mrs. Flanders' imagined alarm.

What is interesting here, aside from the way in which Woolf transfers her anxieties into fictional material, is the consistency with which she views natural fact to be at odds with the desire for order. Sex is terrifying not because it is sinful, but because its manifestations appear so random and discontinuous. That Mrs. Flanders compares her terror to what she might feel at a death or the "birth of a child" seems surprising unless we remember that for Jacob to pin his hopes on Florinda's purity and fidelity is no more illusory than for Mrs. Flanders to center her life on the strength of a young husband or the beauty of her sons as little boys. What Woolf shows, not with moralizing but with tolerance and sympathy, is the common human need for coherence and permanence and the impossibility, in the face of natural fact, of attaining them. Florinda cannot live up to her idyllic name any more than Jacob can forever remain a child running on the beach. Nature changes everything.

Woolf's reticent alarm in dealing with the insanity of Helen Coombe is poignant and easy to understand. What little she does say about it is strikingly like many of her other observations about the effect of natural facts on Fry's life: "The 'beauty of life as a whole' was shattered, and the center upon which he depended was shaken" (p. 104). It seems that madness is the intensification within the individual mind of all that is ungovernable, all the meaningless intrusions of nature that dismantle whatever order has been composed by eliminating or moving its center.

Even while she praises, in good Bloomsbury fashion, Fry's dislike of dogma, his restlessness of mind and spirit, nothing preoccupies Woolf in the biography more than what she refers to repeatedly as his need for a center. In trying to understand what Fry meant when he described his honeymoon with Helen Coombe as "perfect happiness," she interprets his words to mean that at last "everything had fallen into place and all the odds and ends of existence had come together to make a whole, a center of peace and satisfaction" (p. 97). But that peace and happiness proved to be an illusion, and a very temporary one at that, for it appeared neither to be in the nature of things nor—what is of even more concern to Woolf—in the character of Fry to maintain a steady focus. About his first trip to Paris, she writes: "Altogether the months in Paris, though they had a wide circumference, seemed to have lacked a center. He was inquisitive and he was interested, but he found nothing in particular to fasten on" (p. 79).

In her indulgent moods, the biographer summarizes Fry's frantic busyness, his continual turning from theory to theory and project to project, with light-hearted irony: "He was maintaining that a hat suitable for a negress under a tropical sun was fit headgear for Lady Ottoline Morrell in Bond Street; he had discovered a new cure for sciatica, and he was arguing some abstruse point about representation and the aesthetic emotion" (p. 174). But more often, especially as she treats his later years, there is a note of concern. Fame and public responsibilities became nearly as irritating and disruptive as his frequent bouts of illness: "His energy without a center to absorb it was formidable" (p. 254). And near the end of the book, when she tries, perhaps against her own better instincts, to sum him up, Woolf observes the paradox of a man of so much curiosity seeming to have so little interest in himself. She recalls what a good storyteller he was, how much detail he could remember about people and places, but she concludes, in words that define the biographer's problem as well as Fry's view of himself: "The central figure remained vague" (p. 290).

Nowhere in the book does Fry's enigmatic character cry out for interpretation more than during the period immediately following the suicide of the French woman he had met and fallen in love with in Nancy in 1923. And nowhere does Woolf more noticeably absent herself from the narration. She states simply that "in a sudden access of insanity his friend put an end to her life. Far from having caused the tragedy, he had given her, as her family assured him, the greatest happiness she had ever known" (p. 251). Woolf then quotes, without comment, a long passage from Fry's personal papers in which he reflects in French on this episode. In language that is dispassionate and abstract, Fry philosophizes about the different ways in which women and men respond to life, how women tend to live for love whereas men have the "wisdom" to detach themselves and survive life's disappointments. The entire piece is an extraordinary exercise in detachment through which the author achieves a remarkable degree of remoteness from the incident, the reader, and himself:

Il se livre en moi un combat interminable entre deux principes contradictoires. Par l'amour et seulement par l'amour nous touchons ou croyons toucher à une réalité solide, à un monde peuplé de vraies substances . . . indestructibles, éternelles, définitives. Dans tout le reste de notre vie règne une rélativité complète. Là il n'y a que des relations changeantes perpétuellement, et jamais répétées. Tout effort à concilier ces deux expériences semble vain. Les deux mondes n'ont pas une perspective commune. Dans la femme le principe de la vie éternelle de l'amour prime généralement sur l'autre. Souvent elle appartient complètement à l'amour. Je crois que . . . placée comme je suis maintenant et en pleine possession de son entendement elle se tuerait—moi non . . . Est-ce qu'on connait le cas d'une seule femme qui fut vraiment sage? Tandis qu'il y a eu des hommes sages. Et la sagesse consiste dans la complète rénonciation de tout en nous qui réclame la justice.   (pp. 251–252)[12]

Not only does Woolf leave the passage untranslated, she does not comment on it despite the fact that it contains observations that must have been profoundly disturbing to her. That *amour* and *sagesse* are irreconcilable and justice unattainable might, in her darkest moments, have seemed true, but that one of the freest of her free-

12. "There exists within me an unending conflict between two contradictory principles. By love and only by love we touch or we think we touch a solid reality, a world populated with true substances . . . indestructible, eternal, definitive. In all the rest of our life there reigns a complete relativity. There are only perpetually changing relations, and nothing repeated. Every effort to reconcile these two experiences seems vain. The two worlds do not have a common perspective. Among women the principle of the eternal life of love generally takes precedent over the other. Often a woman belongs completely to love. I believe . . . put in my present situation and in full possession of her understanding she would kill herself—Not I . . . Does anyone know the case of one single woman who was truly wise? Whereas there are wise men. And wisdom consists of the complete renunciation of everything in us that demands justice."

spirited friends should have formulated the idea into a rule must have been unnerving. Far more distressing and, at this stage in her life, frightening must have been Fry's assertion—not uncommon at the time, but surely painful to hear from a Bloomsbury friend—that love is the ruling principle in women while men are more capable of wisdom; and therefore that a woman who became aware of the disjunction would probably kill herself, while a man (that is, himself) would survive. Woolf was able to sympathize with Fry's attempt to steady himself and ease his conscience. One also assumes that the creator of Septimus Smith was not intellectually persuaded by Fry's division of human sensibility by sex. But there were vulnerabilities in Woolf that this episode in Fry's life and his reflections on it must have touched deeply.

Woolf must have been sensitive not only as a woman but also as an artist to Fry's insistence on the disjunction between love and wisdom, since it is a variation on a theme that had preoccupied Bloomsbury and other groups of modernist writers and painters, the relationship between engagement and detachment. Did the artist who gave up on art as representation give up all claims to a comprehensible—including the possibility of a moral—link between life and art? It is clear from Woolf's diary and criticism that this was not her aim, but it is also clear that she worried that her experiments would fly off into abstraction or incoherence. That the intensity, movement, and concerns of life might be irrevocably separate from the order of art was a cause of anxiety throughout her career. To hear an old friend, especially an artist and teacher, conclude so near the end of his life that the split between observer and participant was irreparable must have been devastating.

One explanation, then, for the relative lifelessness of the biography and the absence of the central figure (so different from the magnetic absence of Jacob) is that when Woolf saw Fry's life laid out before her, she found in it evidence of all of her worst anxieties about herself. His days were fragmented, divided between projects, obligations, obsessions, affections, habits, ambitions—all interrupted by brief passions, moments of physical pain and depression. Two of the women he loved went mad; another was married to one of his best friends; his paintings were largely ignored; his Omega workshop went out of business; his art criticism brought a notoriety he detested. Near the end of his life, still obsessively busy, he appeared to have concluded—albeit in a time of shock—that there were only two ways of being: the womanly way, to love to the point of self-destruction, and the manly way, to remove oneself from the fray and survive. Insofar as the facts of Fry's life seemed to add up to this, Woolf could only have found herself more and more appalled by them and reticent, for reasons having little to do with respect for the bereaved, about entering fully into the biographical narrative.

Yet it is not like Woolf to allow a mere accumulation of facts, however heavy, to weigh down her judgment altogether. The causes for despair were real and numerous, but she had her way of fighting back. And she had her own Roger Fry—not perhaps the proper subject for a biography, that is, not the public man of the sort Victorian biographers liked to write about at such tedious length, but the man who inhabited her memory, who had become part of herself. At the rare moments when this Fry emerges, Woolf emerges with him, because, of course, they are inseparable. In these inspired moments, she overcomes—as she does in all her best writing—the depressingly apparent divisions between art, life, criticism, and the male and female sensibility.

In praising Fry's criticism, Woolf reveals what is best in her own: "When we read him, we never feel shut off alone in a studio; morality and conduct, even if they are called by other names, are present; eating and drinking and love-making hum and murmur on the other side of the page. And pervading all is the character of the critic himself, with its strange mixture of scrupulous sincerity and fervent belief" (p. 229). Recalling his slide lectures in Queen's Hall, she presents an afterthought, like many in *Jacob's Room,* that leaves an imprint of the person without attempting to fill in every detail:

For two hours [the audience] had been looking at pictures. But they had seen one of which the lecturer himself was unconscious—the outline of the man against the screen, an ascetic figure in evening dress who paused and pondered, and then raised his stick and pointed. That was a picture that would remain in memory together with the rest, a rough sketch that would serve many of the audience in years to come as the portrait of a great critic, a man of profound sensibility but of exacting honesty, who, when reason could penetrate no further, broke off; but was convinced, and convinced others, that what he saw was there. (p. 263)

In citing these moments of vivid recall in the Roger Fry biography, as in *Jacob's Room*, one searches for a better term than *vignette, epiphany, revelation,* all of which imply either a completeness or a dramatic force that is not present. In Woolf's art what is shown is often, in the physical sense, unremarkable and, in any case, only sketched in or suggested; what one is made aware of is not "the thing in itself," but the artist's apprehension of an essential truth, an apprehension that convinces us that what *she* sees is there.

In Fry's study of Cézanne, Woolf's favorite among his books, the critic dwells on the importance of still life as the genre in which "we frequently catch the purest self-revelation of the artist."[13] Fry's aim is not to praise mere technique or the artist's overcoming of his subject with himself. His point is rather that in still life, nature is particularized yet totally available to the viewer in a way that a portrait or a landscape painting of that which the viewer may never have seen cannot be. The artist's design and approach to the subject are, therefore, exposed and engaged with the viewer's in an unusually direct and intimate way. The artist makes a statement that is arbitrary, unmistakable, and fundamental about what is "central." In other words, his bias is an essential aspect of the picture, which the viewer is invited to assess as well as to share. The beauty, if there is any, and the stillness are the product of a joint effort.

Regarded in this light, engagement and detachment, love and wisdom are not incompatible, but interdependent rhythms of the creative life. Woolf comes closest to reflecting the vitality of her friend when she behaves like an artist and allows her own interests, including her impulse toward order, to mingle with the given textures and colorations of her subject. In writing of a new kind of biography, she had said, "The pith and essence of . . . character shows itself to the observant eye in the tone of a voice, the turn of a head, some little phrase . . . The life that is increasingly real to us is the fictitious life; it dwells in the personality rather than in the act . . . Thus the biographer's imagination is always being stimulated to use the novelist's art of arrangement."[14]

One of Woolf's truly memorable presentations of Fry in the

13. Roger Fry, *Cézanne* (New York: MacMillan, 1977), p. 41.
14. *Granite and Rainbow*, p. 155.

biography is novelistic in her own distinctive way—graphic, supple, alternately impressionistic and precise, swift in movement yet *centered* on a carefully arranged composition of objects. Her inspiration was Fry's suffering through the period of the First World War and another of his philosophical efforts to divide things in two—in this instance, art and life, which he had argued in an essay are "distinct, and as often as not play against each other" (p. 214). Woolf does not attack her friend's formulation but undermines it, interprets it in such a way that it becomes her own, and provides the material for a more favorable picture of him than he gives of himself. The contrast Woolf draws is not between illusion and reality but between active and contemplative modes of being, which she refuses to treat as independent. Her definition of detachment does not, like Fry's, emphasize stoic resignation but generosity and compassion:

There were two rhythms in his own life. There was the hurried and distracted life; but there was also the still life. With callers coming, the telephone ringing, and fashionable ladies asking advice about their bedspreads, he went back to his studio at Fitzroy Street to contemplate Giotto . . . If he survived the war, it was perhaps that he kept the two rhythms in being simultaneously. But, it is tempting to ask, were they distinct? It seems as if the aesthetic theory were brought to bear upon the problems of private life. Detachment, as he insisted over and over again, is the supreme necessity for the artist. Was it not equally necessary if the private life were to continue? That rhythm could only grow and expand if it were detached from the deformation which is possession. To live fully, to live gaily, to live without falling into the great sin of Accidia which is punished by fog, darkness and mud, could only be done by asking nothing for oneself. It was difficult to put that teaching into practice. Yet in his private life he had during those difficult years forced himself to learn that lesson. "It was a kind of death to me," he wrote . . . But it was no pale and disembodied ghost who opened the door if one knocked . . . He was huddled in an overcoat over the stove, writing. He was worn; he looked older . . . But he was as eager as ever to talk "about all sorts of things," and the room was if possible still more untidy. Mrs. Filmer had obeyed the command on the placard "Do not touch." Mrs. Filmer had not touched. Rows of dusty medicine bottles stood on the mantelpiece; frying pans were mixed with palettes; some plates held salad, others scrapings of congealed paint. The floor was strewn with papers. There were the pots he was making, there were samples of stuffs and designs for the Omega.

Mr. Carmichael and Lily Briscoe:
The Rhythm of Creativity in *To the Lighthouse*

There is such a thing as being too profound. Truth is not
always in a well. In fact, as regards the more important
knowledge, I do believe she is invariably superficial.
  Dupin, in "The Murders in the Rue Morgue"

Creativity for Virginia Woolf is a matter of an extending or bouyant élan. It is not so much, as I have argued elsewhere,[1] a matter of interpolation, the filling in of gaps between here and there, this and that, as it is a matter of extrapolation, the projection out into the unknown of a life force, a constructive force, whether moral, collective, or artistic. For Virginia Woolf this force, in all its dimensions, is liable to falter, fail, and drop, plunging the one who is dependent on it into an abyss of despondency, even of inexplicable terror, despair, or fear of death, desire for death. "We perished, each alone." Near the beginning of *To the Lighthouse* Mrs. Ramsay thinks:

. . . so that the monotonous fall of the waves on the beach, which for the most part beat a measured and soothing tattoo to her thoughts and seemed consolingly to repeat over and over again as she sat with the children the words of some old cradle song, murmured by nature, "I am guarding you—I am your

1. In "*Between the Acts:* Repetition as Extrapolation," *Fiction and Repetition* (Cambridge, Mass.: Harvard University Press, 1982), pp. 203–231.

support," but at other times suddenly and unexpectedly, especially when her mind raised itself slightly from the task actually in hand, had no such kindly meaning, but like a ghostly roll of drums remorselessly beat the measure of life, made one think of the destruction of the island and its engulfment in the sea, and warned her whose day had slipped past in one quick doing after another that it was all ephemeral as a rainbow—this sound which had been obscured and concealed under the other sounds suddenly thundered hollow in her ears and made her look up with an impulse of terror.[2]

I have interrupted a long sentence in the middle with the "so that" which follows "this sound . . . had ceased": "This sound . . . had ceased; so that . . ." Virginia Woolf's style is characterized by this prolonged, sustained rhythmical movement, drawing breath again just when it seems about to stop, and continuing beyond a semicolon or even beyond a full stop or the numbering or naming of a new section. It is as though Woolf or "the narrator," whoever it is who speaks the words of the novel, were afraid that if she (he? it?) were to stop, the sound of the waves breaking would intervene as the terror of an imminent fall. Woolf's work throughout is dominated by the question of whether there is beneath the manifold human activities of doing, thinking, talking, writing, creating a rhythmical groundswell which is comforting and sustaining; or whether such rhythm as there is outside human constructing beats out no more than the measure of approaching death. To go on talking, thinking, doing, writing, creating is either a way of warding off the fall, of sustaining oneself over the abyss, or if there is somewhere support, comfort, a "wedge-shaped core of darkness," the groundswell before, beneath, or ahead, to rest in that movement and share in it, to incarnate the secret rhythm of creation, out there, in what creates, in here.

To the Lighthouse contains many examples of this effort of rhythmic extrapolation reaching out from what is now and here toward what is there and not yet. The form of the novel is made up of these parallel analogous strands of creativity interacting, wound together, each pursuing its separate course toward its goal. The interpretation of To the Lighthouse is the interpretation of the meanings of each of

2. Virginia Woolf, To the Lighthouse (New York: Harcourt, Brace, 1927), pp. 27–28. Further references to To the Lighthouse will be identified in the text by page numbers from this edition. Reprinted by permission of Harcourt Brace Jovanovich, Inc., The Hogarth Press, and the Author's Literary Estate.

these various examples of creative energy, both separately and in its relation to the others. Mrs. Ramsay gives her dinner party with its triumphant *Boeuf en daube*. She has brought eight children into the world, nurtured and sustained them. She has given her self-pitying and insecure husband "this delicious fecundity, this fountain and spray of life," into which "the fatal sterility of the male plunge[s] itself, like a beak of brass barren and bare" (p. 58). The goal Mrs. Ramsay reaches in the novel, however, is death. The novel turns on the vanishing of her consciousness from the world and from the lives of the other characters. Her vanishing coincides with the vanishing in the catastrophe of the Great War of all that Victorian and Edwardian world of assured social order. The emblematic expression of this vanishing in the novel is that extraordinary representation, in the "Time Passes" section of the novel, of the world without any witnessing consciousness other than the ubiquitous mind of the narrator. There is in this section, to put it more precisely, no witnessing mind watching the gradual decay of the Ramsay's summer house, none but that anonymous mind of the narrator, that and the intermittently present cleaning woman, Mrs. McNab, who comes creaking and groaning now and then to make a momentary stay against entropy.

Mr. Ramsay's sense of failure results from his unsuccessful attempt to reach all the way to Z in his philosophical thinking. He too tries to extrapolate out into the void, but he gets stuck at Q: "A shutter, like the leathern eyelid of a lizard, flickered over the intensity of his gaze and obscured the letter R. In that flash of darkness he heard people saying—he was a failure—that R was beyond him. He would never reach R. On to R, once more. R—" (p. 54). If Mr. Ramsay does not ever reach even R, much less Z, chanter of poetry though he is, he does get finally, with James and Cam, to the lighthouse.

Mr. Ramsay's setting foot on the little island, as any reader of the novel knows, coincides with Lily Briscoe's putting the finishing stroke on her painting, the line that stands for the dead Mrs. Ramsay and substitutes for her, that replaces the missing shadow on the step cast by Mrs. Ramsay, the wedge-shaped core of darkness which had been present there when Lily began her painting and Mrs. Ramsay sat knitting the reddish-brown stocking and reading to James: "With a sudden intensity, as if she saw it clear for a second, she drew a line there, in the centre. It was done; it was finished. Yes, she thought, laying down her brush in extreme fatigue, I have had my vision" (p. 310). Lily's vision, before she has even had it, is proleptically compared to Mrs. Ramsay's establishment of order and stability in chaos by placing herself as the wedge-shaped core of darkness in the midst of the flow. This comparison is proof of that principle of analogy among the various acts of creativity which holds the diverse strands of *To the Lighthouse* together: "Mrs. Ramsay bringing them together; Mrs. Ramsay saying, 'Life stand still here'; Mrs. Ramsay making of the moment something permanent (as in another sphere Lily herself tried to make of the moment something permanent)—this was of the nature of a revelation. In the midst of chaos there was shape; this eternal passing and flowing (she looked at the clouds going and the leaves shaking) was struck into stability. Life stand still here, Mrs. Ramsay said" (pp. 240–241).

Lily's act of painting is presented explicitly as a rhythmical movement which carries her forward through time and seems perhaps to be sustained by an impersonal transcendent rhythm which is beyond her yet in which she nevertheless participates:

The brush descended. It flickered brown over the white canvas; it left a running mark. A second time she did it—a third time. And so pausing and so flickering, she attained a dancing rhythmical movement, as if the pauses were one part of the rhythm and the strokes another, and all were related; and so, lightly and swiftly pausing, striking, she scored her canvas with brown running nervous lines which had no sooner settled there than they enclosed (she felt it looming about her) a space . . .

Then, as if some juice necessary for the lubrication of her faculties were spontaneously squirted, she began precariously dipping among the blues and umbers, moving her brush hither and thither, but it was now heavier and went slower, as if it had fallen in with some rhythm which was dictated to her (she kept looking at the hedge, at the canvas) by what she saw, so that while her hand quivered with life, this rhythm was strong enough to bear her along with it on its current.   (pp. 235–236, 237–238).

The word *rhythm,* one can see, is the key term and concept in this remarkable passage. If "stability" names the fixed stay against chaos, as of a stake planted firmly in the swift current of life, "rhythm" for Woolf is the name for the shaping forward movement through time, scoring it in both senses, of the creative impetus in all its forms. An example is the choreographed and choreographing dance of Lily's hand. The fundamental question is whether, for Woolf, this movement is based on a ground, a fundament or principle outside itself, or whether its power is merely intrinsic, the imposition of a pulsating formal pattern on a formless background, as one scores a piece of music or scores a sign on featureless rock.

There is, however, yet a fourth example of creativity in *To the Lighthouse,* one more covert, muted, obscure: the poetry writing of Augustus Carmichael. If Mr. Ramsay sustains himself by rhythmically chanting poetry, Tennyson's "The Charge of the Light Brigade" or Cowper's "The Castaway," as he paces up and down the terrace, or as they go to the lighthouse, if Mrs. Ramsay brings people together and gives her egotistical husband sympathy, and if Lily Briscoe paints, Mr. Carmichael is presented in the first section of the book, "The Window," as a silent, ineffectual, and not altogether pleasant old man. He shuffles about in yellow slippers, dislikes Mrs. Ramsay, takes opium, and has cat's eyes and a cat's manners. In the last section, "The Lighthouse," the reader learns somewhat to his surprise (to my surprise at least) that Mr. Carmichael has become a successful, even a famous, poet. When Mr. Carmichael sits there catching words out of the air like a cat catching birds, he is gradually assembling words which are perhaps the most successful example of creativity in the novel: "And there he would lie all day long on the lawn brooding presumably over his poetry, till he reminded one of a cat watching birds, and then he clapped his paws together when he had found the word" (p. 145).

I have said that the presentation of Mr. Carmichael's creativity in the novel is obscure. The sign of this obscurity is the curious fact that Mr. Carmichael, almost alone of all the characters in *To the Lighthouse,* is never or scarcely ever presented from the inside by way of that indirect discourse, the consciousness of the narrator married to the consciousness of the character and speaking for it, which is the usual mode of presentation of people in this novel. I note only one time when the reader enters Mr. Carmichael's mind in this way: "And it all looked, Mr. Carmichael thought, shutting his book, much as it used to look" (p. 214). Why this relatively complete effacement of Mr. Carmichael should occur, what significance it may have, can only be speculated about at a later point in this essay.

If these diverse acts of creativity are presented in the novel as they are embodied in the characters, what about the act of representation represented by the novel itself? Is not the novel an act of rhythmic extrapolation out into the future, making form? Should the reader not think of all the forms of creativity within the novel— Mrs. Ramsay's, Mr. Ramsay's, Lily Briscoe's, Augustus Carmichael's—as oblique representations of the act of creativity represented by the novel itself? A distinction must be made here, as always, between Virginia Woolf sitting at her desk with a blank sheet of paper before her, composing *To the Lighthouse,* extending the line of words further and further out into the void of not-yet-written-on paper, and, on the other hand, the imagined and imaginary narrator of the novel. The latter is a different person, is located in a different place, and possesses quite different powers. Whatever may be said of Lily, Mr. Ramsay, Mrs. Ramsay, or Augustus Carmichael, both Virginia Woolf and her imagined narrative voice, in their quite different ways, succeed admirably in fulfilling the creative impetus which carries them out into the future or from one moment in the past up to another moment in the past. The novel creates an imagined world. It gets written, printed, published, reviewed. It makes Woolf famous, more famous than her father. The narrator retraces with patient completeness a stretch of time past, thought of now as having really happened. The narrator retraces this stretch of time all the way from the moment when Mrs. Ramsay sits with James, knitting the brown stocking, up to the moment when Mr. Ramsay, James, and Cam reach the lighthouse at last, and Lily puts the finishing stroke on her painting. All these diverse materials are gathered together, organized formally or rhythmically, and moved forward toward an end, the reaching of the lighthouse, the finishing of Lily's picture. All are recorded and preserved in words for the reader to resurrect once more in his turn.

Exactly who, or what, is the narrator of *To the Lighthouse?* Where is she, he, or it located? What powers does the narrator have? Whatever may be said of Woolf herself, the narrator of *To the Lighthouse* has extraordinary powers. The narrator enters at will into the minds of all the characters, or perhaps it might be better to say that the narrator is located already within all those minds and is able to speak for them in that strange third-person, past-tense form of narration: indirect discourse, *erlebte rede,* or *style indirect libre* (each of these nomenclatures has a different nuance of implications). Indirect discourse, along with dialogue, is the main resource of the tradition in the English novel that Woolf inherited and exploited so admirably. *To the Lighthouse* is a masterwork of exploration of the consciousness of others with the tool of indirect discourse, or to put this another way, it is a masterwork of the creation of the imaginary consciousness of others by means of this technique.

The past tense of the indirect discourse and indeed of all the narration of *To the Lighthouse* places the narrator of the novel at some indeterminate point after the action is over, looking back retrospectively at the events narrated. Exactly how long after or exactly where in space the "now" of the narrator is placed there is absolutely no way to tell. She, he, or it is nowhere and everywhere, located at no identifiable time except at an indeterminate "after." The narrator of *To the Lighthouse* has none of the characteristics of a person except voice and tone. The reader learns nothing of the narrator's history, dress, opinions, or family relations. She, he, it is anonymous, impersonal, ubiquitous, subtle, penetrative, insidious, sympathetic, and indifferent at once, able to plunge into the depths of any character's thoughts and feelings but liable to move without warning out of one mind and into another in the middle of a sentence, as in the shift from James's to Mr. Ramsay's mind in the fourth paragraph of the novel. Or the narrator may move without warning from one time to another time within the mind of a single character or group of characters, as in that sequence in the first pages of the novel in which Mrs. Ramsay reproves her daughter Nancy for saying that the atheist Tansley has chased them all the way to the Hebrides (p. 13). This must have occurred at an earlier time than the "now" in which Mrs. Ramsay sits watching James cut out pictures from the catalogue of the Army and Navy Stores.

The voice of the narrator is subtly subversive of the thoughts and feelings of the characters. The sign of this undercutting is the greater or lesser degree of irony and distance involved not only in repeating these thoughts and feelings in the past tense but also in repeating them in the third person. The signal of this somewhat insolent distance is the locution: "he thought" or "she thought" or "X thought": "[Mr. Ramsay] standing, as now, lean as a knife, narrow as the blade of one, grinning sarcastically, not only with the pleasure of disillusioning his son and casting ridicule upon his wife, who was ten thousand times better in every way than he was (James thought), but also with some secret conceit at his own accuracy of judgment" (p. 10). The narrator, it seems, is a ubiquitous mind, present everywhere at all times of the past, but condemned to know and feel only what the characters know and feel, and condemned also to hollow out these thoughts and feelings in the act of reliving them and repeating them in words.

The narrator, it appears, is a collective consciousness, dependent on the consciousnesses of the various characters for its existence. The narrator is without life, personality, opinions, feelings of its own, and yet is doomed to see all the lives, personalities, opinions, and feelings which it relives from the perspective of that prospective death toward which they all move, and where the narrating mind already is. Woolf's work can in this be defined as a magnificent exploitation and bringing out into the open of the implications of the Victorian convention of the "omniscient narrator," the narrator of *Middlemarch,* or of *The Last Chronicle of Barset,* or of *Our Mutual Friend.* The most disquieting of these conventions, it may be, is the way, if one thinks of it for a moment from the point of view of the characters, it can be seen that each of them is, without knowing it, overlooked, overfelt, if that may be said, penetrated through and through by an invisible, inaudible, wholly undetectable mind. That mind is gifted with terrifying clairvoyant insight, a kind of one-way television, telepathy, telethinking. The location of that "afar," the *tele* in all these words, is the future place of death which sees things as already part of the lost and irrevocable past. There is an indescribable pathos in this instantaneous transformation, by the impersonal conventions of storytelling, of flesh and blood immediacy into long-lost, impalpable ghosts.

Take, as one example of this, the following joining of the narrator's mind to Lily Briscoe's mind. The passage is a segment of extraordinarily supple and expert free indirect discourse from early in the novel. Once again my citation is broken out of a much longer continuous following of Lily's thoughts and feelings as she walks with Mr. Bankes and compares him to Mr. Ramsay:

How then did it work out, all this? How did one judge people, think of them? How did one add up this and that and conclude that it was liking one felt, or disliking? And to those words, what meaning attached, after all? Standing now, apparently transfixed, by the pear tree, impressions poured in upon her of those two men, and to follow her thought was like following a voice which speaks too quickly to be taken down by one's pencil, and the voice was her own voice saying without prompting undeniable, everlasting, contradictory things, so that even the fissures and humps on the bark of the pear tree were irrevocably fixed there for eternity. You [Mr. Bankes] have greatness, she continued, but Mr. Ramsay has none of it. His is petty, selfish, vain, egotistical; he is spoilt; he is a tyrant; he wears Mrs. Ramsay to death; but he has what you (she addressed Mr. Bankes) have not; a fiery un-worldliness; he knows nothing about trifles; he loves dogs and his children. He has eight. Mr. Bankes has none. Did he not come down in two coats the other night and let Mrs. Ramsay trim his hair into a pudding basin? All of this danced up and down, like a company of gnats, each separate, but all marvellously controlled in an invisible elastic net—danced up and down in Lily's mind, in and about the branches of the pear tree, where still hung in effigy the scrubbed kitchen table, symbol of her profound respect for Mr. Ramsay's mind, until her thought which had spun quicker and quicker exploded of its own intensity; she felt released; a shot went off close at hand, and there came, flying from its fragments, frightened, effusive, tumultuous, a flock of starlings.   (pp. 40–41)

In this admirable passage, one among so many similarly admira-ble passages in *To the Lighthouse,* the narrator has entirely pene-trated within the mind and feelings of the character, occupied them from within, down to every crevice, like the tide rising along the shore. The narrator repeats the character's thoughts and emotions for the reader in language composed in the past tense and in the third person, or at least without ever using "I." This repetition alienates the thoughts and feelings from Lily in the act which does her hom-age by so sympathetically identifying with her. That is, the narrator alienates the contents of Lily's consciousness by displacing them into that vast, capacious, impersonal mental-verbal reservoir of the narrator's collective consciousness. Within that manifold mind ev-ery thought and feeling that has ever occurred goes on happening over and over in an eternal repetition of itself in the mode of having always already happened when the reader encounters it. Within that all-embracing collective mind everything is permanently preserved, as even the fissures and humps on the bark of the pear tree seem to Lily "fixed there for eternity," and as her inner voice seems to her to be saying "everlasting" things, but they are preserved as fixed and dead. Within the narration every "I," "is," or "now" becomes "he" or "she," "was," or "then." For Lily the fissures and humps on the bark of the pear tree *are* fixed there for eternity; for the narrator and the reader they *were* so fixed.

I say "for the reader" too. What is performed by the narrator within the novel, the simultaneous alienation and preservation of the characters' affective thoughts, is performed by the novel for the reader in the most concrete and material way. Any copy of *To the Lighthouse* I hold in my hand encloses within itself, like a fly in amber, along with all its other contents, this particular sequence of moments in Lily Briscoe's mental life, eternally preserved in the words on the page, at least as long as this or at least one copy of the novel exists somewhere. The sequence is stored up, ready to be resurrected again in the mind of any reader whenever the paragraph is reread. The two forms of preservation are symmetrical, but they exist on opposite sides of the looking glass of fiction, one performed within the imaginary world of the novel, the other performed by the novel as a strange kind of physical object in the real world, paper marked all over with small black designs and bound in sheaves or stacks with cardboard covers.

The passage I have quoted is especially useful because it contains explicit notations of the mode of existence of the character's mind and a hint of the relation of that mind to that ubiquitous, all-knowing mind of which she is totally unaware. If the major narrative lines of *To the Lighthouse* are large-scale examples of creativity, abortive or unsuccessful, the small-scale existence of each character's mind from moment to moment is no less an example of a specific kind of creative élan, one repeating in miniature the formal structure of the book as a whole. Like the book, Lily's mind in these moments is made up of a large number of separate and contradictory thoughts and feelings all going on at once, a bundle or bunch of fragmentary details. At the same time the human mind, for Woolf, has a constantly acting power of rhythmically unifying these fragments, sweeping them into a measured, ongoing, alternating oneness, and holding them together within it, as all the words of a poem are held within that poem's organizing metrical scheme. This conception of the mind is precisely expressed in the double figure of the dancing gnats and the elastic net: "All this danced up and down, like a company of gnats, each separate, but all marvellously controlled in an invisible elastic net—danced up and down in Lily's mind."

The other crucial formulation here is the one in which the narrator says: "To follow her thought was like following a voice which speaks too quickly to be taken down by one's pencil, and the voice was her own voice saying without prompting undeniable, everlasting, contradictory things." There is no way to tell whether the infinitive phrase "to follow her thought" is to be thought of as Lily's own mental activity following that stream of thoughts which is like a rapid, unprompted, continuous, unstanchable murmur within her, or whether it is to be thought of as the narrator's activity of following and recording that murmuring voice within Lily, not by pencil but by means of that vast, all-inclusive, all-preserving sensorium or ubiquitous bugging apparatus which tapes everything but by some miracle of word-processing turns every present tense to past, every "I" to "he" or "she." The voice within Lily is both those voices at once, her own voice and what her own voice, like the inner voices of all the other characters, participates in without knowing it—the inaudible, all-absorbing voice of the narrator, that voice the reader is uniquely privileged to hear.

I have said that all the characters participate without knowing it in the voice and mind of the narrator, according to the assumption Woolf notes in her diary that a "tunnelling process" deep into the minds of all her characters would reach a point where they all connect, all have the same or similar thoughts, all move to the same profound rhythm, which is the rhythm of that impersonal narrator's way of thinking.[3] Might it not be that this impersonal, all-inclusive, all-keeping, all-annihilating perspective is covertly embodied in the person of Augustus Carmichael? The paradox then would be that although in one sense the mind of Mr. Carmichael is the one mind that the narrator hardly ever recounts from within for the reader in that indirect discourse which is her (or his or its) main resource, in

3. "I dig out beautiful caves behind my characters: I think that gives exactly what I want; humanity, humour, depth. The idea is that the caves shall connect." *A Writer's Diary* (New York: Harcourt, Brace, 1954), p. 59.

another sense there is evidence that Mr. Carmichael's mind coincides (perhaps with the help of opium) more closely than that of any other character with the mind of the narrator. To read the novel, to dwell within the narrator's mind and share the narrator's perspective, is to be within something closely approximating Mr. Carmichael's mind and perspective. Early in the novel the reader is shown Mr. Carmichael "basking with his yellow cat's eyes ajar, so that like a cat's they seemed to reflect the branches moving or the clouds passing, but to give no inkling of any inner thoughts or emotion whatsoever." Mr. Carmichael is unable to respond to Mrs. Ramsay's blandishments, "sunk as he was in a grey-green somnolence which embraced them all, without need of words, in a vast and benevolent lethargy of well-wishing; all the house; all the world; all the people in it" (p. 19). Does this not covertly describe the narrator's perspective, or one aspect of it at least? Much later in the novel, after the reader has been told that Mr. Carmichael has become a famous and successful poet, Lily Briscoe muses about him and his poetry: "She had never read a line of his poetry. She thought that she knew how it went though, slowly and sonorously. It was seasoned and mellow. It was about the desert and the camel. It was about the palm tree and the sunset. It was extremely impersonal; it said something about death; it said very little about love. There was an impersonality about him" (pp. 289–290). The rhythm of successful creativity in Mr. Carmichael, it may be, coincides as closely or even more closely than that of Lily Briscoe to the rhythm of creativity in the novel through which the narrator's impersonal voice transforms everything into pastness and sees everything from the perspective of death.

In what I have said so far I have suggested that the mind of the narrator is dependent on the minds of the characters for its existence. The narrator's mind can appear, can think or feel, can articulate itself, only in terms of what one or another of the characters thinks, feels, or articulates to himself or herself. There is of course a celebrated section of *To the Lighthouse*, "Time Passes," which seems openly and aggressively intended to contradict that generalization. Here the narrator witnesses and narrates the rhythm of gradual dissolution of the Ramsay's summer house when it is left empty, after Mrs. Ramsay's death, bereft of any human presence.

The narrator too, it seems, is bereft, empty of any human presence, and yet still remains as a neutral witness:

> The house was left; the house was deserted. It was left like a shell on a sandhill to fill with dry salt grains now that life had left it. The long night seemed to have set in; the trifling airs, nibbling, the clammy breaths, fumbling, seemed to have triumphed. The saucepan had rusted and the mat decayed. Toads had nosed their way in. Idly, aimlessly, the swaying shawl swung to and fro. A thistle thrust itself between the tiles in the larder. The swallows nested in the drawing-room; the floor was strewn with straw; the plaster fell in shovelfuls; rafters were laid bare; rats carried off this and that to gnaw behind the wainscots. Tortoise-shell butterflies burst from the chrysalis and pattered their life out on the window-pane. Poppies sowed themselves among the dahlias; the lawn waved with long grass; giant artichokes towered among roses; a fringed carnation flowered among the cabbages; while the gentle tapping of a weed at the window had become, on winters' nights, a drumming from sturdy trees and thorned briers which made the whole room green in summer.   (pp. 206–207)

In this extraordinary tour de force of language Virginia Woolf attempts a hyperbolic fulfillment of the project of Mr. Ramsay's books (and no doubt also of Leslie Stephen's books as his daughter thought of them). Mr. Ramsay's work, as Andrew tells Lily Briscoe, is about "subject and object and the nature of reality," and when Lily says she does not understand that, Andrew says, "Think of a kitchen table then . . . when you're not there" (p. 38). How can this be done? It is a genuine double bind. If I think of the table, then I must somehow be "there" to think it, but if I efface myself, then it seems I must efface the table. The "reality" of the table, for me at least, depends on my being there to think it, and yet the table manifestly would go on being there even if I were not there, even if I were dead. And so I try again, like Mr. Ramsay trying to get beyond Q to R, to think of the kitchen table when I am not there. The context of this difficult mental feat is of course those eighteenth-century philosophers, Locke, Berkeley, and Hume, in whom Leslie Stephen specialized, for example in *History of English Thought in the Eighteenth Century* (1876). If a tree crashed in the forest far out of earshot of any living being, would there be any noise? asked Bishop Berkeley. He answered that God's ubiquitous ear guaranteed that there would be everywhere a divine someone to hear every noise. In *To the Lighthouse* Woolf, like her father before her, attempts to do without this way out and to imagine not just the kitchen table but the whole milieu of that version of the table in the Ramsays' house at Skye, and to imagine it without any human consciousness as stay against entropy other than the intermittent and ineffectual presence of the cleaning woman, Mrs. McNab.

Even on a night when the house is full of human inhabitants, darkness and sleep depersonifies these inhabitants and deprives them of the ability to say "I" or of the right to be properly described as "he" or "she": "Nothing, it seemed, could survive the flood, the profusion of darkness which, creeping in at keyholes and crevices, stole round window blinds, came into bedrooms, swallowed up here a jug and basin, there a bowl of red and yellow dahlias, there the sharp edges and firm bulk of a chest of drawers. Not only was furniture confounded; there was scarcely anything left of body or mind by which one could say, 'This is he' or 'This is she' " (pp. 189–190). What persists, in the absence of individual human minds, as witness of the gradual decay of the house is the mind of the narrator or the language of the narrator. Not only does this indicate that, in *To the Lighthouse* at least, the mind of the narrator is *not* dependent on the minds of the characters for its continued existence; it is also evidence that although what the narrator sees when all individual human consciousnesses are withdrawn is a universal and remorseless process of disintegration, a slowing down of the rhythm of creativity and a vanishing of distinctions like that in Swinburne's "A Forsaken Garden," nevertheless for Woolf the traditional "omniscient narrator" is truly omniscient, a fictional replacement of God. This narrative mind exceeds and surrounds all individual minds. It was there before those individual minds, and it is still there when they are all gone. It is anonymous, ubiquitous, impersonal—watching everything, aware of everything, turning everything into all-annihilating, all-preserving past-tense language: "The place was gone to rack and ruin. Only the Lighthouse beam entered the rooms for a moment, sent its sudden stare over bed and wall in the darkness of winter, looked with equanimity at the thistle and the swallow, the rat and the straw. Nothing now withstood them; nothing said no to them. Let the wind blow; let the poppy seed itself and the carnation mate with the cabbage" (p. 208). If only living human beings, working, creating, individually or collectively, can keep nonhuman nature from an irresistible tendency to that dispersal and obliteration of boundaries for which the symbol here is unnatural love, the poppy seeding itself, the carnation grotesquely mating with the cabbage, on the other hand, even if no human being is left to say no to this unnatural propensity in nature, there will still be an inhuman witness of the universal dissolution. There will remain precisely that view and that voice which go on seeing and speaking with such impersonal clairvoyance in "Time Passes."

Is that voice in fact so impersonal, so depersonifying? One form of figuration persists through all the citations from "Time Passes" I have made—in fact it permeates the whole chapter: personification, that trope of prosopopoeia whereby we speak of the absent, the dead, or the inanimate as if they were alive, as if they were possessed of human consciousness and intent. The trifling airs nibble and fumble. They have clammy breaths. The darkness creeps, steals, swallows. The lighthouse beam stares and looks. The carnation mates with the cabbage, as though they were human beings making love. Though this prosopopoeia is present everywhere in "Time Passes," one of the most beautiful of such sequences occurs early in the second part of the section, just after the passage already quoted about the vanishing in darkness and sleep of each "he" or "she." It is as if personality vanishes from the sleeping inhabitants of the house (for in this early section of "Time Passes" the house has not yet been left derelict), only to be displaced to the inhuman entities which remain, in this case the gentle breaths of sea air which circulate through the house. The passage has importance in unostentatiously calling attention to the fictive nature of the prosopopoeia. The night breaths are not really alive, but "almost one might imagine them" to be human. It is "as if" they were able to think and act:

Only through the rusty hinges and swollen sea-moistened woodwork certain airs, detached from the body of the wind (the house was ramshackle after all) crept round corners and ventured indoors. Almost one might imagine them, as they entered the drawing-room questioning and wondering, toying with the flap of hanging wall-paper, asking, would it hang much longer, when would it fall? Then smoothly brushing the walls, they passed on musingly as if asking the red and yellow roses on the wall-paper whether they would fade, and questioning (gently, for there was time at their disposal) the torn letters in the waste-paper basket, the flowers, the books, all of which were now open to them and asking, Were they allies? Were they enemies? How long would they endure?   (pp. 190–191)

What should one say of the personification here? What is its source or justification? What significance does it have? Can "one" not almost say that the dispersed presence of these prosopopoeias, present everywhere in the language of the narration when the narrator tries to think of the kitchen table and all its surroundings when no one is there, is evidence that language itself forbids the carrying out of this project; that the narrator of *To the Lighthouse* is not a ubiquitous mind but language itself; that language therefore takes precedence over consciousness here; or, to put this another way, that the personifications present in ordinary language (so that without necessarily thinking about it one describes the wind as creeping round corners, venturing indoors, questioning, wondering, sighing) are the source of one's ideas of the personalities of "real people" (Lily Briscoe, Mr. Ramsay, Mrs. Ramsay, and the rest)? The evidence for the last point is the way personality will inevitably be ascribed to inanimate objects, animating the wind for example (*anima:* wind, breath, soul in Latin) when all "real people" are asleep, absent, or dead. Wherever there is language there will be personality somewhere. The novel as a genre, "almost one might imagine," is no more than the systematic and highly conventionalized exploitation of the potentiality within ordinary language to generate and project manifold illusions of selfhood, in the wind or in the light if not in some "he" or "she" named "Mr. Ramsay" or "Lily Briscoe."

It is impossible to think of the kitchen table when you are not there not so much because it is impossible to efface consciousness or to imagine the absence of some witnessing mind as because there is no thinking without language. Language always reimports some "you," some "I," "he," or "she" into whatever is turned into language, for example in speaking of the "legs" of that table or in describing the gradual deterioration under the influence of wind and weather of the Ramsays' summer house as time passes.[4] It is not entirely accurate, therefore, to speak of the mind of the narrator of *To the Lighthouse* as dependent on the minds of the characters for its existence. "Time Passes" shows that this is not the case. Language, *To the Lighthouse* implies, preexists everything human as its presupposition, for example in the universal human belief in the existence of minds or selves. Something human might remain if every separate human being were effaced. Language might remain, and with it the conditions of belief in human minds or selves. In the case of *To the Lighthouse* both the personality of the narrator and those of the characters are dependent on that ineffaceable tendency present in ordinary language to project faces and bodies (and minds or feelings behind those faces and bodies). Any speaker or writer inherits language and its pervasive prosopopoeias among all the other things already there in the world into which he or she is born. "Time Passes" is a striking confirmation of this and a demonstration of some of its effects on storytelling or novel writing.

"He or she"? "One"? A final question remains, one that will return to the fundamental question posed earlier of whether there is a fundament or ground for the rhythm of creativity in Woolf. What is the sex of the one who says of the night airs, "almost one might imagine them questioning, creeping, wondering, sighing"?[5] Is the language of narration in *To the Lighthouse* gender-specific? Is the style of *To the Lighthouse* feminine? masculine? androgynous? Does Virginia Woolf "write like a woman"? What would it mean to say, "Virginia Woolf writes like a woman"? How would one tell

---

4. Strictly speaking, "legs" is a catachresis as well as a prosopopoeia. The region of catachresis and the region of prosopopoeia overlap but do not coincide. Their relation is a complex form of chiasmus. "Legs of a table," like "face of a mountain," goes toward effacement in one direction (prosopopoeia) and toward making present in the other (catachresis). I have written in more detail on this topic in "Catachresis and Character: The Example of Clara Middleton in *The Egoist,*" forthcoming in the transactions of a symposium on catachresis and syllepsis held at the University of Toronto in June 1982. And see also, on this topic, Paul de Man, "Hypogram and Inscription: Michael Riffaterre's Poetics of Reading," *Diacritics,* 11 (Winter 1981), 30–35.

5. A preliminary version of this essay was presented at the Woolf Centenary Conference at Brown University, February 26–27, 1982. The conference was supposed to ask, among other things, "whether theories of sexual difference and definition can lead to better understanding of Woolf and her milieu."

certainly about this or persuade another of the truth of one's judgment?

Woolf herself, of course, raised these questions, especially in *A Room of One's Own*. There on the one hand (once more with some embarrassment of pronouns: "room of *one's* own") she asserts that "it is fatal for any *one* who writes to think of *their* sex . . . It is fatal for a woman . . . in any way to speak consciously as a woman" (emphasis mine).[6] On the other hand, Woolf, apparently without irony, praises Mary Carmichael, her imaginary young woman writer, for writing unselfconsciously as a woman: "She wrote as a woman, but as a woman who has forgotten that she is a woman, so that her pages were full of that curious sexual quality which comes only when sex is unconscious of itself" (*ROO*, p. 96). What does this mean? How can one identify this curious sexual quality? Is there any significance in the fact that Woolf gives her aspiring woman novelist in *A Room of One's Own* the same patronymic as she gives the elusive male poet in *To the Lighthouse?* Is Mary Carmichael the daughter of Augustus Carmichael?

At the end of the printed record of the discussion following Jacques Derrida's initial presentation at Cerisy of his essay on Nietzsche and the place of woman, *Éperons: Les styles de Nietzsche,* there is an odd moment. Derrida here affirms in answer to a question that he would like to write like (a) woman and tries to do so: "J'aimerais bien écrire, aussi, comme (une) femme. J'essaie."[7] What does this mean? Can a man write like a woman, or a woman write like a man, as, for example, Mary Anne Evans called herself George Eliot and at least ostensibly "wrote like a man"? Could any writing be beyond sexual difference, truly bisexual or asexual? Would that be desirable?

The issues here are extremely complex, even if one limits oneself

6. Virginia Woolf, *A Room of One's Own* (New York and Burlingame: Harcourt, Brace & World, n.d.; first published in 1929), p. 108; hereafter cited as *ROO*. Reprinted by permission of Harcourt Brace Jovanovich, Inc., The Hogarth Press, and the Author's Literary Estate.

7. *Nietzsche aujourd'hui?* (Paris: Union Générale d'Editions, 1973), I, 299. The discussion at Cerisy of Derrida's lecture is not included in the English translation of the essay. Derrida has more recently returned to his essay on Nietzsche and to the issues it raises about the feminine and about feminine style in "Choreographies," an interview with Christie V. McDonald, *Diacritics,* 12 (Summer 1982), 66–76. This issue of *Diacritics* is devoted to the topic of feminism and literature and is an excellent representation of the state of work in this area.

to the question of sexual differentiation in its relation to style. One must move carefully and tentatively, hypothetically, in these areas. Only the indication of a direction to move toward can be given here. To write like a woman might mean a number of different things, or manifest itself in a number of different ways, for example in straightforward thematic assertion. The latter is certainly present in Woolf's work—in the admirable feminist polemic of *A Room of One's Own,* or in the recurrent treatment of men in her novels as sterile egotists, overdependent on women, such as Mr. Ramsay in *To the Lighthouse* or Peter Walsh in *Mrs. Dalloway.* Writing like a woman might have, and in Woolf's case does have, a number of different possible contexts for discussion: biological, psychological, familial, social, historical, and so on. I suggest that perhaps Woolf's most important contribution to the question of what it might mean to write like a woman or like a man, or like some androgynous combination of the two, is her recognition that at the deepest level it is not a matter of thematic assertion but a matter of rhythm.

The problem for a woman writer, in Woolf's view, is that the rhythm of male style does not fit her natural stylistic stride and pace: "For we think back through our mothers if we are women. It is useless to go to the great men writers for help, however much one may go to them for pleasure. Lamb, Browne, Thackeray, Newman, Sterne, Dickens, De Quincey—whoever it may be—never helped a woman yet, though she may have learnt a few tricks of them and adapted them to her use. The weight, the pace, the stride of a man's mind are too unlike her own for her to lift anything substantial from him successfully. The ape is too distant to be sedulous" (*ROO,* p. 79). As Émile Benveniste has shown,[8] the word and the concept of rhythm arose among the Greeks as an extrapolation from the measured movements of the body in dancing, that is, from just that area from which Woolf draws her figure to explain why the standard masculine style does not work for a woman. Mary Carmichael must therefore in her writing destroy or disrupt the normal male rhythm and replace it with an abrupt, interrupted female style more suited to the biological and social conditions of a woman's life: "The book has somehow to be adapted to the body, and at a venture one would

8. See Émile Benveniste, "La notion de 'rhythme' dans son expression linguistique," *Problèmes de linguistique générale* (Paris: Gallimard, 1966), pp. 327–335.

say that women's books should be shorter, more concentrated, than those of men, and framed so that they do not need long hours of steady and uninterrupted work. For interruptions there will always be" (*ROO*, p. 81).[9] Mary Carmichael in *Life's Adventure* writes like a woman not because of anything she says but because she performs successfully the double act of disrupting the inherited male rhythm and of replacing it with a new feminine rhythm appropriate for her time (as Jane Austen's Mozartean melodies would not have been):

> So I tried a sentence or two on my tongue. Soon it was obvious that something was not quite in order. The smooth gliding of sentence after sentence was interrupted. Something tore, something scratched; a single word here and there flashed its torch in my eyes. She was "unhanding" herself as they say in the old plays. She is like a person striking a match that will not light, I thought. But why, I asked her as if she were present, are Jane Austen's sentences not of the right shape for you? Must they all be scrapped because Emma and Mr. Woodhouse are dead? Alas, I sighed, that it should be so. For while Jane Austen breaks from melody to melody as Mozart from song to song, to read this writing was like being out at sea in an open boat. Up one went, down one sank . . .
>
> I am almost sure, I said to myself, that Mary Carmichael is playing a trick on us. For I feel as one feels on a switchback railway when the car, instead of sinking, as one has been led to expect, swerves up again. Mary is tampering with the expected sequence. First she broke the sentence; now she has broken the sequence. Very well, she has every right to do both these things if she does them not for the sake of breaking, but for the sake of creating.   (*ROO*, pp. 84–85)

"Not for the sake of breaking, but for the sake of creating"—in what sense, exactly, can this broken, interrupted female rhythm be creative? I suggest that there are two possible concepts of rhythm. One is implicitly associated by Woolf with "writing like a man," the other with "writing like a woman." The rhythm of a piece of writing may be a way of participating, or of thinking one participates, in the pulsation of creation already there in the world outside the mind of the writer. An example would be the sprung rhythm of Gerard Manley Hopkins. This rhythm, as Hopkins affirms in "The Wreck of the Deutschland," corresponds to the intrin-

---

9. Peggy Kamuf presented an excellent paper at the Brown Conference entitled "Penelope at Work: Interruption in *A Room of One's Own*."

sic rhythm of God's immanent presence in His creation: "world's strand, sway of the sea," "ground of being, and granite of it." Such a conception of rhythm is constative. It claims to reaffirm, to echo, a pattern already present outside the writing. Woolf tends to associate such a concept of rhythm with the male writer's comforting illusion that he dwells in the truth, that he possesses the truth and sways with its deepest measures. "Indeed, it was delightful to read a man's writing again," says Woolf of Mr. A's novel, her example of male writing in *A Room of One's Own*. "It was so direct, so straightforward after the writing of women. It indicated such freedom of mind, such liberty of person, such confidence in himself. One had a sense of physical well-being in the presence of this well-nourished, well-educated, free mind, which had never been thwarted or opposed, but had had full liberty from birth to stretch itself in whatever way it liked" (*ROO*, p. 103). The problem with Mr. A's novel is that this bland assumption that he is securely in resonance with the deep rhythms of the truth is false. Mr. A's novel is in fact the unjustified assertion of the sterile letter "I" shadowing everything. It expresses the ungrounded imposition of the rhythms of sexual domination over women:

It took place on the beach under sun. It was done very openly. It was done very vigorously. Nothing could have been more indecent . . . There seemed to be some obstacle, some impediment of Mr. A's mind which blocked the fountain of creative energy and shored it within narrow limits . . . When Alan approaches what can he do? Being honest as the day and logical as the sun, there is only one thing he can do. And that he does, to do him justice, over and over (I said, turning the pages) and over again . . . He does it in protest. He is protesting against the equality of the other sex by asserting his own superiority. He is therefore impeded and inhibited and self-conscious. (*ROO*, pp. 104–105)

Against this false rhythm of unjustified solar male superiority may be opposed the more lunar rhythm of writing like a woman. This latter is the free projection of a broken, jagged, hesitant, evanescent measure against the aimless flux and tendency toward entropy of the outside world. This projection is made by the one who writes like a woman in full knowledge of the evanescence of the rhythmic beat of the words thus constructed, and in full knowledge that this rhythm is not grounded on any corresponding rhythm outside. Such a rhythm is extrapolative, performative. It projects a measured form through time out toward an unknown end. It is a way of doing things with words that is not to be measured by its truth of correspondence to any preexisting pattern. Such writing brings something, a repeating and repeatable pattern, into existence through the words, through the autonomous say-so of the writer. To do this, to write performatively rather than constatively, is, it may be, to write like a woman. It is to write beyond or outside the egotistic illusions of "phallogocentrism," that erect male letter "I" shadowing and killing everything, like a giant beech tree, and bamboozled by its confidence that it is in tune with "the truth," the *Logos*.

It will be seen, however, that writing like a woman and writing like a man tend to change places or values in the moment of being defined and enacted. The male thinks he writes constatively, but in fact his affirmations are groundless performatives. The woman writer knows there is no truth, no rhythm but the drumbeat of death, but this means that her broken, hesitant rhythms are in resonance with the truth that there is no truth. Writing like a woman is superior to male writing by being truly constative rather than unwittingly performative. Back and forth from one extreme to the other Woolf's thought alternates; each side is no sooner identified with one pole of the dichotomy than it reverses into its opposite. Nor is this absence or weakness of mind on Woolf's part. Woolf is no more able than any male writer to do without some form, however surreptitious, of the constative notion of authenticity in writing.

It may be that Woolf's well-known intermittent commitment to the idea of androgynous writing, writing like a man and like a woman simultaneously, is no more than a name for this fundamental undecidability in her notion of what would constitute valid rhythms of style, writing with a pen and not with a pickaxe, as she puts it apropos of Mary Carmichael. The good writer writes both performatively and constatively at once, that is, both like a woman and like a man, though the definitions and the values of both kinds of writing change places constantly:

And I went on amateurishly to sketch a plan of the soul so that in each of us two powers preside, one male, one female; and in the man's brain, the man predominates over the woman, and in the woman's brain, the woman predominates over the man. The normal and comfortable state of being is that when the two live in harmony together, spiritually cooperating. If one is a man, still the woman part of the brain must have effect; and a woman also must have intercourse with the man in her. Coleridge perhaps meant this when he said that a great mind is androgynous. It is when this fusion takes place that the mind is fully fertilised and uses all its faculties. Perhaps a mind that is purely masculine cannot create, any more than a mind that is purely feminine, I thought . . .

Coleridge certainly did not mean, when he said that a great mind is androgynous, that it is a mind that has any special sympathy with women; a mind that takes up their cause or devotes itself to their interpretation. Perhaps the androgynous mind is less apt to make these distinctions than the single-sexed mind. He meant, perhaps, that the androgynous mind is resonant and porous; that it transmits emotion without impediment; that it is naturally creative, incandescent and undivided.   (*ROO,* p. 102)

Does not *To the Lighthouse* already fulfill Woolf's desire to write like a woman whose mind is fertilized by the presence of the man in it? In somewhat covertly granting Augustus Carmichael creative power too, along with Lily Briscoe, does Woolf not already express that desire for an equivocal androgynous rhythm of style, beyond or combining the contradictory penchants of sexual difference? And does not the identification of sexual difference in style turn out to be no more than a way of naming these two forms of rhythm in their crisscrossing relation to the presence or absence of rhythm outside language? This constantly reversing rhythm, affirming itself and at the same time interrupting itself, is the dominant measure of *To the Lighthouse* and of Woolf's work generally. An example is the quotation I made at the beginning of this essay describing Mrs. Ramsay's sense of the double meaning of the beat of the waves, sustaining and devastating at once.

RONALD BUSH

Modern/Postmodern: Eliot, Perse, Mallarmé, and the Future of the Barbarians

One must hide depth. Where? On the surface.
  —Hugo von Hofmannsthal

Peering into the future, T. S. Eliot wrote, is most likely to produce "a document upon the present time."[1] Yet when the present time is one of the turning points of the century's poetry, there is reason to attend to its oracles, especially when their ambivalence voices the coming change. And so a forgotten review Eliot wrote in 1927 of John Rodker's *The Future of Futurism* and Gertrude Stein's *Composition as Explanation* may now be worth rereading. One of the four dozen occasional pieces Eliot churned out in 1927, "Charleston, Hey! Hey!" puts our present account of twentieth-century literature in question. It suggests, among other things, that the *Four Quartets,* whose stylistic roots begin in Eliot's writing of the late twenties, are not simply Eliot's "last testament," which "founded no idiom [and] fathered no school;"[2] they are on the contrary one of the significant predecessors of postmodernist poetry.

1. This and subsequent citations are from T. S. Eliot, "Charleston, Hey! Hey!" *Nation and Athenaeum,* 40 (29 January 1927), 595.
2. Lawrence Lipking, *The Life of the Poet: Beginning and Ending Poetic Careers* (Chicago: University of Chicago Press, 1981), p. 74.

In "Charleston, Hey! Hey!" Eliot adds his own reflections on the evolution of twentieth-century literature to those of John Rodker:

Mr. Rodker seems to think, in short, that the future of literature lies in two directions: in the line of "Blake, Mallarmé, Roussel, and the development of those qualities we have called mental agility," and the other the line of "the sublimity of the bowels as in Tchekhov and Dostoevsky." Or, to put it crudely . . . the direction of abstraction ("pure poetry"), and on the other hand the investigation of the subconscious . . . He seems to think that we "shall grow more refined, our nervous antennae more delicately aware of new vibrations," &c. We shall produce, on the one hand, a pantheon of super-Mallarmés for a smaller and smaller public, and on the other hand we shall have a popular literature—if literature it be—for a completely Americanized Russia and a more and more Russianized America.

Responding to this "vaticination," Eliot is of two minds. He agrees that Rodker is essentially correct, but he is troubled all the same. Some years earlier Eliot had founded his fame on the assertion that "poets in our civilization, as it exists at present, must be *difficult*. Our civilization comprehends great variety and complexity, and this variety and complexity, playing upon a refined sensibility, must produce various and complex results. The poet must become more and more comprehensive, more allusive, more indirect, in order to force, to dislocate if necessary, language into his meaning."[3] Now, however, Eliot expresses uneasiness that such complexity should exist for its own sake, and wonders "whether complication of syntax always implies complexity of thought or sensibility, whether the thought and sensibility of the [refined literature] of the future may not become more simple and indeed more crude than that of the present." "There is," he says, "something . . . *ominous* about Miss Stein." Exactly what we may guess from his 1936 essay on Milton, which complains that Milton's "tortuous style" had turned poetry into a "solemn game" and compares Milton's style with that of Henry James, whose more benign intricacies reproduce the "by-paths of mental movement."[4]

3. From "The Metaphysical Poets" (1921). See T. S. Eliot, *Selected Essays* (1932; reprinted, New York: Harcourt, Brace and World, 1960), p. 248.

4. See T. S. Eliot, *On Poetry and Poets* (1957; reprinted, New York: Noonday, 1969), pp. 163, 160.

The force of Eliot's uneasiness, it seems, is that twentieth-century literature is after thirty years at the point of decadence. According to his way of thinking, the two streams of Rodker's vision had once been united. Before the decadence, Henry James had harnessed refinement to a profound investigation of the subconscious. And James was followed, as the "Milton" essay points out, by James Joyce, at least by Joyce "in his early work, and . . . in [the first] part of *Ulysses.*"[5] We need only complete Eliot's thought to add that, faithful to James's ideal, Joyce was also typical of the modernist movement. It is the very essence of the high modernism of the early twenties that the currents Rodker associated with Dostoevsky and Mallarmé were somehow made to reinforce one another. Thus the representative modernist masterpieces (the *Cantos, The Tower, Ulysses, Women in Love, To the Lighthouse*) yoke together elements of symbolist music and psychological exploration. There is, however, no better example than *The Waste Land,* which drew heavily on a study of Dostoevsky for its nightmarish intensity even as it orchestrated its fantasies with the craft of *la poésie pure.*[6] *The Waste Land* has come to stand as the archetypal modernist work because in it we find the perfection of what Eliot found in Ezra Pound's *Cantos:* a "nearly continuous identification . . . of form and feeling."[7] This is what Helen Gardner had in mind in her recent Norton lectures when she observed the nostalgia of the contemporary scene for a time when there were giants on the earth.[8]

Still, the discomfort and confusion Eliot vents in "Charleston, Hey! Hey!" were unavoidable. By 1927 modernism really had begun to split apart, and to split along the lines Rodker indicated. Eliot himself would later remark that after the middle of *Ulysses,* Joyce turned "from the visible world" to a "music" relatively unrelated to speech and to "an auditory imagination abnormally sharpened at

5. Ibid., p. 162.

6. On Eliot and Dostoevsky, see John C. Pope, "Prufrock and Roskolnikov Again: A Letter from Eliot," *American Literature,* 18, no. 4 (January 1947), 219–221. See also Eliot's remarks on Dostoevsky in "Beyle and Balzac," *Athenaeum,* 30 May 1919, 392–393, and in "London Letter," *The Dial,* September 1922, 330–331).

7. Introduction to *The Selected Poems of Ezra Pound* (1928; reprinted, London: Faber and Faber, 1973), p. 19.

8. See Helen Gardner, *In Defence of the Imagination* (Cambridge, Mass.: Harvard University Press, 1982), chap. 1 ("Present Discontents").

the expense of the visual."[9] And by 1927 the same unhinging of sound from sight and music from speech and psychological nuance could be illustrated in many of Joyce's contemporaries. To clarify what happens to Joyce after the middle of *Ulysses,* we have only to recall what happens to Yeats after *The Tower* (1928), to Woolf after *To the Lighthouse* (1927), to Lawrence after *Women in Love* (1920), or to Stevens after *Harmonium* (1923). In each case, a balance between psychological depth and musical organization tilts toward the latter and leads to a literature of the surface, whether the surface be a toccata of myth and history (late Joyce or Lawrence) or a symphony of disembodied abstraction (late Stevens). The result, as F. R. Leavis bemoaned, was reprehensible to modernist taste. In 1933, measuring the just published "Byzantium" against the earlier "Sailing to Byzantium," Leavis noted that the tension in Yeats's work had "slackened," and that the poetry betrayed a "relaxed grasp."[10] His judgment marks the passing of an era.

Trying hard not to acknowledge any of this in "Charleston, Hey! Hey!" Eliot is patently uncomfortable. On the one hand he disdains the power of Gertrude Stein's "kinship with the saxophone" and remarks that "her work is not improving, it is not amusing, it is not interesting, it is not good for one's mind." Aware of his contemporaries' flirtation with incantatory rhythms, however, he finds himself forced to acknowledge that Stein's writing has "a peculiar hypnotic power not met with before." He concludes, "If this is of the future, then the future is, as it very likely is, of the barbarians." From the perspective of 1982, though, there is more interest in his resigned acceptance ("as it very likely is") than in his censure. As the intervening years have shown, not only the future of literature but the future of Eliot's own poetry belonged to the barbarians. But to make sense of that assertion, I want to review what happened to the line of "the sublimity of the bowels": why it was originally so central to modernism and why it lost its authority in the mid-twenties; and finally why, in the work of later modernism, the loss of its authority led both to the production of "a pantheon of super-Mallarmé's" and to the relegation of psychology to the demimonde of popular literature. All of these questions, it seems to me, point

9. Eliot, *On Poetry and Poets,* p. 162.

10. From a 1933 review of *The Winding Stair and Other Poems.* See F. R. Leavis, *A Selection from Scrutiny* (Cambridge: Cambridge University Press, 1968), I, 89–90.

to an anterior question—the question of what the modernists thought about literary sincerity.

Characteristic of a paradoxical time, the keystone of Eliot's early work can be found in an essay on Blake and glossed with a passage from Wordsworth:

It is important that the artist should be highly educated in his own art; but his education is one that is hindered rather than helped by the ordinary processes of society which constitute education for the ordinary man. For these processes consist largely in the acquisition of impersonal ideas which obscure what we really are and feel, what we really want, and what really excites our interest . . . Tennyson is a very fair example of a poet almost wholly encrusted with opinion, almost wholly merged into his environment. Blake, on the other hand . . . was naked, and saw man naked, and from the centre of his own crystal . . . there was nothing to distract him from sincerity.

[Where may we find our best measure of human nature?] I answer, [from with] in; by stripping our own hearts naked.[11]

Disavowing Romantic sentimentalism at every turn, Eliot nevertheless roots himself in nineteenth-century notions of the self. For Eliot as for Wordsworth, the conventions of polite society and polite literature are to be viewed as encrustations. Both writers assert that the aim of poetry is to show the heart stripped naked—to reveal, from the center of the poet's crystal, "what we really are and feel, what we really want, and what really excites our interest." What, however, happens to this ideal in an age when, to quote Virginia Woolf, "character is dissipated into shreds?"[12] To express sincerely *this* complex life, literature, in Eliot's words, must become "difficult." It must be witty, so that it comes to involve "a recognition, implicit in the expression of every experience, of other kinds of

11. The first citation is from "Blake" (1920); see Eliot, *Selected Essays*, p. 277. The second comes from Wordsworth's letters, as quoted in David Perkins, *Wordsworth and the Poetry of Sincerity* (Cambridge, Mass.: Harvard University Press, 1968), p. 56. (The first two chapters of Perkins' book provide an excellent gloss on the problems of Romantic and modernist sincerity, and should be used to supplement the brief discussion of the subject given below.)

12. Virginia Woolf, *A Writer's Diary* (1953; reprinted, New York: Harcourt Brace Jovanovich, 1973), p. 56.

experience."[13] It must, in its ironies, mirror the uncertainty of discontinuous being.

And yet, at the bottom of all this sophistication, the literature of early modernism continues to reflect a belief in what Arnold called the "buried life"—the seat of "what we really are and feel" and the perpetual antagonist of our conventional selves. This belief is one of the major supports of Eliot's famous assertion of impersonality, as E. M. Forster brings out when he alters Eliot's usage slightly and proclaims the virtues of "anonymity":

Modern critics go too far in their insistence on personality.

They go too far because they do not reflect what personality is. Just as words have two functions—information and creation—so each human mind has two personalities, one on the surface, one deeper down. The upper personality has a name. It is called S. T. Coleridge, or William Shakespeare, or Mrs. Humphrey Ward. It is conscious and alert, does things like dining out, answering letters, etc., and it differs vividly and amusingly from other personalities. The lower personality is a very queer affair. In many ways it is a perfect fool, but without it there is no literature, because unless a man dips a bucket down into it occasionally he cannot produce first-class work. There is something general about it. Although it is inside S. T. Coleridge, it cannot be labelled with his name. It has something in common with all other deeper personalities, and the mystic will assert that the common quality is God, and that here, in the obscure recesses of our being, we near the gates of the Divine. It is in any case the force that makes for anonymity . . . The poet wrote the poem, no doubt, but he forgot himself while he wrote it, and we forget him while we read. What is so wonderful about great literature is that it transforms the man who reads it towards the condition of the man who wrote, and brings to birth in us also the creative impulse.[14]

Unlike Forster's anonymous creator, however, the early modernists regard their buried lives as idiosyncratic. Eliot, for one, allowing a character in one of his plays to assert something he once believed, envisions a "tougher self":

13. From "Andrew Marvell" (1921). See Eliot, *Selected Essays,* p. 262.

14. From "Anonymity: An Inquiry" (1926). See E. M. Forster, *Two Cheers for Democracy* (1938; reprinted, New York: Harcourt, Brace and World, 1951), pp. 83–84.

The self that can say "I want this—or want that"—
The self that wills—he is a feeble creature;
He has to come to terms in the end
With the obstinate, the tougher self; who does not speak,
Who never talks, who cannot argue;[15]

(p. 326)

Similarly, in his 1904 sketch "A Portrait of the Artist," Joyce announces his intention to become one of those artists "who seek through some art . . . to liberate from the personalised lumps of matter that which is their individuating rhythm, the first or formal relation of their parts . . . for such as these a portrait is not an identificative paper but rather the curve of an emotion."[16] Lawrence gets at the same thing in a more polemical way. Writing to Edward Garnett in 1914 that he is interested in the individual vicissitudes of "the inhuman will," Lawrence advises that "you mustn't look in my novel for the old stable ego of the character. There is another ego, according to whose action the individual is unrecognizable." (Two years earlier, in his "Study of Thomas Hardy," Lawrence had called this other ego the "real, vital, potential self.")[17]

Thus although in the beginning of their careers the modernists disavow a belief in the old stable ego of character, they do not despair of discovering something analogous. In this first phase of modernism's revaluation of the self, sincerity resides not in dis-

15. T. S. Eliot, *The Complete Poems and Plays 1909–1950* (1950; reprinted, Harcourt, Brace and World, 1962). Unless otherwise indicated, all citations from Eliot's verse are from this edition and are identified by page numbers in the text. The author is grateful to Harcourt Brace Jovanovich, Inc., and Faber and Faber Ltd, for permission to reprint lines from *Collected Poems 1909–1962, Four Quartets,* and *The Cocktail Party,* all by T. S. Eliot, and from *Anabasis* by St. John Perse, translated and with a preface by T. S. Eliot, copyright 1936, 1938, 1949 by Harcourt Brace Jovanovich, Inc., copyright © 1943, 1950, 1963, 1964 by T. S. Eliot, copyright 1966, 1971, 1977, 1978 by Esme Valerie Eliot.

16. See Chester G. Anderson, ed., *A Portrait of the Artist as a Young Man: Text, Criticism and Notes* (New York: Viking Critical Library, 1968), p. 258.

17. The letter to Garnett is reprinted in Julian Moynahan, *The Deed of Life: The Novels and Tales of D. H. Lawrence* (Princeton: Princeton University Press, 1963), pp. 38–40. For the "Study of Thomas Hardy," see Edward D. McDonald, ed., *Phoenix: The Posthumous Papers of D. H. Lawrence* (1938; reprinted, New York: Viking, 1974), p. 410.

owning but in finding indirect ways to imply this invisible "tougher self," this "individuating rhythm," this "real, vital, potential self." And, as Freud was not the only one to notice, perhaps the best way was via a theater of dreams. So we find Eliot as early as 1917 observing the "dreamlike" quality of Noh drama:

Dreams, to be real, must be seen. When we speak of the Noh as dreamlike, we do not imply any attenuation of emotion, nor imply that the emotions of dreams are essentially different from the emotions of waking . . . but the ways of approaching these emotions are diverse. The Japanese method is inverse to that with which we are familiar. The phantom-psychology of Orestes and Macbeth is as good as that of Awoi; but the method of making the ghost real is different. In the former cases the ghost is given the mind of the possessed; in the latter case the mind of the sufferer is inferred from the reality of the ghost. The ghost is enacted, the dreaming or feverish Awoi is represented by the "red Kimono." In fact, it is only ghosts that are actual; the world of active passions is observed through the veil of another world.[18]

Carrying these remarks to their poetic conclusion, Eliot produced a poem which, even more than *Sweeney Agonistes,* is a "cream of a nightmare dream."[19] In *The Waste Land,* Eliot taps, as he said no novelist had dared to do, "the atmosphere of unknown terror and mystery in which our life is passed and which psychoanalysis has not yet analysed."[20] The unifying voice of *The Waste Land* consequently has no identity. Its narrator (if we can apply that locution to a voice without a name whose utterance comes from below the level of ordinary speech) "never talks [and] cannot argue." Yet he dreams, and his dreams are charged with an "atmosphere of unknown terror and mystery" which comprises the authentic "personality" of *The Waste Land:*

> There I saw one I knew, and stopped him, crying: "Stetson!
> "You who were with me in the ships at Mylae!
> "That corpse you planted last year in your garden,
> "Has it begun to sprout? Will it bloom this year?
>
>   (p. 39)

18. See T. S. Eliot, "The Noh and the Image," *Egoist,* 4, no. 7 (August 1917), 102–103.

19. Eliot, *Complete Poems and Plays,* p. 84.

20. T. S. Eliot, "London Letter," *The Dial,* September 1922, p. 330.

Having completed *The Waste Land,* however, Eliot changed his course. In November of 1922, he wrote Richard Aldington that "*The Waste Land . . .* is a thing of the past so far as I am concerned and I am now feeling toward a new form and style."[21] And the work he turned to demonstrates what he meant. Reaching, in *Sweeney Agonistes,* toward the cartoon clarity of popular drama, in *The Hollow Men* toward spiritual X-ray, in "A Song for Simeon" toward a more traditional kind of dramatic monologue, Eliot devalued both the psychological resonance of *The Waste Land* and its concomitant technique. That kind of radical sincerity was something he no longer cared about, as he suggested in 1929 when he recorded his nostalgia for "an age . . . when human beings cared somewhat about the salvation of the 'soul,' but not about each other as 'personalities,' "[22] Nor was Eliot's change-about entirely attributable to a shift in religious belief. There were two other considerations involved, only one of which was peculiar to Eliot.

There was first of all the force of Eliot's psychological situation, which I have written about elsewhere.[23] *The Waste Land* was written in a time of temporary personality disorder when a deep-seated anxiety somehow broke through the defensive walls of Eliot's character and his style. Afterwards, when Eliot regained his equanimity and realized how transparently he had recorded his inner terror, he was horrified. Returning from therapy in Lausanne to consult with Ezra Pound in Paris, he reread his fragments without pleasure. Though it was neither, he remembered his manuscript as a "sprawling, chaotic poem" and a "mess."[24] Then he put it in Pound's hands and together they did their best to contain the energies of a nightmare in an aesthetically and morally acceptable frame. Later Eliot dissociated himself from *The Waste Land,* and abandoned further attempts to fathom certain levels of his psyche. Eventually, he came

21. Valerie Eliot, ed., *The Waste Land: A Facsimile and Transcript* (New York: Harcourt Brace Jovanovich, 1971), p. xxv.

22. From "Dante" (1929). See Eliot, *Selected Essays,* p. 233.

23. *T. S. Eliot: A Study of Character and Style* (New York: Oxford University Press, 1983). The present essay is intended as a bridge between that book and another on the passing of modernism.

24. See "Ezra Pound" (1946) in Walter Sutton, ed., *Ezra Pound: A Collection of Critical Essays* (Englewood Cliffs, N.J.: Prentice-Hall, 1963), p. 19, and "From T. S. Eliot" (1933), in *The Cantos of Ezra Pound: Some Testimonies* (New York: Farrar and Rinehart, 1933), pp. 16–17.

to regard the idea of a buried self, an unchanging authenticity below the level of conventional consciousness, as repellent. To cling to it was to acknowledge that certain impulses and cruelties of his past could never be outgrown. This burden Eliot could not bear, and in "The Dry Salvages" his distress is apparent as he figures the self as a river swollen with debris:

> Time the destroyer is time the preserver,
> Like the river with its cargo of dead Negroes, cows and chicken coops,
> The bitter apple and the bite in the apple.
>
> (p. 133)

But by that time, Eliot had affirmed his faith in another kind of self. In the *Quartets,* being is not "contained in time past"; the river is transfigured as it flows into the sea. "A world of speculation," we are shown, can transform us. "Caught in the form of limitation / Between un-being and being," our existence is not a timeless authenticity but a project, in play until death.[25]

Yet, though colored by the particulars of his life, Eliot's evolving conception of the self corresponds to a larger pattern. Having been driven to explore the Romantic conception of sincerity to its absolute, not only Eliot but Yeats, Lawrence, Woolf, and Joyce finally saw the inadequacy of any notion of an inalienable and unchanging self, and grew weary of exploring the intensities of the individual psyche. In *Last Poems, The Plumed Serpent, Between the Acts,* and *Finnegans Wake,* they reduced the importance of dramatic voice, immersed themselves in history and myth, and delighted in complex musical organizations that had little to do with the hope put forward in *To the Lighthouse* that literature might "express . . . the emotions of the body."[26] Once again, it is Joyce who throws the meaning of Eliot's career in highest relief: as Michael Groden observes, in "the first nine episodes of *Ulysses* . . . the narration seems to limit itself to the perception and frame of reference of the character, either Stephen or Bloom." But "during his writing . . . and beyond it,"

25. Citations are from "Burnt Norton," pp. 117 and 122. For a Heideggerian reading of the *Four Quartets,* see William V. Spanos, "Hermeneutics and Memory: Destroying T. S. Eliot's *Four Quartets,*" *Genre,* 11 (Winter 1978), 523–573.

26. Virginia Woolf, *To the Lighthouse* (1927; reprinted, New York: Harcourt, Brace and World, 1955), p. 265.

Joyce tired of his characters. His "vision expanded; individual and even national history gave way to a larger view in which any specific individual or situation recreates archetypal patterns from the past."[27] (An additional example may prove the rule by its very unlikelihood: according to Richard Wollheim, near the end of his life Freud himself deprived the unconscious of much of the authority with which he had originally invested it. In his last work he concluded that "our unconscious life may be powered by strong bursts of energy, it may contain rigid and deathless concatenations of belief and desire, but it seems not to be the locus of complex or evolved emotions. For emotions, like the traits of character, like man's cultural capacities, evince the workmanship of the ego.")[28]

As in the literature that followed the Second World War, then, late modernist writing locates the authentic self in "workmanship," in construction. No wonder that by 1927 the "investigation of the subconscious" was no longer a proper subject for serious literature, and the novels of Dostoevsky looked decidedly dated. But if the true self is a construction, it is, as the postmodernists would say, open to deconstruction and reconstruction. Amenable and even demanding the whimsy and caprice of a Barthelme or an Ashbery, with the works of late modernism the self is no longer to be approached as seriously or as solemnly as Joyce addressed his "individuating rhythm." The music of *Finnegans Wake* is the music of the nursery. How, though, did all this accord with the Anglican Eliot of the thirties and forties? As we may infer from his mid-life apprenticeship to two great French masters of caprice, surprisingly well.

Eliot's main line of evolution after *The Waste Land* can be read out of his 1923 confession that the only verses of the poem he no longer considered "ephemeral" were "the 29 lines of the water-dripping song of the last part."[29] Confirming his drift toward incantatory verse, ultimately the remark points toward his reappraisal of the symbolist tradition, particularly of Stéphane Mallarmé. In the

27. Michael Groden, *Ulysses in Progress* (Princeton: Princeton University Press, 1977), pp. 33–36.

28. Richard Wollheim, *Sigmund Freud* (1971; reprinted, Cambridge: Cambridge University Press, 1981), p. 249.

29. *Facsimile*, p. 129.

late teens, Eliot had been skeptical about Mallarmé's importance. He had praised Pound's sharp images at the expense of Mallarmé's "mossiness," and he had suggested that beside the "sincere" prose of Rimbaud, the "laboured opacity of Mallarmé fades colourless and dead."[30] But by 1920 Eliot's opinion began to change. In the *Athenaeum* for that year, he directed his readers to Dujardin's study of Mallarmé, and two years later he was commending Mallarmé along with Dryden "for what he made of his material."[31] Writing in the 1921 *Chapbook*, he elaborated:

Verse is always struggling . . . to take up to itself more and more of what is prose, to take something more from life and turn it into "play". Seen from this angle, the labour of Mallarmé with the French language becomes something important; every battle he fought with syntax represents the effort to transmute lead into gold, ordinary language into poetry; and the real failure of contemporary verse is its failure to draw anything new from life into art.[32]

In 1921, though, Eliot went no further. Busy with other things (the summer of 1921 was the summer of *The Waste Land*), he did not begin to study Mallarmé for several years. According to what Eliot told Edward Greene, it was 1925—at the time he was preparing the Clark lectures on metaphysical poetry—when he began to reread him seriously.[33] It is conceivable, in fact, that Eliot's interest was quickened as he wrote the eighth of the Clark lectures, which treats Laforgue and Corbière as metaphysical poets because their verse acquires emotional coloring by entertaining metaphysical beliefs.[34] It was only the limitations of the occasion, I suspect (the lecture on Laforgue was the last in the series), that

30. For the first citation, see "Ezra Pound: His Metric and Poetry," in T. S. Eliot, *To Criticize the Critic* (New York: Noonday, 1965), p. 170. The second is from "The Borderline of Prose," *New Statesman*, 19 May 1917, p. 158.

31. See Eliot, "Artists and Men of Genius," *Athenaeum*, 25 June 1920, 842, and *Selected Essays*, p. 269.

32. T. S. Eliot, "Prose and Verse," *Chapbook*, 22 (April 1921), 3–10.

33. Edward J. H. Greene, *T. S. Eliot et la France* (Paris: Boivin, 1951), p. 137.

34. Eliot's eight "Lectures on the Metaphysical Poetry of the Seventeenth Century" were presented at Cambridge University in early 1926 and then never published. Two manuscripts of them have survived, however: a typescript in the Eliot collection, Kings College, Cambridge, and a carbon in the Houghton Library at Harvard. The lectures display Eliot searching for a model for philosophical poetry and chronicle his turn from Donne and Laforgue to Dante. At the time of this writing, Mrs. Valerie Eliot is preparing the lectures for publication.

prevented him from speaking of Mallarmé. We know, at any rate, that Eliot published a "Note sur Mallarmé et Poe" a few months later, and that he introduced it as an appendix to a "suite d'études encore incomplète [sur] . . . *la poésie métaphysique.*"[35] Accordingly, Eliot wrote, he wished to consider a poet who relied on philosophy "pour raffiner et pour développer [son] puissance de sensibilité et d'émotion." The work of Donne, Poe, and Mallarmé, Eliot explained, "était une expansion de leur sensibilité *au-delà des limites du monde normal,* une découverte de nouveaux objets propres à susciter de nouvelles emotions."

It is clear from the "Note sur Mallarmé et Poe" that what attracted Eliot to Mallarmé was the way the French poet anchored a spiritual vision in local matters of lineation and syntax. Though Eliot wrote in his "Note" that he did not wish to explore the subtleties of Mallarmé's craft, he ascribed Mallarmé's "nouveaux objets propres à susciter de nouvelles emotions" to a syntax so difficult that it "empêche le lecteur *d'avaler d'un coup* leur phrase ou leur vers." Through mastery of syntax, Eliot says, Mallarmé transmutes "de l'accidentel en réel." It is all, according to Eliot, the product of "*incantation* . . . qui insiste sur la puissance primitive du Mot."

At the center of Eliot's argument, then, is "le Mot"—the Word. By 1926 Eliot had seen that in Mallarmé's incantatory syntax, every word dislocates the expectations of discourse with a new beginning even as it liberates reality from our conditioned sense of it. Installed in its "puissance primitive," Eliot tells us, the word can conduct us from "[le] monde tangible" to a world beyond: "[le] monde des fantômes."

But having written the "Note sur Mallarmé et Poe," Eliot did not put himself immediately under Mallarmé's guidance. Like Shakespeare, the French poet was at first too daunting a master, and Eliot at first felt more comfortable studying under the great man's followers. Thus, acknowledging the powers he had attributed to Mallarmé, Eliot turned to the work of St.-John Perse. Beginning with a translation of Perse's *Anabase,* over several years Eliot incorporated lines from Perse into "Journey of the Magi," *Ash Wednesday,* and *The Rock.*[36] The note that sounded loudest in these appropri-

35. For this and the following citations, see "Note sur Mallarmé et Poe," *La Nouvelle Révue Française,* 14 (1 November 1926), 524–526.

36. For details, see Richard Abel, "The Influence of St.-John Perse on T. S. Eliot," *Contemporary Literature,* 14, no. 2 (Spring 1973), 213–239.

ations, however, was the one that Eliot had first heard in Mallarmé: the syntactic battle "to take something more from life and turn it into play."

Anabase, which Eliot began to translate in 1926, is a poem whose haunting beauty is impossible to describe to anyone not acquainted with it. Combining concrete detail with narrative indeterminacy, it achieves the "jeu, très allusif et mysterieux . . . à la limite du saisissable" that Perse said he had aimed at.[37] The poem was inspired by Xenophon, but, as Eliot points out in his introduction, it has "no particular reference" to the external world—neither to history's journey of the Ten Thousand nor to the map of Asia Minor.[38] Instead, it renders what Perse called "la solitude dans l'action. Aussi bien l'action parmi les hommes que l'action de l'esprit envers autrui comme envers soi-même. J'ai voulu rassembler la synthèse non pas passive mais active de la ressource humaine."[39] To do so it assembles, to again use Eliot's terms, a sequence of images, ideas, stresses, and pauses. And, concentrated to evoke an eternal moment of the human soul, the sequence helped Eliot find himself once again. At least, his effort at translation made an impact such that recalling it in 1949, he confessed, "On voit son influence dans quelques-uns des poemes que j'écrivis aprè̀s avoir achevé la traduction: influence des images et peut-être aussi du rythme. Ceux qui examineront mes derniers ouvrages trouveront peut-être que cette influence persiste toujours."[40]

But perhaps the best way to demonstrate what translating *Anabase* meant to Eliot is to look at a particularly influential section along with Eliot's translation. The beginning of canto VI follows:

TOUT-PUISSANTS dans nos grands gouvernements militaires, avec nos filles parfumées qui se vêtaient d'un souffle, ces tissus,

37. "Une Lettre de St.-John Perse," *The Berkeley Review* (Winter 1956), 40. Cited by Arthur J. Knodel in "Towards an Understanding of *Anabase,*" *PMLA* (June 1964), 331.

38. T. S. Eliot, Preface to *Anabasis: A Poem by St.-John Perse* (1930; reprinted, New York: Harcourt, Brace, 1949), p. 9.

39. From *Le Figaro littéraire,* 5 November 1960. See Knodel, "*Anabase,*" p. 329.

40. "Une feuillet unique," a letter to Jean Paulhan in *Honneur à St.-John Perse: Hommage et témoignages littéraires* (Paris: Gallimard, 1965), p. 19. The volume also contains the letter to Perse that Eliot enclosed along with his first-draft translation in January 1927. In the letter, Eliot says the poem "me semble un des plus grands et plus singuliers des temps modernes . . . [un] chef-d'oeuvre" (p. 419).

nous établîmes en haut lieu nos pièges au bonheur.

Abondance et bien-être, bonheur! Aussi longtemps nos verres où la glace pouvait chanter comme Memnon . . .

Et fourvoyant à l'angle des terrasses une mêlée d'éclairs, de grands plats d'or aux mains des filles de service fauchaient l'ennui des sables aux limites du monde.

Puis ce fut une année de souffles en Ouest et, sur nos toits lestés de pierres noires, tout un propos de toiles vives adonnées au délice du large.

OMNIPOTENT in our great military governments, with our scented girls clad in a breath of silk webs,

we set in high places our springes for happiness.

Plenty and well-being, happiness! For so long the ice sang in our glasses, like Memnon . . .

And deflecting a crossing of lights to the corners of terraces, great chargers of gold held up by the handmaidens, smote the weariness of the sands, at the confines of the world.

Then came a year of wind in the west and, on our roofs weighted with black stones, a whole business of bright cloths abandoned to the delight of wide spaces.[41]

In this excerpt Perse conjures up a state of mind ("nos filles parfumées qui se vêtaient d'un *souffle, ces tissus*") and then alters the coloring of the images to suggest a shifting mood ("Puis ce fut une année de *souffles* en Ouest et, sur nos toits lestés de pierres noires, tout un propos de *toiles* vives, adonnées au delíce du large"). His combination of concreteness and suggestiveness reminded Eliot of the extended mythological passages in Pound's *Cantos*,[42] but that association is as deceptive as it is helpful. Whereas in Pound's *Cantos* images are allowed to assert their own claims, here they are amplified with the apparatus of bardic chant. Perse shares with Pound an incantatory parataxis and an ability to suggest the visionary present through participial constructions ("Et fourvoyant à l'angle . . ."). But his breathlessness and the ease with which he deserts metonymy for metaphor ("l'ennui des sables aux limites du monde") suggest not the *Cantos* but Dylan Thomas's "Fern Hill." Eliot's translation, moreover, emphasizes precisely this element of

41. From the original (1930) edition.

42. See Eliot's unpublished lecture "Hopkins and Others," given in the undergraduate course ("English 26: English Literature from 1890 to the Present Day") he taught at Harvard in the spring of 1933. His notes can be consulted in the archives division of the Harvard University Library.

rhapsodic fluidity. In Eliot's hands "se vêtaient d'un souffle, ces tissus" loses its caesura and becomes "clad in a breath of silk webs." He also alliterates "tout un propos de toiles vives" to "all the business of bright cloths."[43] Eliot is concerned, in other words, with heightening the opacity of the verse and emphasizing the exoticism and otherworldliness of Perse's central images. In the original, and even more in the translation, Perse's substantives approach the status of musical themes and combine with what Eliot's Preface to his translation calls the poet's "*declamation, the system of stresses and pauses*" (p. 11) to transform a passage of natural description into a self-conscious poetic confection. (Perse in fact complained to Eliot about his liberties, but his protest had no effect.)[44]

The sixth canto of *Anabase* is particularly significant because it inspired a section of "Journey of the Magi":

> 'A cold coming we had of it,
> Just the worst time of the year
> For a journey, and such a long journey:
> The ways deep and the wather sharp,
> The very dead of winter.'
> And the camels galled, sore-footed, refractory,
> Lying down in the melting snow.
> *There were times we regretted*
> *The summer palaces on slopes, the terraces,*
> *And the silken girls bringing sherbet.*
> Then the camel men cursing and grumbling
> And running away, and wanting their liquor and women,
> And the night-fires going out, and the lack of shelters,
> And the cities hostile and the towns unfriendly
> And the villages dirty and charging high prices:
> A hard time we had of it.
> At the end we preferred to travel all night,
> Sleeping in snatches,
> With the voices singing in our ears, saying
> That this was all folly.
>
> (p. 68; emphasis mine)

43. This kind of thing is emphasized even more in Eliot's drafts, copies of which are available in the Houghton Library, Harvard University. In a letter attached to the drafts, Perse complained to Eliot about "bright" and suggested the more precise "flashing," or "lively" or "living." Eliot, however, insisted.

44. See note 43.

I am not the first to notice that Perse was the source of Eliot's
serving girls, nor that the syntax and the figurative thrust of *Anabase* give Eliot's lines their idiosyncratic flavor.[45] "Journey of the
Magi" begins by borrowing from Lancelot Andrewes' sermon, and
like the sermon sharpens the gospel's detail. But the developing
incantatory power of the passage transforms Andrewes' liturgical
repetition and creates a Persean world of imagination. It is true that
Eliot is more precise about his images than Perse, and that we find
nothing in his poem that resembles "adonnées au délice du large."
But no less obviously Eliot establishes and repeats his images to
suggest a series of delicate emotional shifts. (Notice, for example,
the way "we regretted . . . the silken girls bringing sherbert" is
repeated in another key as "the camel men . . . wanting their . . .
women".) As in Perse or Pound, Eliot's syntax suspends images in
a world of enclosed vision. Thus the incantatory series, "And the
camels . . . And the silken girls . . . And the night-fires going out,"
makes us almost forget the gritty realism of the scene. As Perse had
admonished Eliot on the draft of his translation of *Anabase,* the
purpose of such poetry is not to call up a single journey in the mind's
eye but to provide at once the geographical and spiritual significance of an expedition into the interior.[46]

But these reminiscences in the poem's first stanza only begin to
suggest its debt to Perse. Its most distinctive Persean elements
emerge in what is to follow, and turn it into a more difficult kind of
poem than it first appears. A companion piece to "A Song for
Simeon," "Journey of the Magi" dramatizes the period in Eliot's
life that followed his official conversion, when his old ways of
thinking and feeling seemed irrevocably alien and his new life as a
Christian existed more in intention than fact. Like Simeon's recognition of the Christ child in the temple, its Christmas epiphany
corresponds to Eliot's own moment of spiritual vision. Yet "Journey of the Magi" transcends its fiction in a way that "A Song for
Simeon" does not. In it, Eliot undermines the dramatic monologue
form almost as soon as he announces it. Instead of cultivating the
illusion of an objective speaker, for example, Eliot suggests that the
events of the monologue are convenient but inadequate represen-

45. After a number of critics guessed as much, Eliot confirmed the fact to Edward
Greene. See *T. S. Eliot et La France,* p. 136, n. 2.
46. Perse's comments are on the title page of Eliot's draft. See note 43.

tations of an experience that lies outside of the dramatic frame. In doing so he calls into question the continuity of the private experience to which the frame corresponds. Thus though composed a year earlier than "Simeon," "Journey" is a less conventional poem. It is also a better guide to where Eliot was going.

Like "Animula," "Journey of the Magi" begins with a self-conscious citation, signaling that the account that follows is not a dramatic monologue but a meditation that centers around the assumption of a role. As stanza 2 begins, this becomes clearer, and Eliot's setting turns problematic. Departing from the story of the Magi, he introduces images from two unexpected sources—from accounts of the Passion and from his own storehouse of private imagery. ("Why, for all of us . . . do certain images recur, charged with emotion, rather than others . . . six ruffians seen through an open window playing cards at night at a small French railway junction where there was a water-mill: such images may have symbolic value, but of what we cannot tell, for they come to represent the depths of feeling into which we cannot peer.")[47]

> Then at dawn we came down to a temperate valley,
> Wet, below the snow line, smelling of vegetation;
> With a running stream and a water-mill beating the darkness,
> And three trees on the low sky,
> And an old white horse galloped away in the meadow.
> Then we came to a tavern with vine-leaves over the lintel,
> Six hands at an open door dicing for pieces of silver,
> And feet kicking the empty wine-skins.
>
> (pp. 68–69)

Noticing that the story's frame of reference has been broken, most readers feel compelled to do one of two things: either they invoke the authority of Christian allegory and gloss the entire section by reference to the traditional commentaries about the Passion; or they emphasize the pressure of Eliot's own inner life.[48] But to do either is to ignore the fact that the poem flaunts its indeterminacy. Eliot's

47. T. S. Eliot, *The Use of Poetry and the Use of Criticism* (1933; reprinted, London: Faber and Faber, 1967), p. 148.

48. See, for example, R. D. Brown, "Revelation in T. S. Eliot's 'Journey of the Magi,' " *Renascence*, 24 (1972), 137, and Elizabeth Schneider, "Prufrock and After: The Theme of Change," *PMLA*, 87 (1972), 1114.

symbolic configuration conflates three realms of reference—the fictional frame, the correspondences of Christian typology, and his own deepest and most troublesome feelings. And far from asserting the dominance of any of them, the poem opens up a field in which the question of reference is deliberately deferred.[49]

What allows Eliot to perform this act of prestidigitation, of course, are the effects he had appropriated from Perse. In the incantatory magic of stanze 2, the boundaries between the dramatic and the allegorical blur and even the phrase "three trees on the low sky" jars but a little. The vegetation, the running stream, the water mill, the three trees, the old white horse, and the rest seem to come from two different worlds of significance—the world of preconscious experience and the world of Christian exegesis. Doubt is cast by the poem on the significance of both. Both worlds represent different ways of apprehending the decomposition and death that Eliot inevitably associates with spring and the natural world. But here Eliot is willing to bestow the name of reality on neither his private fears nor Christianity's promises.

In *Ash Wednesday* and some of the shorter pieces that followed it, Eliot would experiment further with the possibility of a symbolism that is not simply the correlative of powerful feeling. He would allow poetry to be more than the expression of states of feeling that antecede it and thus to become more of a game. In Perse's words, he would create "un jeu, très allusif et mysterieux,"[50] in which feelings lead the self beyond *what is* to *what might be*. These poems will be dreams, but not in the manner of *The Waste Land*. Their dreams will be hallucinatory fields, open areas where the attractions of the ideal are as pressing as sorrow. They will, in short, be fields of crossing; or as the conclusion of *Ash Wednesday* has it, places "of solitude where three dreams cross." For the strength to create them, however, Eliot would have to return to the poet who had originally sent him to *Anabase*.

In January of 1933, Eliot interrupted his Norton professorship at Harvard to travel to Baltimore and give the Turnbull lectures at

49. See Daniel Harris, "Language, History and Text in Eliot's 'Journey of the Magi,' " *PMLA*, 95, no. 5 (October 1980), 838–856. Harris points out much the same thing, but applies his observations to a very different reading of the poem.

50. See above, note 37.

Johns Hopkins University.[51] These lectures, entitled "Varieties of Metaphysical Poetry," were in fact an abbreviated version of the Clark lectures he had given eight years before. Cutting and rearranging his original eight lectures into three, however, Eliot did enlarge his text to accommodate a single subject—French symbolism, and more particularly the symbolism of Stéphane Mallarmé.

The second Turnbull lecture is especially interesting because it shows how Mallarmé had entered Eliot's technique. Speaking of Crashaw and defending a kind of figuration that had found little place in his early verse, Eliot advises that it is a mistake to suppose that a simile or a metaphor always has to be visible to the imagination. Taking Mallarmé's *M'introduire dans ton histoire*, he points out that in the sonnet we find four or five images that it is impossible to imagine or conceive simultaneously and one that cannot be visualized at all:

> Dis si je ne suis pas joyeux
> Tonnerre et rubis aux moyeux
> De voir en l'air que ce feu troue
>
> Avec des royaumes épars
> Comme mourir pourpre la roue
> De seul vespéral de mes chars

Tell me if I am not glad, thunder and rubies at the axle, to see, in the air that this fire pierces, amid scattered realms, as if dying purple, the wheel of my only vesperal chariot.   (My translation.)

The line "Tonnere et rubis aux moyeux," Eliot says, demonstrates how effective vagueness can be when employed in a controlled context. The truth is that in poetry the word, each word by itself, has absolute value. Poetry is incantation as well as imagery, and the images of thunder and rubies, though they cannot be seen, heard, or thought together, when conjoined bring out the connotation of each word.

Focused on lines he later absorbed into "Burnt Norton," these remarks contain one of those discriminations Eliot made to "prepare

51. The manuscript of the Turnbull lectures is now in the Houghton Library, Harvard University.

the way for his own practice. "[52] As in his 1926 "Note sur Mallarmé et Poe," he ends by affirming the radical potential of each word. But here he is thinking through his insight, and along the way he connects his claim to several other notions he had been toying with since he finished *The Waste Land*. For the poet to preserve the absolute value of each word, for example, Eliot recognizes that he must rely on context. In the early twenties, feeling himself into his second period, Eliot had put it baldly: "A creation, a work of art, is autotelic"; "it is essential that a work of art be self-consistent, that an artist should consciously or unconsciously draw a circle beyond which he does not trespass."[53] Now the implications of those remarks for a new kind of poetry began to make themselves felt.

Also, just as the notions of connotation and incantation were essential for *Anabasis* and "The Journey of the Magi," they are central here. In the Turnbull lectures, Eliot connects the terms in a near-comprehensive neo-symbolist statement of the musical characteristics of poetry. In part, the statement corresponds to what Eliot later said in an essay on Valéry: that the essence of music as the symbolists understood it was a striving "towards an unattainable timelessness . . . a yearning for the stillness of painting or sculpture."[54] "Burnt Norton," shading "silence" as Mallarmé does in his "Crisis of Poetry,"[55] puts it this way:

52. That is, the beginning of "Burnt Norton, II": "Garlic and sapphires in the mud/Clot the bedded axle-tree." On the evidence of a typescript at the Houghton Library, Eliot used these lines earlier in a draft of "Lines for an Old Man" which he dedicated "To Mallarmé." (In its final version, "Lines for an Old Man" retains remnants of Mallarmé's poem, both in the phrase, "tell me . . ." and in its syntax.)

53. See Eliot, *Selected Essays*, pp. 19, 93.

54. T. S. Eliot, Introduction to Paul Valéry, *The Art of Poetry* (1958; reprinted, New York: Vintage, 1961), p. xiv.

55. See Bradford Cook, ed., *Mallarmé: Selected Prose Poems, Essays and Letters* (Baltimore: The Johns Hopkins Press, 1956), p. 41: "The inner structures of a book of verse must be inborn; in this way, chance will be totally eliminated and the poet will be absent. From each theme, itself predestined, a given harmony will be born somewhere in the parts of the total poem and take its proper place within the volume; because, for every sound, there is an echo. Motifs of like pattern will move in balance from point to point. There will be none of the sublime incoherence found in the page-settings of the Romantics, none of the artificial unity that used to be based on the square measurements of the book. Everything will be hesitation, disposition of parts, their alternations and relationships—all this contributing to the rhythmic totality, which will be *the very silence of the poem*, in its blank spaces, as that silence

> Words, after speech, reach
> Into the silence. Only by the form, the pattern,
> Can words or music reach
> The stillness, as a Chinese jar still
> Moves perpetually in its stillness.
> Not the stillness of the violin, while the note lasts,
> Not that only, but the co-existence,
> Or say that the end precedes the beginning,
> And the end and the beginning were always there
>
>   (p. 121)

Yet the music of Eliot's poetry goes beyond stillness, and these lines represent only one mood of "Burnt Norton." In the *Quartets,* even as in the passage from the Turnbull lectures I have para-phrased, Eliot's heaviest weight falls on a *jangle* of dissonant words—phrases and images that are, Eliot says, impossible to imag-ine or conceive simultaneously. The thought is elaborated in "The Music of Poetry" (1942), where Eliot counsels that the phenomenon of his title is at least as much a matter of tension as of resolution. For one thing, Eliot said, poetic structure demands it: "Dissonance, even cacophony, has its place: just as, in a poem of any length, there must be transitions between passages of greater and less intensity, to give a rhythm of fluctuating emotion essential to the musical structure of the whole." For another, the music of individual words occurs "at a point of intersection: it arises from its relation first to the words immediately preceding and following it, and indefinitely to the rest of its context."[56]

What is perhaps most striking about Eliot's emphasis on dis-sonance, however, is how well it dovetails with his religious dispo-sitions. Consider what Eliot's friend Joseph Chiari wrote in an essay Eliot introduced as "the first book in English on Mallarmé and his art of poetry":

[Mallarmé] came to realise that the *logos*—God's expression—was behind the human, and could not be heard or apprehended, for it was silence—the absolute, source of all things—and the poet, if he were absolutely logical, could only remain silent . . . In Mallarmé's poetry, each word anticipates and

---

is translated by each structural element in its own way" (emphasis mine). The same essay also glosses the overtones of "vagueness" and "nuance" as Eliot used those words in the Turnbull lectures.

56. Eliot, *On Poetry and Poets,* pp. 24–25.

merges into the next, therefore only exists in its dual capacity of projection backward and forward axled on a state of virtuality which is the continuous becoming of the word . . . the words [that is to say] are used as much as possible like musical notes or signs; they have been deprived by various syntactic distortions of their logical meaning so that they never produce a static picture in the Parnassian style; their aim is to give life by continuity and movement . . . Language is used both symbolically and also musically as a kind of magic aimed at creating a state of trance whence will rise the unheard music, the vision of the absolute . . . Yet such an ideal is condemned to failure, for the words, part of creation, can never be rid completely of the contingent, and therefore they cannot destroy *le hasard*.[57]

As Chiari implies by his reference to the *logos,* Mallarmé's symbolist aesthetic fits Eliot's Anglican belief without a wrinkle. How better to convey the Christian's humble awareness of his inability to apprehend or characterize the *logos*—what *The Rock* was to call the "Light Invisible . . . / Too bright for mortal vision" (p. 112)—than through a poetry yearning toward silence yet conscious that failure is inevitable?

Consider further: for Eliot to affirm poetry's fundamental inadequacy was also to affirm its open-endedness. On the one hand, this points toward a deplorable condition. It means that every attempt to use words

> Is a wholly new start, and a different kind of failure
> Because one has only learnt to get the better of words
> For the thing one no longer has to say, or the way in which
> One is no longer disposed to say it.
>
> ("East Coker," p. 128)

But it also means something more positive, something that had been asserted by Eliot's earlier struggle against convention. It implies that the self, which stands in no less provisional a relationship between man and God than speech does between words and an ideal language, cannot be fixed. As man is forced constantly to revise his speech, so he is forced constantly to revise himself. He is permanently in question, but he is also *free* to recast his history of unhappiness and guilt; he can, in the play of "a world of speculation," renew himself. Curse or blessing, that is his lot. And to

---

57. Joseph Chiari, *Symbolisme from Poe to Mallarmé: The Growth of a Myth* (1956; reprinted, New York: Gordian Press, 1970), pp. 142–144. Eliot's praise appears in his Foreword. p. xx.

Eliot, who was approaching middle age burdened with the psychic load of an old man, at times it seemed a very great blessing indeed— one that more than compensated for the difficulties it made for his Flaubertian ideals of shapeliness, harmony, and finish.

Still, the poetic consequences were considerable. As is apparent from the trouble Eliot had tying up the *Quartets*,[58] to follow Mallarmé down this road meant abandoning the hope of poetic closure. If the poem, like the self, is condemned never to reach wholeness or stillness, if it exists in a state of continuous becoming, if the word by itself, like each successive act of choice, has absolute value, then literary closure is always self-conscious and arbitrary.

I wonder, though, whether Eliot ever put the proposition to himself as nakedly as that; I suspect he did not. The logical extension of endorsing the importance of open-endedness in the self and in poetry is to identify wholeheartedly with "the future . . . of the barbarians," and that Eliot would not willingly do. Yet, drawing close to Mallarmé and Perse, Eliot managed it despite himself. Insisting on "la puissance primitive du Mot," Eliot invites comparison not only with John Ashbery but with the American who most anticipates Ashbery, William Carlos Williams in his Dadaist phase. In fact, if we seek a contemporary guide to the premises of Eliot's late work, we could do worse than to turn to Williams' *Spring and All*. The affinities are close enough so that when Williams' best critic, James Breslin, instructs us how to read Williams, he does so in phrases haunted by the *Four Quartets*. The poems of *Spring and All*, Breslin writes, should be read "in a voice that is more flat than dramatically expressive—giving equal weight to each of the words." He continues, to approach Williams properly is "to discover a new world, one that is open, fluid and shifting . . . Ends dissolve into beginnings. Each poem . . . becomes a series of lines, each of which . . . pulls toward isolation, independence, at the same time that it is pulled back by syntax, by recurrences, toward all the other lines. At the edge of chaos, containing the pressure of its pushing and pulling, the poem trembles with force."[59]

58. See Helen Gardner, *The Composition of Four Quartets* (London: Faber and Faber, 1978), p. 21.

59. James Breslin, *William Carlos Williams: An American Artist* (New York: Oxford University Press, 1970), pp. 85–86.

Instances of Modernist Anti-Intellectualism

Not rarely, modernist writers have appeared to lose their aim, or perhaps (as they certainly felt) to widen their aim: an assault upon the supposedly sterile, self-important academy might, for instance, turn into a bitter denunciation of intellectuals in general, including the very writer making the accusation. William Carlos Williams' *Paterson* starts with such a mode of social analysis and interpretation. We are to be offered "a local pride," a pointed reference to those who leave America for places such as London or Paris—or who leave small towns within our country for cultural centers, either big cities or celebrated universities. Next comes this: "a reply to Greek and Latin with the bare hands."[1] A not very obscure effort to make a claim for a proud, contemporary, intellectual excitement, worthy of attention and approval: one of W. C. Williams' several versions of modernism—in this case, a working-class machismo appeal to folk wisdom, to the polyglot ethnic intuitions which a Paterson, New Jersey, general practitioner had come to know so well.

1. William Carlos Williams, *Paterson* (New York: New Directions, 1946), p. 2. Copyright 1946, 1948, 1949, 1951, 1958 by W. C. Williams; copyright 1963 by Florence Williams. Reprinted by permission of New Directions Publishing Corporation. All further quotations, identified by page numbers in the text, are from this edition.

But Williams was not only taking on an arid classicism. He used the word "daring" provocatively, a truculent response to Eliot's Prufrock; a tough challenge to enemies in the present, never mind those lost in the ancient world. He repeats his animus in these lines, meant to raise the eyebrows of those familiar with the fifth and last section of Eliot's "Little Gidding":

> For the beginning is assuredly
> the end—since we know nothing, pure
> and simple, beyond
> our own complexities.
>
> (p. 3)

Then he escalates his assault even further, takes on "ideas," the entire ambitious enterprise of Theory—abstract formulations as a means of removing oneself from countless human experiences, including those a poet ought to know and address in his or her writing:

> and the craft,
> subverted by thought, rolling up, let
> him beware lest he turn to no more than
> the writing of stale poems . . .
> Minds like beds always made up,
>   (more stony than a shore)
> unwilling or unable.
>
> (p. 4)

A harsh broadside: Williams the antagonist, who uses Paterson, New Jersey, as a base of operations in a fiercely ambitious military campaign. A few lines further the commanding general sounds his clarion call, to be repeated again and again: "Say it, no ideas but in things" (p. 6). Let others become swollen-headed with thoughts, interpretations, extended reifications. This poet and, he hoped, his readers would, in the powerful intimacy of a particular American lyrical celebration, cling tenaciously to the infinite, exuberant reality of the concrete, the everyday, the tangible and visible and audible.

> Sniffing the trees,
> just another dog

among a lot of dogs. What
else is there? And to do?
The rest have run out—
after the rabbits.

(p. 3)

With such lines as these Williams escalated his polemics even further: the artist as a street dog. Not a prissy human being, locked in
a library, removed from the flesh's vitality; and speaking of human
beings, not an aesthete, chasing rabbits in some far removed, all too
"pretty" field. A mongrel in a factory town, out to survive today,
then tomorrow: find the food, have some sex if it's available, empty
the bladder and the bowels—and no highfalutin pretenses or postures. Man is an animal, and if he forgets that, denies that, he is
living a big lie, and soon enough other lies get going.

Nor is Williams himself, for all his daring criticism of others,
immune to the skeptical poet's eye. A question is posed which
contains a devastating self-indictment, rendered decades before the
subject of "narcissism" became yet another (narcissistic?) preoccupation of the American intelligentsia:

Who are these people (how complex
the mathematic) among whom I see myself
in the regularly ordered plateglass of
his thoughts, glimmering before shoes and bicycles?

(p. 9)

Literary smugness, the writer's preening egotism, the poet knew,
cannot be banished by a few slaps at others. Modernism meant
taking chances—with language, images, forms; but also, with the
range and depth of one's self-observation. Williams uses the word
"divorce" (p. 18) as a signal of sorts in book 1 of *Paterson;* and he
knows that one form of "uprootedness" or "alienation," those
fashionable twentieth-century statements, is the divorce of the social critic from the objects of his criticism: so long as I tear into a
"them" with my words and speculations and grim approximations
(sometimes amounting to not so flimsily disguised denunciations),
I am myself safe, protected, clean, and wholesome. No, a truly
radical survey of a world and its language demands a lacerating
introspection, and an earthy return to origins:

> A delirium of solutions, forthwith, forces
> him into back streets, to begin again:
> up hollow stairs among acrid smells
> to obscene rendezvous. And there he finds
> a festering sweetness of red lollipops—
> and a yelping dog:
> Come YEAH, Chichi! Or a great belly
> that no longer laughs but mourns
> with its expressionless black navel love's
> deceit.

(p. 28)

In the event that anyone should fail to notice the determined nature of such a return to the elementary, the urgently physical (again, the dog!), Williams lifts his flag of battle again (a version of it), "No ideas but in the facts" (p. 28), and a little further on, lances yet again the boil of his own self-centeredness: "How strange you are, you idiot!" (p. 30). Then, a few pages on, he fires off this blast:

> We go on living, we permit ourselves
> to continue—but certainly
> not for the university, what they publish
>
> severally or as a group: clerks
> got out of hand forgetting for the most part
> to whom they are beholden.
>
> spitted on fixed concepts like
> roasting hogs, sputtering, their drip sizzling
> in the fire

(p. 32)

Some of us who got to know Dr. Williams, even across the distance of age and residence, remember that the above could be considered an understatement of his, if placed in the overall spectrum of sentiments professed during a lifetime—especially those uttered among friends. But for his poetry, this was one of the blunter moments; the imagery intensifies rather than mollifies an argumentative statement. Clerks, as in *trahison des clercs:* the intellectual is charged with arrogance, with bullying pushiness. Moreover, there is another bill of divorcement entered in the growing annals of *Paterson*—heady professors who are removed in heart and mind and soul from others in a given community or region or nation.

Lest the reader (not to mention the first reader, who wrote the words) be troubled by the self-serving nature of such anti-intellectualism (yet another *them* which affords protection to an *I,* a *we*) a prose segment follows immediately—in sum, a devastating portrait of the self-preoccupied, if not selfish, practicing doctor. His own idle reveries take precedence over the specific, here-and-now complaints of a vulnerable, needy, ailing group of patients, whose number and condition gets spelled out: "Twenty and more infants taking their turn from the outer office, their mothers tormented and jabbering" (p. 33).

This was an unflinching look inward, a spell of Augustinian self-scrutiny—part of an intellectual tradition, actually, that has both a religious and a secular aspect. Williams desires membership in that tradition. He jabs at his own kind, writers and thinkers; then for good measure, gives himself a good kick in the pants—but quickly moves to the poor of New Jersey in the Depression years, to the dreary banalities of a general culture saturated with materialism, much of it crooked: commerce and its discontents. We begin to wonder whether he is simply flailing—a poet anxious to be a wise philosopher, a shrewd observer of his fellow human beings, but unable to summon the necessary, sustained cohesion, the required largeness of outlook. When, toward the end of book 1, a line "the knowledgeable idiots, the university" appears (p. 34), we notice a dangerous repetition—and wonder why, given the careful ambitiousness of this major modernist statement.

Williams begins to redeem himself in that last section of the first book with a kind of candor that transcends the constraints of bitterness and invective. Here is Augustine improved upon—the way Pascal tersely, if not poetically, managed to do in some of his *Pensées:*

> Moveless
> he envies the men that ran
> and could run off
> toward the peripheries—
> to other centers, direct—
> for clarity (if
> they found it)
>   loveliness and
> authority in the world—

(p. 36)

The references to Pound and Eliot are obvious—they both escaped, leaving the doc to tend the patients he found stimulating and nourishing, but also wearing, distracting. Anyway, he was himself unable to follow suit; only able to confront lyrically his envy—and in a startling reference a few lines further, acknowledge the "ice bound" quality to his mind that kept him confined (p. 36). Ice and glass—both elements of a writer's imprisonment within himself: "vanity of vanities," as it is put in the famous passage of *Ecclesiastes*. Here is poignant release through scrupulous self-arraignment—the jail as an anteroom, where the glass will break, the ice melt, so that William Carlos Williams may begin to do his dancing and singing in unashamed earnest, free of the malignant self-consciousness a poet has been ascribing to everyone, it seems—a way, of course, to acknowledge the eager intellectual who is himself.

But repeated self-accusation can be a coy form of the very egotism being condemned. After a while self-rebuke reveals its narcissistic origins, as does an overworked humility. True enough, Williams would no doubt have been the first to admit. Still, there *is* a difference between a narcissism of self-importance and a narcissism of self-criticism as a corrective for (as well as expression of) that self-importance. The only release from such endless psychological inquiry is in others, in the outside world—hence the admonition at the very start of book 2 of *Paterson:*

> Outside
>   outside myself
>   there is a world,
> he rumbled, subject to my incursions
> —a world
>   (to me) at rest,
>   which I approach
> concretely—
>
>   (p. 43)

That last word is no offhand adverb thrown in as the poet rushes along to his subject matter. Again he is at it: the "approach" of *Paterson* must be distinctively at odds with the kind of comprehension congenial to other writers, cultural observers, social theorists, and yes, political polemicists or activists; all those for whom the "world" is a means to one or another overriding purpose—an essay or treatise (or poem) or book, a big conclusion, a series of definitions, a plan or objective or program.

Williams was not without the above; he embraced his own, idiosyncratic American populism. He dipped into the Social Credit movement, so influential, for a while, with his old friend Ezra Pound. Nor was Williams unable to reach out *generally* to a given population. *Paterson* is full of a writer's social indignation, his sense that injustice rules the day, his compassionate yearning for more equity in America. The poor were his patients, after all; and plenty of times he worked for nothing. He could be, on their behalf, enthusiastically nonconcrete:

> Minds beaten thin
> by waste—among
>
> the working classes SOME sort
> of breakdown
> has occurred. Semi-roused
>
> they lie upon their blanket
> face to face,
> mottled by the shadows of the leaves
>
> upon them, unannoyed,
> at least here unchallenged.
>
> (pp. 51–52)

That collective "they"—and, needless to say, "the working classes": Dr. Williams is distanced, as have been countless sociologists, reformist advocates, revolutionary organizers. True, he is usually ironic, at the very least, when he generalizes. He moves from "picnickers" to "voices! / multiple and inarticulate" (p. 54), then to this line: "The 'great beast' come to sun himself" (p. 55). He is taking on, politically, Alexander Hamilton and his class-conscious capitalism; but he is also struggling with his own situation—the Rutherford physician/writer who lived in a quite pleasant Victorian home on Ridge Road, and who was educated and traveled and in so many ways a lucky, privileged man: not Hamilton's kind of aristocrat, and not with Hamilton's social views, and not (or not yet) Harvard's kind of poet, still not prized, still not covered with honorary doctorates, but on his way—and aware that he had always been, from birth on, all things considered, a singularly blessed animal (socially, economically) rather than an anonymous cell of the "great beast."

Such awareness was not denied the author of *Paterson;* rather, such awareness fuels his intermittent rage, his episodic anti-intellectualism. He cannot escape himself; does not desire to do so. He wants a cleansing change in the way people get on—a shared vision that somehow enables a successful triumph over certain of his long-standing foes, and academic snobbery was only one of them. He detested materialism, the debasement of human affairs (language, sex, the environment, learning) at the hands of modern exploitive industrialism: the story of the city of Paterson's demise. Yet he had no confidence, really, in any of the proposed twentieth-century solutions other intellectuals have found attractive: statism, be it in the name of socialism or fascism; psychoanalysis; the withdrawal into art; religion; personal adventurism and fulfillment of one kind or another. Even his much announced inclination to the particular, as opposed to the schematic, the theoretic, was by no means an unqualified source of solace or hope to him. When, in book 1 of *Paterson,* he denounces "the whole din of fracturing thought" (p. 23), he quickly has to insist: "the particular / no less unique" (p. 24). There are few consolations offered *this* intellectual; hence, perhaps, his despair—based not only on a dislike for others, but on a gnawing knowledge of one's own inadequacies.

The second book of *Paterson* is full of a poet's frustration. The problem is utterly contemporary. Paterson is "debased by the divorce from learning, / its garbage on the curbs, its legislators / under the garbage, uninstructed, incapable of self instruction" (p. 81). Again, the teacher is impotent: what language, what manner of education, what effort of will and analysis can turn around such an impossible state of affairs? Some of Williams' anti-intellectualism is an expression of his moody bafflement. His modesty, too, expresses his hesitancy, his doubt. He could, on occasion, mobilize the very impatient hauteur he criticized so strenuously in others, especially professors and critics. But in book 2, especially, he is down-and-out, skeptical, worried about everyone and everything, and not in the least able to see a way through the general impasse he has been documenting, line after line—a lyrical social history, but spiraling downward without letup.

That second book ends with a long letter from a rejected correspondent of Dr. P.; the correspondent is Williams himself, of course—sparing himself and his kind little. This resort to sustained prose, rendered in the form of the letter, brings to mind Pascal's *Provincial Letters,* and the structure of Georges Bernanos' novel *The Diary of a Country Priest.* Both Pascal and Bernanos knew the dangers of prophetic insistence, yet were sorely tempted, as all writers are. Pascal put limits on himself through an aphoristic style and through the medium of the letter, which lends itself to the pastoral, the reflective, as opposed to the declamatory and the exhortative. Bernanos was rescued by the novel's demands— though he knew that other novelists had used stories as a means of collaring readers with *this* or *that* idea, and he also knew how strongly his mind was drawn to political journalism, the social essay, religious controversy. In *The Diary of a Country Priest* he finds a solution in the diary—a means by which grace can be given an incarnation without embarrassment. The priest's writing reveals him to be (like Dr. Williams in *Paterson*) troubled, confused, self-critical. The priest lacks the fire in Williams' belly, but he shares with him a distrust of the high-and-mighty, in and out of the church. There is, too, a streak of anti-intellectualism, easily recognized as that of Bernanos, but worked tactfully into the ruminations of this somewhat desolate curé, a tragic figure indeed. And yet, he is a figure whose dignity and courage we gradually come to realize and admire. Even his admitted mistakes and blunders and moments of excess somehow adorn him in our minds. His words are honest; they are meant for no one else's eyes. We can be kind and generous to him—as he cannot be to himself without the severe risks of manipulative self-regard.

Similarly with *Paterson,* and in particular the long, complaining letter that closes the second book: "You've never had to live, Dr. P.—not in any of the by-ways and dark underground passages where life so often has to be tested," she tells him (p. 91). Then she strikes at his vulnerable, writing self: "The very circumstances of your birth and social background provided you with an escape from life in the raw; and you confuse that protection from life with an *inability* to live—and are thus able to regard literature as nothing more than a desperate last extremity resulting from the illusionary inability to live. (I've been looking at some of your autobiographical works, as this indicates.)" (p. 91).

She spells out her differences with Dr. P. further in a devastating paragraph that gets to the very center of Williams' felt tension, in *Paterson,* between art and conduct. Living, she stresses, is not something one plans, constructs, *decides* to do. Life happens: "in a small way, like measles; or in a big way, like a leaking boat or an earthquake." He "brings to life," she charges, "purely literary sympathies and understandings, the insights and humanity of words on paper *only*—and also, alas, the ego of the literary man." He is the imposter who knows others of his own ilk; abandons their sinking ship through angry verbal blasts at them; tries to masquerade as an enraged ordinary Paterson citizen—yet, by his own admission, makes "incursions" (p. 91). Anti-intellectualism, she implies, is a form of manipulation as well as an indication of self-loathing. The *expression* of anti-intellectualism is, at its best, confessional; at its worst, an act of illusionary self-purification. The resort to "her" letter in *Paterson* represents, it would seem, a penitential exercise— the poet saying: I know the aforementioned, all of it, and can only use words, once again, in the service of a self-critical truth about the writer and those who read him devotedly.

Williams, we know, was constantly attracted to autobiography. Little in his own life, including the life of his beloved Flossie's family (the Stecher trilogy) escaped the writer in him. But his anti-intellectualism seemed also to be a constant attraction—and when used, subject to his writer's censoring skills: intelligence, a sense of proportion, a respect for factuality, the desire to be clear, pointed, convincing. Modernism, so proximate, historically, with psychoanalysis and the devastating social satire of, say, Expressionist painters—never mind the probing of such political, intellectual, and literary figures as Kurt Weill, Gramsci, and Lukács—would naturally welcome Williams' socially conscious, morally earnest, emotionally relentless self-scrutiny. The intellectuals become, for Williams, a foil, a means of being all the tougher on himself. Without his vigorous explication of their sins, we would be tempted to dismiss his enunciation of his own failings, if not misdemeanors, as overwrought and unnecessary. Instead, we take him seriously with respect to himself, feel rather pained about ourselves, and maybe even tempted to follow suit: to use that exclusively human disposition, language, as a weapon against someone, anyone, a bit like ourselves, who works in a library, a classroom.

One final function of anti-intellectualism in the modernist canon: it is a means of both connecting with and dispensing with a tradition. The Williams who assaults intellectuals is also the Williams who quotes them with evident interest and favor—as in the reference to John Addington Symonds' *Studies of the Greek Poets* (vol. 1, p. 284) given us at the end of book 1 of *Paterson* (p. 40). Williams did, after all, write *In the American Grain,* showing thereby that his writing makeup included the learned social historian. He was not barbarous; rather, a polemical enthusiast who wanted his intellectual allies to fight hard against their enemies. Modernism has been, in so many instances, a recourse to past invigorations, too brusquely and completely set aside by various "principalities and powers," so the particular, agitated modernist claims. Let the bullying interpretations be set aside, let the original voices be heard, or new ones in this fresh linkage with those original ones: Williams, through Symonds, to Hipponax and his iambics ending with a spondee or a trochee, rather than the compulsory iambus.

Similarly with James Agee's agitated, exalted, burdensome, fuming, penetrating, vexing, and triumphant *Let Us Now Praise Famous Men,* a major tirade against all forms, all sorts and conditions of language; and curiously, at times, despite the dramatic, rebellious indulgences and discursive tirades, an effort that offers, finally, rather traditional lyrics—biblical not only in title, and Shakespearean not only by virtue of a significant, introductory reference to *King Lear.* This prose-poem, like *Paterson,* is fairly saturated with self-lacerating, titillating, provocative anti-intellectual passages—which feed grandly anyone's iconoclastic fires. *Let Us Now Praise Famous Men* is not only a young writer's piece of work, a masterpiece of the literary-documentary tradition (and perhaps, in it, the very last improvisation possible), but also a young reader's exercise. The energy is catching—an exhilaration to those starting out, but wearying, one suspects, to many well along in this life. Agee himself aged considerably under the burden of this, his one major book. As for its anti-intellectualism, it is as brazen and unguarded and punishing as anything Williams has given us: "Most children prefer pleasure to boredom, lacking our intel-

ligence to reverse this preference"; or, also in connection with
children, "They are much too innocent to understand the profits of
docility"; or with regard to academic people, "Disregarding the
proved fact that few doctors of philosophy are literate, that is, that
few of them have the remotest idea how to read, how to say what
they mean, or what they mean in the first place . . ." These are some
choice moments of but one, comparatively short section titled "Education"—wherein the author, as a sort of bonus, tells us this with
regard to his "subjects," the Alabama sharecroppers of Hale
County: "I could not wish of any one of them that they should have
had the 'advantages' I have had: a Harvard education is by no means
an unqualified advantage."[2]

No need to dredge up more examples; they abound. They also
uncannily resemble, in their sum, those of Dr. Williams—the references to "vanity," the surly self-denigration, rendered so tren-
chantly one cannot but be reminded that here is a first-rate writer
whose self-imposed lashing is being done with great and singular
panache. Agee's anger is directed at New York intellectuals; at the
Partisan Review in its late 1930's, early 1940's heyday; at his beloved alma mater, Harvard; at Franklin D. Roosevelt, not exactly an
enemy of America's Depression-era poor; at schoolteachers and
college professors; at everyone, it seems, but his tenant farmer
hosts, whose ignorance he acknowledges, but then (almost a tic)
contrasts favorably with the deadness and deceit that characterize—
well, the life he lives, the kind of people he knows to call friends,
colleagues, lovers. All in all a great performance: the privileged
intellectual as a tormentor, a villainous spy, a phony, a pompous
ass, an unknowing, pretentious fool—thereby springing James
Agee, sending him into the company of the Alabama damned, the
last who will one day be first.

And why not? James Agee did, indeed, belong spiritually with his
Southern country people, the "famous" ones he tried so hard to
love, warts and all (to repeat, there is a price for his modernist
romanticism: the warts of Alabama folk go significantly unnoticed,
or perhaps, unmentioned). His heart was large, even as his pride
was (he knew) great and assertive. He wanted to conquer a certain
world, and his "three families" were in bad need of someone who

2. James Agee and Walker Evans, *Let Us Now Praise Famous Men* (Boston:
Houghton Mifflin, 1939), pp. 300, 303, 301, 310–311.

could help them fight, and with some chance of victory. On the other hand, words, even the brilliant, summoning juxtapositions of them in this extended oratorio, do not beat politicians and plantation owners and factory owners; not even foundation executives (the Guggenheim people also get it from Agee) or magazine editors can always be won over with language, however sublime. Anti-intellectualism becomes, therefore, a balm for the hurt frustration of basically gentle, giving souls: a kind of hate that seems therapeutic yet inconsequential (only the intellectuals will notice, and they can be counted on to understand, excuse, even to enjoy themselves). Of course, there is always a boiling point—not to mention a point of no return: Ezra Pound's references to American education as full of "syphilis," to American cultural life as full of "dry rot," were sad enough (and of a different order of animus than either that of Williams or Agee), but his sallies against American academics (and, as a matter of fact, against the same President, F. D. Roosevelt, to whom Williams and Agee were not always kind) eventually became unforgivably mean, wild, and in the end, as sadly incomprehensible as crazy talk can often be.

As Flannery O'Connor let us know in her letters (*The Habit of Being*), a writer's anti-intellectualism can be a variant of self-examination, self-parody—and an indirect call for mercy, an appeal for forgiveness in the Christian tradition. She lets us know that the Joy who turned into Hulga of "Good Country People" needs no gratuitous psychiatric interpretation from us. An author had done some sweating about herself and her kind. In story after story, as a matter of fact, O'Connor gives us pitiable, pretentious renderings of "interleckchuls"—the unpleasant spelling, used in her letters, is a sort of added boost. One thinks of poor Asbury in "The Enduring Chill" and poor Julian in "Everything That Rises Must Converge" and poor Sheppard in "The Lame Shall Enter First"—all the same character, really: heady (as in Mr. Head of "The Artificial Nigger") and so headed for comeuppance if not perdition. Modernism outside Dixie has given us grotesquerie in the short story, and so why not a few Southern oddball thinkers or pseudo-thinkers who try to read books and go North or become shrinky and reform-minded in their approach to life! There is, as always with O'Connor, a tough, astringent side to such portraits, but as one considers her own brave yet vulnerable life, one realizes that with her, too, as with W. C.

BRUCE ROBBINS

Modernism in History, Modernism in Power

In the first chapter of Henry Roth's *Call It Sleep* (1934), the six-year-old protagonist stands, thirsty and reflective, next to the sink of his immigrant family's New York tenement, too small to reach the "distant tap" and bring water out from its source in the "strange world . . . hidden behind the walls of a house."[1] Afterwards, when the novel plunges into the turbulent, disorienting current of up-rooted images and half-submerged meanings that makes up the child's consciousness, the initial tableau sticks in the mind as a helpful landmark. It indicates where this turbulent subjectivity— "the typical condition of the modernist outlook"—comes from.[2] The child's stream of consciousness flows with such violence, one might say, because he cannot make the tap water flow at all. The world seems to break up into private fragments only because children—and immigrants, for the son's helplessness stands for that of the entire family—cannot control its public forces. Fragmentation is not in the nature of things, nor in the nature of perception, but is produced, the scene suggests, as an effect of the distribution of power.[3]

1. Henry Roth, *Call It Sleep* (New York: Avon, 1962), p. 17.
2. Irving Howe, ed., *The Idea of the Modern in Literature and the Arts* (New York: Horizon, 1967), p. 14.
3. In the same way, it suggests that modernism's history-canceling use of myth

229

In addition to situating this characteristic modernist motif in a field of force, *Call It Sleep* also inserts the process of psychological maturation into the larger social chronology that is sometimes referred to antiseptically as "modernization"—the transition from rural precapitalist to urban capitalist society, here as so often partly concealed by the other more visible adaptations facing the immigrant.[4] In two senses, then, and despite its narrow focus on what a child can register of one brief act in a classic Oedipal drama, the novel can be said to restore to modernist fiction some of the historical awareness that modernism had notoriously expelled, repressed, or displaced. In short, it helps reconcile modernism with history. Of course, a shorthand statement like this one inevitably contains some ambiguity. History, like modernism itself, is a bulky composite term, and appeals on its behalf tend to run together a number of divergent notions—in addition to chronology and force, for example, there are narrative linearity, trusteeship of the past, ethical and social responsibility. If modernism is to make its peace with history, this portmanteau word will have to be unpacked. And this unpacking has recently come to seem more urgent. First, because modernism's alleged "negation of history," at issue both in the so-called Brecht-Lukács debates of the 1930's and in the troubled contemporary reception of *Call It Sleep* (modernist or proletarian?), clearly needs an update in the light of the fifty years of history that have passed.[5] Second and perhaps more important, because modernism, declared dead, is now felt to "belong to history," and the consequences of this putative proprietorship would bear some looking into.

---

belongs to the realm of the relative and the contingent. David's adored mother swells to mythic proportions in her son's eyes not because humankind is condemned to reenact the myth of Oedipus but because it is she who answers the call for water, who represents to her helpless child the awesome powers of the world "behind the walls of a house."

4. On the weakness of the concept of modernization, see, for example, Immanuel Wallerstein, *The Capitalist World-Economy* (Cambridge and Paris: Cambridge University Press and Editions de la Maison des Sciences de l'Homme, 1979), pp. 132–137.

5. The phrase cited comes from Georg Lukács, "The Ideology of Modernism," in *Backgrounds to Modern Literature*, ed. John Oliver Perry (San Francisco: Chandler, 1968), p. 252. The best English introduction to the modernism/realism debates is *Aesthetics and Politics* (London: New Left Books, 1977) with "Reflections in Conclusion" by Fredric Jameson.

In the years following the publication of *Call It Sleep* in 1934, the revising of modernism in the direction of history became a central activity. The previous generation had received the epithet "modernist" in recognition of its commitment to the new over and against the authority of the past. The next, spanning roughly the middle third of the century, reasserted the authority of history over it. In mid-century works like Kazin's *On Native Grounds* (1942), Kermode's *Romantic Image* (1957), Williams' *Culture and Society* (1958), and Ellmann's and Feidelson's *The Modern Tradition* (1965), rupture and schism were woven into seamless continuity, the abyss that had seemed to divide modernism from romanticism was filled in, the sudden explosion was eased into a sedate tradition. When *The Modern Tradition,* following earlier declarations by Harry Levin and Irving Howe, concluded that modernism "has passed into history," it was both referring to the end of a great period of creative endeavor and describing its own reinterpretation of that period. Modernism was now seen as "more than a cultivation of immediacy," as "also a containment of the resources and perils of the present by rediscovery of a relevant past."[6] In two senses, modernism now belonged to the past.

In the last third of the century, however, this way of putting modernism into history has come to seem somewhat premature. To a number of recent observers it has become necessary to affirm that modernism is very much alive: not as a self-conscious creative movement (though that case could be made), nor as a set of early twentieth-century texts that continue to speak to us (though they do), but as a strong presence within the tacit paradigms and routine functioning of institutions that once seemed and may still seem its polar opposites, including both the media, transmitter of "mass culture," and the university department of literature, preserver of "high culture." This affirmation implies a different relation between modernism and history. If the earlier generation insisted on modernism's continuity with the past, this one lays new stress on its

6. Richard Ellmann and Charles Feidelson, Jr., eds., *The Modern Tradition: Backgrounds of Modern Literature* (New York: Oxford, 1965), pp. vi, vii. On the dating of modernism's demise see Harry Levin, *Memories of the Moderns* (London: Faber and Faber, 1981), pp. 6–7. On the relation of Kermode and Williams to the modern tradition see Jonathan Arac, "History and Mystery: The Criticism of Frank Kermode," *Salmagundi,* 55 (Winter 1982).

complicity with the present. In taking institutional form, the suggestion is, modernism has also taken power.

One might even suggest, more particularly, that the insistence on continuity was a means of bringing about complicity, and that historical contextualization—taking historical context both as "tradition" and as "wider social determination"—did not so much overwhelm modernism as help carry it to an unforeseen position of prominence. Consider, for example, the sentences of context with which one popular and influential anthology of American literature opens its section on modernism: "In the early decades of the twentieth century the United States emerged as a major power whose actions in diplomacy, warfare, and political and economic affairs had profound consequences on the international scene. There was a comparable accession of power in American writing."[7] This double use of the word "power," which aligns the emergence of modernist literature with the rise of America's influence on the world beyond its borders, is neither a mere rhetorical convenience nor an innocent act of historical placement. On the one hand, it uses the authority of history to validate the cosmopolitan, universalistic claims with which modernism is associated; once the United States has stepped onto the "international scene," American literature is justified in speaking for the whole world, for example via the supposed universals of psychology and mythology. On the other hand, it offers the undeniable greatness of the modernist achievement to the United States as a sort of cultural reward for acting in the role of world policeman.

It is a commonplace of American literary scholarship that modernism was a specifically and uniquely *international* phenomenon, but the complacency with which this internationalism is acknowledged in America is not the rule for other nations. A Soviet critic argues that the "denationalization" of American literature by American theorists has permitted the United States to insinuate that its "extranational, 'universal' " works, like other products stamped "Made in U.S.A.," are superior to the homely native equivalents they are designed to supplant: "Their support of a Modernist literature, which usually lacks an authentic national character . . . serves the claims of the United States to a literary and, beyond this, an

7. Ronald Gottsman et al., eds., *The Norton Anthology of American Literature* (New York: Norton, 1979), II, 1015.

ideological rule over the world."[8] Modernism would thus be Americanism in sheep's clothing. It would be easier to dismiss this notion out of hand (it does not square well with Eliot's defection to Anglo-Royalism or Pound's to Mussolini) if the American critical rhetoric that helped consolidate modernism did not so often echo the uncritical internationalism of the multinationals, crusaders for "the internationalization of human society" whose slogan has become "Investment abroad is investment in America."[9] Leon Edel introduces Henry James's "transatlantic vision of the New World's relations to the Old" as a foreshadowing of "the central fact of the twentieth century—America's assumption, among the nations of the world, of those international responsibilities from which it had once isolated itself."[10] But an English observer is unlikely to regard this "central fact" with the same enthusiasm. What "the student of Henry James" should know, one critic declares, is "reactions to the penetration of Europe by American finance and capital," the so-called "American invasion" that "dominated press headlines in the 1890s."[11] It seems telling that the combination of anti-modernism with a nervous defensiveness about "authentic national character" occurs in more than one place. In 1961 Philip Hobsbaum had already written that "modernism in English poetry is beginning to seem something of an American imposition."[12]

The possibility of correlating the literary movement of modernism with movements of world power was most clearly anticipated, however, not in criticism but in two best-selling novels of the middle of the century, Orwell's *1984* (1949) and Heller's *Catch-22* (1961). Reacting directly to their modernist predecessors, both novels, like *Call It Sleep,* took pains to anchor certain floating elements

8. A. N. Nikolyukin, "Past and Present Discussions of American National Literature," *New Literary History,* 4:3 (1973), 587. Edmund Wilson's *Axel's Castle,* which did so much to introduce modernism in America, offers a (highly critical) counterexample.

9. Cited in Richard J. Barnet and Ronald Miller, *Global Reach: The Power of the Multinational Corporations* (New York: Simon and Schuster, 1974), pp. 13, 17.

10. Leon Edel, *Henry James* (Minneapolis: University of Minnesota Pamphlets on American Literature, no. 4, 1960), p. 7. The role of Pound and of his critical supporters is probably more important in this regard than that of James and his.

11. Fred Reed, "The Disintegration of Liberalism, 1895–1931," in *1900–1930,* ed. Michael Bell (London: Methuen, 1980), pp. 97, 95.

12. Graham Martin and P. N. Furbank, eds., *Twentieth-Century Poetry: Critical Essays and Documents* (Milton Keynes: Open University Press, 1975), p. 212.

of modernist sensibility in a well-mapped field of social forces. The destruction of the past, the relativizing of knowledge and morals, the domination of empirical fact by language and subjectivity—these motifs are traced by Orwell to the totalitarian use of a new technology of surveillance and thought-control, by Heller to the internal victory of Special Services, a self-sustaining bureaucracy charged with propaganda, over that portion of the military engaged in fighting the war. For each, in other words, our new, characteristic form of subjectivity results from our new, characteristic form of power—one that operates not by open coercion, which can be re-sisted, but by dissolving reality itself into a discontinuous succes-sion of images, thus leaving no solid ground for resistance. From their point of view, one might say, imagism was not a short-lived literary movement but an essential mode of obtaining consent from the governed in modern society.

If modernisn is not to be found in a museum, but in power, then it becomes more elusive and must be sought in unaccustomed places—for example, in advertising. It is no accident that adver-tising plays an important part in the thinking and the careers of Orwell and Heller, for to many observers the image-making indus-try seems one institution in which their unhappy vision of modernist power has been realized. Here modernism and modernization come together.

Since the debates of the thirties, the terms of the modernist/realist confrontation have come to require reformulation, Fredric Jameson suggests, largely because of "the fate of modernism in consumer society": "For what was once an oppositional and anti-social phe-nomenon in the early years of the century, has today become the dominant style of commodity production . . . a once scandalous 'perceptual art' has found a social and economic function in sup-plying the styling changes necessary to the *société de consommation* of the present."[13] The techniques of the modernist classics have been incorporated into modernist commercials. By the 1960's, An-dreas Huyssen writes, "the use of visual montage, one of the major inventions of the avant-garde, had already become standard pro-cedure in commercial advertising, and reminders of literary mod-ernism popped up in Volkswagen's beetle ads: 'Und läuft und läuft

13. Jameson, "Reflections in Conclusion," p. 209.

und läuft.' "[14] As Raymond Williams points out, the two also share a commitment to antirealism. In the "magic system" of advertising, which is "the official art of modern capitalist society," it can never be enough to describe the object as in itself it really is. If consumption is to be stimulated, referentiality must be undermined: "The attempt is made, by magic, to associate this consumption with human desires to which it has no real reference."[15] In addition, like Orwell's Ministry of Truth and Heller's Special Services, advertising hides or distorts the past in the interest of what John Berger describes as "a future continually deferred."[16] It creates, that is, a continuous present cut off from the possibility of development. The modernist conception of time thus both obeys and is put into practice by the staccato rhythm of acquisition, obsolescence, novelty, and reacquisition. It should not be surprising that many students, having grasped the modernist project of collapsing history into a perpetual present of mythic repetition, "go on to work in advertising, where they put to good use what the tradition teaches them; by celebrating the endlessly recurring, which is also endlessly disposable."[17] Leopold Bloom, advertising canvasser, is thus prophetic of what the literary modernism he embodied would become.

But modernism does more than lend its services to the advertising industry. Working in the cause of consumption, it also sells a false promise of power that diverts attention from the real sources of power—and it thus exercises power. On this point too a number of recent writers have converged. "Since consumption is within its limits a satisfactory activity, it can be plausibly offered as a commanding social purpose," Raymond Williams declares, and can thus ratify "the subjection of society to the operations of the existing social system."[18] John Berger argues that "publicity turns consumption into a substitute for democracy. The choice of what one eats (or wears or drives) takes the place of significant political

14. Andreas Huyssen, "The Search for Tradition: Avant-Garde and Postmodernism in the 1970s," *New German Critique,* 22 (Winter 1981), 24.

15. Raymond Williams, "Advertising: The Magic System," in *Problems of Materialism and Culture* (London: Verso, 1980), pp. 184, 189.

16. John Berger, *Ways of Seeing* (London: BBC and Penguin, 1972), p. 153.

17. Alan Wall, "Modernism, Revaluation and Commitment," in *The Politics of Modernism,* ed. Francis Barker et al., Proceedings of the Essex Conference on the Sociology of Literature, July 1978 (University of Essex, 1979), p. 188.

18. Williams, "Advertising," p. 188.

choice."[19] Similarly, Gerald Graff describes how the modernist media redescribe actual alienation as "a revolutionary form of freedom and potency," thus furnishing "a model by which social powerlessness can be experienced as gratification."[20] Modernist reflexivity put to work, consumerism sells itself over and above any particular content. Its most important effect is indirect: the creation of a depoliticized public sphere where, as in a hall of mirrors, the shocking novelty of an infinite proliferation of images both conceals an underlying sameness and, more important, precludes any glimpse of the controlling machinery outside. In an imagistic society, spectacle becomes, as Guy Debord puts it, "the sun that never sets on the empire of modern passivity"—or, in other words, "the self-portrait of power in the epoch of its totalitarian management of the conditions of existence."[21]

Susan Sontag, retreating from the "make it new" militancy of *Against Interpretation* (1966), has recently offered a similar revaluation of the politics of novelty. In *On Photography* (1977) she takes the extraordinary expansion of the photograph into all areas of private and public life as strong evidence of a modernist takeover of twentieth-century perception. "Photography is the most successful vehicle of modernist taste in its pop version."[22] By wrenching things from their context in order to taste the gratification of seeing them afresh, photography makes of reality "an array of casual fragments." The consequence is an enormous, unconscious aestheticism: "The camera makes everyone a tourist in other people's reality, and eventually in one's own." "Marx reproached philosophy for only trying to understand the world rather than trying to change it. Photographers . . . suggest the vanity of even trying to understand the world and instead propose that we collect it."[23] Installed in a series of perceptual practices, technologies, and industries, photography is modernist aestheticism in action, or rather inaction.

19. Berger, *Ways of Seeing,* p. 149.

20. Gerald Graff, *Literature against Itself: Literary Ideas in Modern Society* (Chicago: University of Chicago Press, 1979), p. 92.

21. Guy Debord, *La Société du spectacle* (Paris: Buchet/Chastel, 1972), pp. 14, 18. My translation.

22. Susan Sontag, *On Photography* (New York: Delta, 1977), p. 131.

23. Ibid., pp. 80, 57, 82.

The notion of modernism's witting or unwitting collusion with contemporary social institutions would seem to be a new commonplace of the twentieth century's final third. "The seven major characteristics of modernism or their postmodernistic variation as formulated by Ihab Hassan described New York just as well as . . . Beckett's prose." "Modernism is . . . the art of modernization." "One might ask whether the uncompromising attack on tradition, narration, and memory which characterizes large segments of the historical avant-garde, is not just the other side of Henry Ford's notorious statement that 'history is bunk.' " "The real 'avant-garde' is advanced capitalism."[24] Like other commonplaces, this one points toward a large truth. Its main weakness lies in not engaging with the large and opposite commonplace that modernism can be critical as well as indicative of our epoch. Its main strength is in suggesting that what is at stake in the matter of literary modernity is power. As Jürgen Habermas argues in a critique of Daniel Bell's *The Cultural Contradictions of Capitalism,* it makes little sense to disavow the symptom and yet cling to the disease: "Neoconservatism shifts onto cultural modernism the uncomfortable burdens of a more or less successful capitalist modernization of the economy and society. The neoconservative doctrine blurs the relationship between the welcomed process of societal modernization on the one hand and the lamented cultural development on the other."[25] This argument also brings out a certain disingenuousness in familiar "high culture" complaints about "mass culture"—complaints that it otherwise resembles. In this view, the very temple of high art, modernism, jealously guards the same modernity that circulates promiscuously in the marketplace.

In *Memories of The Moderns* (1981), Harry Levin speaks of the "ironic fate that wafted the books of the *avant-garde* from Bohemia to Academe."[26] This may seem a lesser irony than that which now associates modernism with urban mass culture, "the dark Other

---

24. Heiner Müller, "Reflections on Post-Modernism," *New German Critique,* 16 (Winter 1979), 56; Malcolm Bradbury and James McFarlane, *Modernism* (Harmondsworth: Penguin, 1976), p. 27; Huyssen, "Search for Tradition," p. 37; Graff, *Literature against Itself,* p. 8.

25. Jürgen Habermas, "Modernity versus Postmodernity," *New German Critique,* 22 (Winter 1981), 7.

26. Levin, *Memories of the Moderns,* p. 8.

against which Modernists like T. S. Eliot and Ortega y Gasset emphasized time and again that it was their mission to salvage the purity of high art."[27] To a number of critics, in any case, this incongruity too can now be seen to reveal an underlying complicity. If modernism lights up the show windows of late capitalism with its dazzling defamiliarizations, it is in part because it never ceased to be "the art of modernization." And if it has found a strong institutional base in university departments of literature, it is in part because, creating the taste by which it could be enjoyed, it helped form the modes of reading responsible for canonizing it.

As Edward Said points out, modernism is roughly contemporary with the existence of academic departments of English in their present shape: "The intellectual hegemony of Eliot, Leavis, Richards and the New Critics coincides not only with the work of masters like Joyce, Eliot himself, Stevens, Lawrence, but also with the serious and autonomous development of literary studies in the university, a development which in time becomes synonymous with 'English' as a subject."[28] It comes as no surprise to learn that the New Criticism was a wing of the modernist vanguard. The point that deserves attention is the extent to which the procedures that the New Criticism helped install, in order to transmit and interpret the modernist canon, have remained intact—the extent to which, in other words, English has remained a modernist discipline. Long after the disappearance of the New Criticism itself, and despite the newer criticism's changing fashions and permanent pluralism, a tendency persists, for example, to value the emotive over the rational; psychological and mythic universals over historical particulars; an idealized preindustrial past or highly selective tradition over a present that is judged, in the "modern tradition," to be sordid, chaotic, meaningless. Questions of literary value and inclusion in the canon are still decided according to the modernist touchstones of disinterestedness, hermeticism, and structural unity. Whether or not one is suspicious enough to see "Eliot, Faulkner, Joyce, and their imitators" as "deliberately providing occasions for the complex critical explications of the New Critics," it is difficult not to see some truth

27. Huyssen, "Search for Tradition," p. 27.
28. Edward Said, "Reflections on Recent American 'Left' Criticism," *Boundary 2*, 8:1 (Fall 1979), 17. For several years *Boundary 2* has been regularly furnishing outstanding contributions to the theme of modernism-in-criticism.

in Gerald Graff's somewhat overstated conclusion: "If English has an ideology today, it is the anti-bourgeois ideology of literary and cultural modernism."[29]

Even the advent of so-called poststructuralist criticism—usually taken as the academic variant of literary postmodernism—has not disturbed the deep-seated aestheticism that pervades the modernist heritage. Whether texts are processed for organic form and unified sensibility or for indeterminacy and reflexive self-consumption, the product is a discourse that is autotelic and hermetic. In this sense, postmodern criticism might be said to have taken modernism out of its period and spread it over the entire canon. What could be more faithful to modernism than the current practice by which the reflexivity that supposedly marked its break with the past is now routinely unearthed in whatever text and whatever period the critic happens to be discussing? In finding modernity everywhere, this newer criticism takes up the modernist gesture of farewell to history and generalizes it, institutionalizing literature itself as a departure from history. If to be human involves living in history (in any combination of several senses), then such criticism has a good claim to be, as Ortega y Gasset wished modern art to be, "dehumanized."

This is not to say that criticism lacks either a theory or a practice of history. (The older conventions of contextualization, realism, linear narrative, and assumed omniscience of course remain in service alongside criticism's modernist modes.) It is, on the other hand, to see in criticism the same paradox with regard to history that Irving Howe finds in the modernist classics: "Modernism despairs of human history, abandons the idea of linear historical development, falls back upon notions of a universal *condition humaine* or a rhythm of eternal recurrence, yet within its own realm is committed to ceaseless change, turmoil, and recreation. The more history comes to be seen as stable . . . the more art must take on a relentless dynamism."[30] Like the dynamism of modern art, the cheerful professionalism of modern criticism is also founded on a despair of history. This is the burden of Francis Mulhern's historical analysis of the "cultural power" of *Scrutiny,* first as a major influence on the nascent branch of English studies at Cambridge after the First World War, and later, despite its apparent disintegration, as "the spontane-

29. Graff, *Literature against Itself,* pp. 33, 110.
30. Howe, *Idea of the Modern,* p. 17.

ous ideology of academic literary criticism" throughout Britain.[31] In the period of acute economic and cultural "modernization" from 1890 to 1920, Mulhern says, when existing disciplines like political economy and philosophy seemed either complicit with or irrelevant to the general collapse of tradition, the way was open to Leavis and company to offer the study of the national literature as a sanctuary for the common past uprooted by urban, cosmopolitan, "Americanized" civilization, a powerful stay against "the progressive atrophy of organic wholeness in individuals and in society."[32] If history is atrophy, then initiative passes from society to the Scrutineer, one of the happy few who recognize and nourish the sacred remnants of earlier and better ways of life preserved in the canon. Thus the modernist move against modernity was embodied in an institution.

Even when the myth of a lost preindustrial Eden had fallen before the scholarly critique of primitivism, and Leavis himself had fallen from his controversial eminence, his vision of historical decline survived. Abandoned as theory, it was retained as a series of practices. Disputed as a reading of sixteenth-century history, the undissociated sensibility could live on as the premium on "organic form" and the "resolution of tensions" in countless textual readings. If the particular canon was questioned, canon-formation itself lent literary criticism the authority of the national past. The specifics of the great tradition were less important than the institutional permanence of *a* tradition, whose greatness—propped up by the institution—could be taken for granted and would cast a giant shadow over the empty and unredeemed present.

In institutional form, Leavis' gesture could become a powerful routine: a past tradition of "humane" or "eternal" values was continually thrown up against urban-industrial society, declaring it sterile and decayed. Stephen Spender has given a much-quoted definition of modernism as "the vision of a whole situation," a "confrontation of the past with the present" in "a single vision that restores wholeness to the fragmentation, even by realizing it as disaster."[33] As far as criticism is concerned, the key word here is

31. Francis Mulhern, *The Moment of "Scrutiny"* (London: New Left Books, 1979), pp. 328, 9.

32. Ibid., p. 306.

33. Stephen Spender, "The Modern as Vision of a Whole Situation," in Perry, *Backgrounds to Modern Literature,* p. 232.

"disaster." Since the one thing the institution cannot lay open to question is the value of the past it preserves, and that gives it its *raison d'être,* the past must appear as some version of the "great tradition," and its "confrontation . . . with the present" condemns the latter to appear as disastrous loss, a seeping away of value. In order for past culture to be seen as perfection, present civilization must be seen as chaos. The result is a structural or procedural pessimism, an institutionalizing of that "*rentier* despair" that Orwell felt in "Prufrock."[34] Indeed, the pattern of allusions from a nobler past that Prufrock brings to bear on his futile and meaningless present, only to crush the present further beneath their weight, makes the poem something of an allegory of the academic modernism that Eliot did so much to establish. There is no doubt that this sacrifice of respect for the present has been energizing for criticism, but only at the cost of keeping it away from overwhelming questions about contemporary society and the possibilities of action within it.

If the media represent modernism in its antitraditional mood, bartering action and change for the aesthetic pleasures of disinterested, decontextualized observation, the more traditional modernism of the academy, founded on the cultural despair of an elite, produces much the same effects. In historical perspective it seems natural enough that similar structural motifs can be detected in the modernist classics, in modern mass culture, and in the literature departments that grew up along with the former and in reaction to the latter. To describe modernism in these expanded terms—that is to say, in an institutional context—is first of all to bring out the presentness and the continuing powers of what might otherwise seem a cluster of past and impotently "adversary" movements. It is emphatically not to repeat the accusations of the thirties, like that of Lukács, against modernist ideological decadence. The two sorts of historical analysis can be distinguished by their fruits. In pinning modernism to the wall of capitalist ideology, Lukács encouraged the conclusion, in Bloch's words, "that there can be no such thing as an avant-garde within late capitalist society."[35] Like today's historical contextualization, this use of historical context runs the risk of eliminating contingency, and thus of reproducing that fatalistic sub-

34. George Orwell, *The Collected Essays, Journalism, and Letters,* ed. Sonia Orwell and Ian Angus (Harmondsworth: Penguin, 1970), II, 276.
35. Ernst Bloch, "Discussing Expressionism," in *Aesthetics and Politics,* p. 20.

mission to the status quo that it most wants to avoid. On the other hand, to focus on institutions rather than ideologies is to reject the spurious implication of necessity (which can serve equally well to dismiss or to empower modernism) and to recuperate what has been called "the activism of modernity."[36] For the term "institution," unlike more monolithic expressions, "enables the sense of 'being instituted,' and thus the possibility of resistance and trans-formation."[37] In this sense, historical analysis makes room for the present tense of agency and slips by some of the rigidities by which "history" has been beset. Here it approaches the useful if some-times mystifying term "power," one of whose advantages is its suppleness. In power, if not always in history, modernism does not belong to any providential plan, and is neither to be spurned nor to be embraced.

Examining the conjunction of modernism and criticism with this more versatile instrument, it is possible to draw conclusions of an unaccustomed order. Consider for instance the argument that "wholeness" is an essential source of the power of their combina-tion. "In a culture which everywhere repressed the notion of totality," Perry Anderson writes, "literary criticism represented a refuge."[38] The implication is that in a fragmented, divided, "mod-ernized" society, "totality" is not merely an ideological illusion but a necessary counter of thought and mobilizer of feeling, a precon-dition of political action. If wholeness, in mythic and procedural forms, underlies the power that Leavis and the New Critics claimed for criticism, then perhaps the most *powerful* answer to their legacy is not *Ideologiekritik* but more and other wholes. The suggestion that what is called for is a version of what we have already learned to do echoes the surprising conjunctural twist that Fredric Jameson gives to his update of the modernism/realism controversy: "In these cir-cumstances, indeed, there is some question whether the ultimate renewal of modernism, the final dialectical subversion of the new automatized conventions of an aesthetics of perceptual revolution

36. Paul de Man, "Literary History and Literary Modernity," in *Blindness and Insight* (New York: Oxford, 1971), p. 184.

37. English Studies Group in Stuart Hall et al., eds., *Culture, Media, Language: Working Papers in Cultural Studies, 1972–1979* (London: Hutchinson and the Centre for Contemporary Cultural Studies, 1980).

38. Perry Anderson, "Components of the National Culture," in *Student Power: Problems, Diagnosis, Action,* ed. Alexander Cockburn and Robin Blackburn (Har-mondsworth: Penguin and New Left Books, 1969), p. 276.

might not simply be . . . realism itself! For when modernism and its accompanying techniques of 'estrangement' have become the dominant style whereby the consumer is reconciled with capitalism, the habit of fragmentation itself needs to be 'estranged' and corrected by a more totalizing way of viewing phenomena."[39] As Lukács' call for realism was a call for a literature that would *not* reflect the experience of daily life under capitalism, which was fragmentary, so too, rather than any sort of return to naive mimesis, Jameson asks for "the forcible reopening of access to a sense of society as a totality, and . . . the reinvention of possibilities of cognition that allow social phenomena once again to become transparent."[40] Repudiating "history" as inexorable linear progression and as simple reflection of objective reality, Jameson invokes it in another sense, as a vision of human interrelatedness. Historical criticism, in this sense, would also have to become visionary.

This program for literature and criticism has points in common with what is sometimes claimed for postmodernism. Against modernism's elitism and exclusive canon, postmoderns often call for a reintegration of art and life. In order to achieve a resacralizing of present-day life, emptied both by the system of commodities and by the withdrawal of modernism to the high ground of tradition, it calls for a desacralizing of the artwork. Similarly, seeing that the inwardness of modernism simply confirms in retrospect the privatization and fragmentation of the world of commodities that it tried to escape, postmodernism wills for itself what Jerome Rothenberg describes as a "new public and political poetry."[41] The results of this impulse seem less sure, but it has had its successes. Edward Mendelson praises Pynchon, for example, for his turn outward from modernism's "hermetic self-referentiality" and psychologism to the "large vision of political interconnectedness" of *Gravity's Rainbow,* a vision that reaches out to comprehend new wholes, "self-sustaining bureaucracies" and "a new international culture of electronic communication and multi-national cartels."[42]

At the same time, there are risks for anyone who would speak

39. Jameson, "Reflections in Conclusion," p. 211.

40. Jameson, "Reflections in Conclusion," p. 212, and *The Political Unconscious: Narrative as a Socially Symbolic Act* (London: Methuen, 1981), p. 234.

41. Jerome Rothenberg, *Revolution of the Word: A New Gathering of American Avant-Garde Poetry 1914–1945* (New York: Seabury, 1974), p. xxi.

42. Edward Mendelson, ed., *Pynchon: A Collection of Critical Essays* (Englewood Cliffs, N.J.: Prentice-Hall, 1978), pp. 15, 14, 9–10.

confidently in postmodernism's name, beyond the obvious one of falling in with the consumerist adoration of pure novelty. For Gerald Graff, the critical move from modernist organicism to postmodernist deconstruction is nothing but the mark of a further "acquiescence in the agreeably meaningless surfaces of mass culture," that is, a further acceptance of the phenomenal world of late capitalism.[43] Terry Eagleton notes that the approach to the sign in contemporary semiotics involves an uncanny duplication of "the very structure of the commodity," and he goes on to accuse deconstruction, despite its radical pretensions, of further depoliticizing the already shaky framework of public discourse: "Political quietism and compromise are preserved, not by a Forsterian affirmation of the 'personal,' but by a dispersal of the subject so radical as to render it impotent as any kind of agent at all."[44] Postmodernism proposes to reverse modernist despair by climbing back onto the wave of the future, but it seems late in the day for such confidence as to where history's waves will break.

Foregoing the luxury of a free ride on historical authority, we can still generate power in and out of the modernist classics. "Prufrock," for example, that canonical expression of modernist despair, has yet to be read, after the modernist fashion, against the grain. So read, the poem can be seen to contain, alongside "that fragmentation which is characteristic of human experience generally" (J. Hillis Miller) what might be called fragments of totality, and it is these, like the final vision of the mermaids, that add to the poem's "futility" its "wonderful vitality and power" (Orwell).[45] And in *Call It Sleep,* too, the aspiration to totality is a path to power. Like Prufrock, the child protagonist is engaged in a process of vision and revision by which he tries to break out of the fragmented subjectivity to which his powerlessness condemns him. Unlike Prufrock, he succeeds. By the end of the novel he has touched power, if not controlled it. He does this in two ways. The first strategy, stressed in modernist readings of the novel, is textbook Freud. Piecing together fragments of what he has seen and heard, he creates a myth of his own origin, providing his mother with a Gentile lover,

43. Graff, *Literature against Itself,* p. 58.

44. Terry Eagleton, *Walter Benjamin, Or Towards a Revolutionary Criticism* (London: Verso, 1981), pp. 30, 138.

45. J. Hillis Miller, *Poets of Reality: Six Twentieth-Century Writers* (New York: Atheneum, 1969), p. 148; Orwell, *Collected Essays,* II, 276.

making himself illegitimate, and freeing himself from his father's terrible authority. But like Pynchon's postmodern Oedipa Maas, this detective work gives us something more than Oedipus, more than the mythic repetition of entry into the status quo characteristic both of American Freudianism and of much modernism. The child's second strategy is to carry the quest for power over the heads of his parents and out into the world. If one quest leads back to the past, the other leads out into America, the "strange world . . . hidden behind the walls of a house" where the water comes from, and where his father is less a tyrant than a victim.[46]

Collecting the leaves of a calendar, playing with the pieces of an alarm clock, the child studies the force that sends his father to work so early in the morning. In his search for power and light, he mounts a sort of cult of the public utilities; chasing telegraph poles into the distance or contemplating the world from behind the gas-works, he finds in the public face of power the sources and limits of his private tyranny. A syncretist, he translates the religious imagery of the Old World, whose power his parents acknowledge, into the modern language of New World utilities, which tbey have not yet learned to master. Isaiah helps him see that the black coal in the cellar that so terrifies him is nothing but stored-up light. The power of the Cross becomes that of electricity in the telegraph wires. By the last scene of the novel, the fragments have come together in a single vision, and he knows where to find the power to light up his darkened home. He thrusts the dipper of his milkman father—symbol of private potency but also of the public powerlessness of a former cow-herder in industrial New York—into the tram tracks, thus plugging into the system that rules the New World: "Power! Power like a paw, titanic power, / ripped through the earth and slammed / against his body and shackled him / where he stood. Power! Incredible, / barbaric power! A blast, a siren of light / within him" (p. 419). He is burned (like Oedipus, he suffers a "swollen foot," p. 440), but he has also incinerated the dipper, stopped the frenzied motion of the street, permanently shifted the balance of power in his family. Among the results of his research that can be generalized is the simple notion that power is dangerous but graspable, and not terminal.

46. On the specific weakness of the modernist father, see Robert Kiely. *Beyond Egotism: The Fiction of James Joyce, Virginia Woolf, and D. H. Lawrence* (Cambridge: Harvard University Press, 1980), p. 50.

JUDITH WILT

Behind the Door of *1984:*
"The Worst Thing in the World"

Modern police states, proud of their techniques and pure in their moral stances, have given us the closest look since Dante at the structural operation of one of our most enduring fantasies: "The thing that is in Room 101," the inquisitor of *1984* tells the quailing, desiring Winston Smith, "is the worst thing in the world."[1] What is the worst thing in the world? Dante's imagination structured this fantasy as a downward spiral, humiliation under humiliation, a falling sickeningly toward the huge frozen agonized bulk in whom "the worst" lived and breathed and, vaccuumlike, exercised upon all Being its dire charism. Reports from the Gulag Archipelago, its outposts in P.O.W. camps and police stations east and west, south and north, confirm this carefully organized downward-spiraling structure. Exquisite orchestrations of the experience of falling, being kicked down, pushed under, forced to drop, result, according to the testimony of prisoners, in a hatred not of the interrogator, not even of the falling, but of the coming up, the being stopped from falling.

This movement is the dark opposite to the ladder of Being which Joyce's Stephen Dedalus climbs, for instance, when he signs his

1. I quote from the easily available Signet edition of George Orwell's *1984* (New York: New American Library, 1961); this scene occurs on p. 233. All further quotations, identified by page numbers in the text, are from this edition.

247

name Stephen Dedalus, Class of Elements, Clongowes Wood College, Sallins, County Kildare, Ireland, Europe, The World, The
Universe. The best things in the world augment the self. The worst
thing in the world is whatever unmakes the self, dispersing it or
devouring it. And Dante's fundamental insight about this process,
confirmed by Freud and articulated by Dostoevsky's Grand Inquisitor, and Orwell's and Arthur Koestler's and all the many inquisitors
who are empowered by governments, not artists, is that the soul
somewhere *desires* this unmaking, this worst. Encountering this
worst, after a long series of small unmakings have brought it within
view, most people must recoil into the last solid grain of that de-
spoiled self, no matter what betrayals or abandonments, what awful
discoveries of the nature of that last grain, result. To embrace this
worst, on the other hand, is the most ambiguous act of all—triumph
or surrender? suicide or martyrdom? losing the self on the knowable
level to gain it on some unknowable level? Dante had such a mystic
paradox to provide him with a map through the territory beyond
"the worst." Lacking such a map, or disposed to think twice even
if we do possess a map, our century pauses, irresolute, guarded,
before the last circles of the inferno, on the threshhold of Room 101,
mesmerized by another Dantean insight also explored by Orwell—
whatever "the worst" is, it is different for each person, and belongs,
like a lover, to him alone.

Like many others, perhaps, I remember being a tiny bit disap-
pointed as a teenager when the door of Room 101 finally opened in
book 3, chapter 5 of Orwell's *1984*. Being buckled into a face-cage
with two starving rats—that was bad, certainly, but was it the worst
thing in the world? I was unconvinced, and the apparent eccentricity
of Orwell's fantasy triggered alternate fantasies of my own, as
Orwell no doubt partly intended. Teaching *1984* twenty years later,
however, I come to feel more strongly Orwell's primary purpose: to
establish the cage, the rat, the face, the specific tableau of Room
101, as the inevitable, the imperative, worst of our world. And the
fantasy seems more appropriate every year that that future approaches us.[2]

2. "The date itself," notes David Kubal, "has become a general metaphor . . .
calling up an emotion of apprehension about the future" (*Outside the Whale: George
Orwell's Art and Politics* [South Bend, Ind.: University of Notre Dame Press, 1972],
p. 132). And Christopher Small more recently remarked that "already something

Let us think first for a moment about the rat, the underminer, the garbage dweller, the bright-eyed guest at the last dinner table of man, not, as Hamlet said of Polonius, where he eats, but where he is eaten. The sly and toothless worm was the ultimate scavenger for the medieval imagination, for Dante and Shakespeare, but the rat, a savager playfellow, haunts the modern imagination. Joyce's Stephen Dedalus was shouldered into a ditch of cold slimy water while a boy at Clongowes school, and the rats in the "scum," slimy, damp, and cold, "sleek slimy coats, little little feet tucked up to jump, black shiny eyes to look out of," become the permanent emblematic companions of the cold-water side of himself, arousing disgust, recognition, horror.[3] Better acquainted with the "meat" that is his flesh, Leopold Bloom suffers only a momentary check at Paddy Dignam's funeral when "Rtststr! A rattle of pebbles" signals the presence of the obese grandfatherly rat, the "grey alive" for whom the dead man is "a regular square feed."[4] But the spooked intelligencer of T. S. Eliot's *The Waste Land* recognizes a less amiable companionship, an identification. Whether in his wife's bedroom or fishing in the garbage-canal of his culture, he is still, he affirms, quivering in recognition and in self-loathing, "in rats' alley."[5]

---

like a countdown has started" (*The Road to Miniluv: George Orwell, the State, and God* [London: Victor Gollancz, 1975], p. 13). The question of how far it is personal is much debated. Kubal asks the question—"Has Orwell touched a nerve unique to our own time? Or has he given expression to a universal anxiety about man's inability to control his own nature?" (*Outside the Whale*, p. 133)—in such a way as to emphasize the general. Small's account stresses recent speculation about Orwell's own "severely repressed" attraction to sadism and homosexuality, calling the scene in Room 101 a personal fantasy of "narrowly averted homosexual rape" (*The Road to Miniluv*, pp. 167, 168).

3. James Joyce, *Portrait of the Artist as a Young Man* (New York: Viking, 1956), p. 22. Reviewing the posthumously published "Such, Such Were the Joys . . . ," Stephen Spender noticed that "the resemblance of the world of his preparatory school to that of *1984* is striking" (*New Republic*, 10 March 1953, quoted in *George Orwell: The Critical Heritage*, ed. Jeffrey Myers [London: Routledge and Kegan Paul, 1975], p. 314). One of the things that links Orwell's memoir of his childhood to Joyce's *Portrait* (and to Dickens as well) is the adult-retained sense that fundamentally "only child life is real life."

4. James Joyce, *Ulysses* (New York: Vintage, 1961), p. 114.

5. I quote from "The Waste Land," in T. S. Eliot, *The Complete Poems and Plays* (New York: Harcourt, Brace and World, 1971), p. 400, II, l. 115.

What is the special modern dread that the rat embodies for Eliot, Joyce, and Orwell, and for D. H. Lawrence as well? It is that we are essentially *already* a race of living corpses, and thus are fated to meet the rat corrupted body to body, maimed soul to soul, open eye to eye, inside the grave-cage of the twentieth century. The frantic analysis of Lawrence is that mind and will have spun madly out of control in this century, leaving the flesh-soul to rot; the only vitality he sees left in London is in the working-class man of *Women in Love,* "a creature that the towns have produced, strangely pure-bred and fine in one sense, furtive, quick, subtle," with "some of the fineness and stillness and silkiness of a dark-eyed silent rat." With this "dark suggestive presence, gutter presence," Lawrence says provocatively, his protagonist Birkin shares a "male, outlawed understanding."[6] He shares it, inevitably, with the furtive Loerke too, the German artist who lives "like a rat in the river of corruption," the "wizard rat" (p. 419) who takes the principle of modern mechanism, rathood, death-in-life, to its ultimate brilliant negating conclusion—the root of self is work and the root motive of work is, simply, darkly, beyond mere survival, hunger. Ursula instinctively loathes this hungry rat in Birkin, shouting at him her famous epithet—"eater of corpses!" (p. 298). And Birkin nods in momentary despairing corroboration. Even his philosophical abstractions, his cosmic new construction of reality, partook of the bright-eyed joy of the underminer, the self-devourer: "There really *was* a certain stimulant in self-destruction for him—especially when it was translated spiritually" (p. 301).

Even Virginia Woolf marked the rat briefly at the point where modern man sees, seeks, the death, and the death-eater, in himself. In the first draft of the first pages of *The Waves,* where six sensitive children play in the Edenic garden, Louis and Jinny "together killed" a rat. "And kissed there." Submerging her image almost immediately, Woolf changed the phrase to "together saw the dead rat—the innumerable maggots," a sight that stayed "in the hearts" of those children. By the second draft the passage buries the rat entirely. Louis sees instead, vision of time passing in the underworld, women carrying water on the banks of the Nile, and Jinny, breaking his contact with the dead like a sword of "steel upon the

6. D. H. Lawrence, *Women in Love* (New York: Viking, 1960), pp. 350–351. All further quotations, identified by page numbers in the text, are from this edition.

nape of the neck!" so that "the line is cut!" This becomes in the published novel a death trance for Louis, dangerous but in its way promising, "self"-destructive but spiritually potent with para-human possibilities as it was for Lawrence, a trance which Jinny breaks with her kiss, fearful for him as Ursula was for Birkin—"Is he dead? I thought"—awakening him, and the other children who observe or learn of the kiss, to the warm, restless, limited human "life" which is their dwelling place.[7]

Lawrence and Woolf share this half-yearning, half-contemptuous respect for and curiosity about the vital death and the insights within its destructive, dissolving avatar, the rat. Joyce, interested in the contradictory upward strivings of the spirit, allows Stephen and Bloom only a mordant glimpse of the fundamental rat before firmly averting the eye to the elemental stars and skies. As modernists, blowing up the Victorian foundations, admitting (and admitting to) the rat, these authors offer half-glimpsed neo-Romantic alterna-tives. But Orwell's reduced and beleaguered Everyman, from the perspective which the beautifully imagined postmodernist gener-ation of *1984* affords, commands the bleakest truth: "we are the dead men," says Winston Smith, and "we are the dead," echoes his lover "dutifully," and "you are the dead" confirms the "iron voice" of the secret policeman who has been watching all along their doomed struggle to add a spark of life to their death by making love (p. 182).

Now it is important to note that this recognition of the death which one *is,* is at the beginning of *1984* the condition for regen-eration, as it is for Lawrence. It is the modernist neo-Romantic alternative, the existential confrontation which ought to make possi-ble the life one may *become.* As Winston contemplates the unbear-able yet hypnotically beautiful void of the "creamy-white" diary page which he has begun to disfigure with his personal writing mark, his thought, his thought-crime (these are the same thing in the police state), he makes two more of the vital connections which begin existential regeneration. He commits the crime, that is, makes the commitment to an expressed (and exposed) selfhood, equates

7. See Virginia Woolf, *The Waves: The Two Holograph Drafts,* ed. J. W. Graham (Toronto: University of Toronto Press, 1976), draft I, p. 4., and draft II, pp. 406–408; and Virginia Woolf, *Jacob's Room and The Waves* (New York: Harcourt, Brace and World, 1958), p. 183.

the crime, that is, the fact that thought is crime, with the death that each thinking member of the police state lives in, and then makes a curious discovery: "Now that he had recognized himself as a dead man it became important to stay alive as long as possible" (p. 27).

This recognition expresses itself immediately afterwards in a complex dream of three women, a dream which displays both the worth and the price of the recognition, both the tragedy and the beauty of it. His mother, with his baby sister in her arms, sinks down and down below him, "in some subterranean place, the bottom of a well, or a very deep grave, or the saloon of a sinking ship"; in any case "it was a place which, already far below him, was itself moving downwards." Then suddenly, in a lovely, silent, natural setting which in his waking thoughts he calls The Golden Country, a girl with dark hair comes toward him, flinging off her clothes with a confident gesture which arouses not sexual desire but a still more fundamental emotion, "admiration for the gesture, which with its grace seemed to annihilate a whole system of thought, as though Big Brother and the Party and the Thought Police could all be swept into nothingness by a single splendid movement of the arm" (pp. 28–29). The gesture of the girl, and that of his mother pressing his sister to her, link with the peculiar feeling that overcame Winston in a movie theater earlier, watching a film of a "prole" mother in a doomed boatload of refugees putting her arms in futile protection around a child, "all the time covering him up as much as possible as if she thought her arms would keep the bullets off him" (p. 11).

All these gestures, women's gestures, belong to "the ancient times," Winston senses, because they speak outwardly of an inner world which is private, self-maintained and self-maintaining, concerned not with public but with personal standards and hence paradoxically not with the isolated self, so manipulable by the Party, but with individual relationships. Alone, one is naked to the Thought Police, but selves rooted in relationship, he reasons, are always covered, each by the other, each by his feeling for the other. And since the feeling, mother for child, lover for lover, is ancient and necessary to the species, he reasons further, though it will be challenged, though it must, when challenged under torture, be confessed and perhaps even abjured, it cannot actually be changed, any more than one's body chemistry, one's brain waves, can be changed. Therefore, "since they can't get inside you" to alter that fundamental chemistry, relationship, it is that which makes one human. And, Winston concludes in shaky relief, in daring thought-crime, though "life" and "death" remain surely in the grip of the Thought Police, "humanity" is out of their power to reach, is even out of his own tarnished reach: "They could not alter your feelings, for that matter, you could not alter them yourself, even if you wanted to . . . the inner heart, whose workings were mysteries even to yourself, remained impregnable" (p. 138). And so, though we are dead men and futile, it is only necessary to remain alive long enough to become human; after that, when life is destroyed by the Thought Police, as it inevitably will be, life will take with it, tragic and glorious and futile but unharmed, the inner heart, the impregnable mystery.

In the world of *1984,* mystery, like eroticism, is a crime.[8] The technicians of society are working to strip language and action of both these qualities, not only because both qualities reinforce the private world but also because deprivation of these qualities in human beings "induced hysteria, which . . . could be transformed into war fever and leader worship" (p. 110). The intolerable pressure on language to invert meaning, and on eroticism to convert to suspicion, is indeed splitting the atom of the private heart and releasing huge quantities of energy for the state to use in its economy of destruction, an economy which the state understands perfectly well. We know they understand it, that they are knaves rather than fools, when we find that the "revolutionary" analysis of the economy has been written by the chief technician himself, O'Brien. And since the analysis also includes the perception that so monstrous a channeling of the energies of man directly into destruction is making visible the operation of the second law of thermodynamics, is dramatizing in all economies an increasing death-of-heat, we know that "life" in this world is futility, not only from

8. It is in this context, I think, that it is proper to see the various "conversion" processes of *1984* as "a monstrous parody . . . of religious conversion" (Small, *The Road to Miniluv,* p. 160) and the novel itself as "suffused with religious imagery" (Robert A. Lee, *Orwell's Fiction* [South Bend, Ind.: University of Notre Dame Press, 1969], p. 135). A world without mystery, or with only fake mysteries (like the contrived rebellious underground "Brotherhood" that Winston joins only to find it is virtually a department of the Party), exposes the purely material basis of "conversion" imagery, that is, the conversion of (Winston's) energy into dead "food" which becomes (O'Brien's) energy.

Winston's "human" viewpoint but also ultimately from the technicians'. This is a world ending.

But there is one value-act left in it—to preserve the heart, in both
senses of the word, the inner mystery of human things, and the spark
of eroticism that creates new heat. Three hiding places emerge in the
novel, three enclosures or cages where "they can't get in." Ah, but
they can, and they do.

The first secret place is the past. Whatever else "they" can alter,
we think, the past remains itself, unchangeable repository of "ancient" gestures and motives, safe in its unreachable pastness. But
Winston Smith works in the Ministry of Truth, whose job it is to
alter the writings that sustain the only certainties about the past.
This is a Herculean task (Tristram Shandy's gallant effort to recap-
ture all his past, even the past that flies by while he is recapturing
earlier moments, is as nothing compared to the effort required to
erase the past, even the past that is accumulating while one is
erasing it!). The task is stimulating technicians to veritable miracles
of technique. But the task seems nearly accomplished in *1984,* a
mere generation after it was begun. The old "facts" along with the
instructions changing them to the new old "facts" proceed steadily
to the furnaces, down chutes nicknamed, "for some reason,"
memory holes (p. 35). The reason, no mere accident or sloppy
"abuse" of language but a part of a planned reversal of all-important
word concepts, is that the holes are not places where memories are
stored but places where memory itself is stored, and cosmetized,
and finally transformed into a void, a hole. Given this control of the
paper of the past, is not the hiding place of "the past" breached?

Not entirely. For there is an oral culture still alive, among the
Proles. And though it is perverted and sometimes inane and always
unconscious of itself, the oral tradition seems to preserve a sense of
the power of the past, of its continuing quirky aliveness and its
contribution to present identity. An expression of this, primitive and
corrupt and "drivelling" as Winston finds it, occurs in the "pop
song" sung by the Prole woman hanging clothes outside Winston
and Julia's "love nest." The song was composed, of course, by
computer, to feed the subhuman needs of this subparty group, and
yet it "haunts" the streets, even overpowering the songs composed
for Hate Week. The song, now we come to look at it, is a powerful
recovery of pastness, a hymn to that unbreachable hiding place of
the heart:

> It was only an 'opeless fancy,
> It passed like an Ipril dye,
> But a look an' a word an' the dreams they stirred,
> They 'ave stolen my 'eart awye!
>
> They sye that time 'eals all things,
> They sye you can always forget;
> But the smiles an' the tears acrorss the years,
> They twist my 'eartstrings yet!

(pp. 114, 117)

So song and rhyme resist the mechanism of "healing" and "forget-ting" which is now in the hands of the state, resist the underminer, the rat. But documents do not; in the cubicles of the Ministry of Truth, connected to the destroying furnace by a long tube "pro-tected by a wire grating" (p. 34), sit the "rectifiers" of the past, engaged in "that process of continuous alteration" whose ultimate perfection is "the creation of dead men" (p. 43). And one of the alterers, underminers, rats, one of the best, is Winston Smith himself. We shall have occasion to remember this when Winston sits in Room 101 at the end of the novel, confronting another destroyer through another wire grating.

No wonder that when he enters the second of the novel's secret hiding places for the heart, Winston brings the rat with him. The second hiding place is the lover, for Winston, the woman—erotic feeling for his woman. This place of feeling takes to itself the lost safety of the past as well, in the symbolic object Winston picks up in the antique shop, the heavy glass paperweight containing the fragment of coral, the "strange pink convoluted object" which, being both "old" and "beautiful," is doubly dangerous for a Party member to identify with (p. 80). The erotic charge of that pink convoluted object, lying enclosed, dreamily sufficient and "mag-nified" in its "rainwatery" curves of glass, oddly uniting in its shape the human organs of brain, heart, vagina, lifts Winston's heart with a vague promise which is fulfilled in Julia. Julia is engaged in an animal erotic-aesthetic rebellion against the gray of Party life; she is the agent of the secret place. She calls him to her. She associates herself first with the "golden place" in Winston's rather exalted sexual fantasy and then with the pink object in a clear representation of woman as (temporary) hiding place. After meeting Winston in several outdoor or open and abandoned places, she agrees to a permanent enclosure for their lovemaking, the room above the antique shop, and then buys forbidden cosmetics to make herself the coral at its center: "her lips were deeply reddened, her cheeks rouged" (p. 118). The bravery of her gesture calls forth an important one from the man—"it was the first time that he had stripped himself naked in her presence"—and marks him with the colors of their mutual hiding place of sex; after sleep that evening "most of her make-up had transferred itself to his own face or the bolster, but a light stain of rouge still brought out the beauty of her cheekbone . . . A yellow ray from the sinking sun fled across the foot of the bed" (p. 119). The pink place is also the golden place; the place of color is the holding place, and "the paperweight was the room he was in, and the coral was Julia's life and his own, fixed in a sort of eternity at the heart of the crystal" (p. 122).

Yet the rat is there, inside the enclosure. Julia sees it and, unconcerned, frightens it back into its deeper hole, flinging a shoe with the same superb, self-expressive, mindless, unhaunted gesture which attracted him when it meant flinging off her clothes, and alarmed him when it meant flinging the Newspeak dictionary at the filmed face of "Goldstein" during the Two Minute Hate. Winston does not see the rat in his love nest, but reacts with unusual horror to Julia's sight of it. For he has had, we then learn, a recurring nightmare about a "something unendurable, something too dreadful to be faced" on the other side of a "wall of blackness," which he now connects briefly with the rat, and more, "with what Julia had been saying before he cut her short." The nightmare had, importantly, included an element of self-deceit, for despite the darkness "he did in fact know what was behind the wall." His cutting Julia short extends the deceit, for by it he signals that he knows not only whom he fears, but what rat-action he fears. Julia's chatter about the rat was going in this dangerous direction: "In some of these streets a woman daren't leave a baby alone for two minutes. It's the great brown ones that do it. And the nasty thing is that the brutes always—" (p. 120). Winston's guilty boyhood memory of the mother and little sister he lost in "these streets" is here; and deeper, his memory of the food he snatched ratlike from the child, and devoured before coming back to find them gone. But deeper still: "*Don't go on!*" Winston shrieks, with his "eyes tightly shut," and then, recovering, deceiving, "It's nothing. I don't like rats, that's all" (p. 120).[9] That isn't all. The brutes always—attack the face, go for the eyes, was what Julia left unsaid, what Winston understands about rat-action and walls off in darkness.

This fear O'Brien will later deduce from Julia's confession of their life together and use against Winston, putting together the last of the elements of the tableau that waits behind the door of Room 101. A man's last hiding place, after memory becomes a "hole," after erotic feeling breaks down, is behind his own face, under the fragile eyes, inside the egg of the skull. And the beast he fears most, knows best, is the rat that rips off the face. Julia knows about Winston's desire for enclosures—the golden place, the glass paperweight, the room, even the four-poster bed—and she remembers casually from Winston's outburst the rat, and the rat's attack. But it takes a technician of the faceless society, the unfaced society, to squeeze from the imprisoned woman not only the details, but the meaning of the details, to arrange them in their proper order in Room 101, to make of the face, the cage, the rat, the very duplicate of the world inside the skull. And manipulate it.

The deadpan face contradicted by the living eyes, the lying face undermined by the truth-telling eyes, the defended wall of face rent, sapped, humanized, by betraying eyes—this is man in *1984*. On the first page of the novel we meet the prime fact of life in Oceania: "The enormous face gazed from the wall . . . one of those pictures which are so contrived that the eyes follow you about when you move." Big Brother exists on, as, a wall; he imparts fear, controls other men's faces, through his eyes, "hypnotic eyes" exerting "some huge force . . . something that penetrated inside your skull, battering against your brain" (pp. 68–69). Big Brother wants to make sheer face, sheer wall, out of everyone else; his eyes put out everyone else's, they "told you to reject the evidence of your eyes" (p. 69). In one sense Winston's eyes bring his brain evidence of an alternate reality to Party logic, and he struggles to defend his eyes for that reason. In another terrible sense Winston's eyes are evi-

9. My personal favorite Winston-Smith-like evasion among Orwell's early reviewers is Julian Symons' dainty scolding of Orwell's final meeting, at last, with the rat: "This kind of crudity . . . will never do; however great the pains expended upon it, the idea of Room 101 and the rats will always remain comic rather than horrific" (in the *Times Literary Supplement,* 10 June 1949, quoted in Myers, *The Critical Heritage,* p. 256).

dence of his brain, bring evidence against him. "To control your face, was an instinctive reaction" during the routine Two Minute Hate of the Enemy which was required activity for all Party members, but Winston's mixed feelings escape out his eyes: "There was a space of a couple of seconds during which the expression of his eyes might conceivably have betrayed him," and the affable, mysterious colleague O'Brien notices. Winston "caught O'Brien's eye," a "flash of intelligence" passes between the men "as though their two minds had opened and the thoughts were flowing from one into the other through their eyes" (p. 18).

Winston thinks he has caught O'Brien through the eye, has found a kindred soul; in fact, O'Brien is a watcher for the Thought Police and has caught Winston through the eye. The face of O'Brien ("O'Brien was on his side," p. 69) reassures Winston. It is for O'Brien's imagined eye that he writes his secret, therefore criminal, diary. The consoling face of O'Brien displaces the glaring face of Big Brother in the mind's eye of Winston Smith (p. 69), though in moments of acute fear "the face of Big Brother swam into his mind displacing that of O'Brien" (p. 87). "Something" in the face attracted Winston to O'Brien, and to Julia too, and something in his face "caught" their eyes; something betraying live thoughts behind the "inscrutable" faces everyone wears (p. 18), live desires behind the dead flesh. When O'Brien admits/traps Julia and Winston into the Anti-Big Brother "Brotherhood" he warns them that he may at any moment "become a different person with a different face" (p. 144); when the man who supplied the bedroom to Julia and Winston reveals himself as an agent of the Thought Police, "his face had undergone only tiny changes, that had nevertheless worked a complete transformation" (p. 185). When Winston is finally caught by the police and imprisoned in the Ministry of Love he confronts a fellow prisoner who has already confessed everything, renounced everything, betrayed everyone; his face is gone, "emaciated," thinned down, demolished so that "it looked like a skull" (p. 194).

Yet something remains even when the face is lost; as Winston, despairing, but obscurely comforted, understood at the very beginning, "nothing was your own except the few cubic centimeters inside your skull" (p. 26). The prisoner has forgotten that he has those living "owned" few centimeters inside; but Big Brother has not, and the man is dragged off to Room 101, to be turned fully into skull, inside and out. The next thing Winston learns is that the face of Big Brother and of O'Brien are the same, the face of O'Brien and of the rebel "Goldstein" are the same. And the two men settle down, face to face, eye to eye, O'Brien to try to penetrate the opening of the eyes, Winston to resist by his puny force, then by guile, then by sincere self-renunciation, the catching of his eye, the devouring of his "own."

But his antagonist wants not self-renunciation but self-annihilation, and in the end ("You knew this, Winston—you have always known it," O'Brien chides, p. 197), the wish of the victim is found to coincide with the will of the tormentor. O'Brien holds up four fingers and "for a fleeting instant . . . thirty seconds, perhaps, of luminous certainty," Winston's own eyes, disowned, repossessed, see the five fingers that O'Brien orders him to see (p. 213). In the grinding encounter of eyes and faces both men lose a little face— "Winston was struck by the tiredness of O'Brien's face . . . there were pouches under the eyes, the skin sagged from the cheekbones" (p. 217)—but Winston is the bigger loser: "The creature's face seemed to be protruded, because of its bent carriage. A forlorn, jailbird's face with a nobby forehead running back into a bald scalp, a crooked nose, and battered-looking cheekbones . . . the mouth had a drawn-in look. Certainly it was his own face, but it seemed to him that it had changed more than he had changed inside" (p. 223). The outside has become skull but the inside few centimeters remain, barely, alive; the creature's eyes remain "fierce and watchful."

Using the uncomplicated methods of pain and torture, O'Brien has almost won, but only almost. Therefore he has lost. He changes his tactics, gives Winston more food, more freedom. The victim's face fills out, takes "a new shape," behind which unfamiliar but still useful "camouflage" the few centimeters of brain keep alive on one last cry of hatred. Winston imagines, with joy, the day they will rip off his face, again, "the camouflage would be down, and bang! would go the batteries of his hatred" (p. 231). They would return their own bullet into his exposed brain, and he would die, defeating them—"the heretical thought would be unpunished, unrepented, out of their reach forever" (p. 231). And O'Brien, having tenderly coaxed that last spark of freedom, that last heretical thought, out of the skull and onto Winston's face, denies him the final hiding place, death. Instead he takes him to Room 101, where "the worst thing in the world" waits.

The new face that O'Brien fits to him in the dire tableau of Room 101 is a mask that radically reverses outside and inside. Locked in one cage, divided by a thin partition of wire, or skullbone pierced by eyeholes, Winston's "own" few centimeters of brain-self confront two rats, "enormous . . . fierce," an "old scaly grandfather" of a force brimming with "astonishing intelligence" (p. 235). The terror of the rats, O'Brien clarifies in his "schoolmasterish manner," is that they hunger to get inside the skull, they will shoot out "like bullets . . . leap onto your face and bore straight through it . . . attack the eyes first . . . burrow through the cheeks and devour the tongue" (p. 235). The horror is of demonic possession, a ghastly substitution of their intelligence for his, the final physical usurpation of the ultimate hiding place.

Two sharp clicks punctuate this encounter. The first encloses Winston in the mask and provokes a "screaming animal" cry that seems to come indistinguishably from "inside" him and "outside" him, from "them" and from "him." Is it only "the rat" trying to get in, or has Winston harbored another rat all along, a screaming animal inside, one that seized food from his starving baby sister and now leaps to interpose Julia's body and brain as food for its enemy? This dweller inside, this inhabitor of his dreams, this secret sharer on the other side of the "wall of blackness" whom he desperately tried not to know, shows himself: "Julia . . . Tear her face off, strip her to the bones!" (p. 236). And "another metallic click" ends the episode. But, crucially, "the cage door had clicked shut and not open." Winston is alone, alive, with his untouched face, and the rat feeds within, behind the door of the face, on the few cubic centimeters of spoiled selfhood. The cage is permanent. The rat is home, and the rat's name, most horrible of all, is "love"—"he loved Big Brother," the rat-eaten human exults at the end, "oh stubborn, self-willed exile." And with that "admission," says Orwell, "the long hoped-for bullet was entering the brain" (p. 245).

With this word, exile, we begin to understand why the dreadful work of Room 101, the worst thing in our world, puts Orwell in the company of the other Western modernists who struggled away from rats' alley, and allows him to complete politically their aestheticopsychic insight. It was by stubborn, self-willed exile from their home-cultures that Lawrence, Joyce, and Eliot kept their private centimeters of self distanced from the rat of what they saw as the Western Wasteland, dust-heap, garbage pile. This is a bad thing to know of your own culture, but the worst thing is to know you bring the rat with you wherever you go. Orwell had known this in his essay of the early 1930's, "Shooting an Elephant," that description of his early days as a servant of Empire, a master of civilization, doing "the dirty work of Empire at close quarters" in Burma (p. 235).[10] "With one part of my mind," Orwell says, he had hated the British Raj, knowing it to be, like the Party of *1984,* "an unbreakable tyranny . . . clamped down . . . upon the will of prostrate peoples." But behind the wall of darkness he knows the love of that hated thing, feels the rat-emotion: "With another part I thought that the greatest joy in the world would be to drive a bayonet into a Buddhist priest's guts" (p. 237). These divided feelings are "the normal by-products of imperialism," Orwell understands. But even the schizophrenia is healthy compared with what follows. A man can only wear a mask, live in two compartments, for so long; finally "his face grows to fit the mask" (p. 241). And the man who "knows with perfect certainty," with the few cubic centimeters inside the skull which are his own, that he should not shoot the lost and inoffensive elephant, shoots the elephant, "poured shot after shot into his heart" (p. 241), plays the killer "they" make him play, the killer he is brother to, the killer he is.

The tableau of "the worst" that occurs in Room 101, the rats in the cage that fits the face like a mask—and the brain like a face— made its first appearance in "Shooting an Elephant" and its most memorable, but not its last, appearance in *1984.* And it is still appearing at the corners of our eyes. Did I not catch a glimpse of it again in "The Deer Hunter"? In the middle of that film the Everyman, Nick, is imprisoned by the enemy. He confronts the rat caged with him in the river-pen, and receives an obscure but permanent injury. And a "truth." The cage door clicks, and he is saved from the rat by his friend. But not really. For he is shut into the

10. The essay can be found in *The Collected Essays, Journalism, and Letters of George Orwell,* ed. Sonia Orwell and Ian Angus (New York: Harcourt Brace, Jovanovich, 1968), I, 235–242. Quotations from the essay will be identified by page numbers in the text.

Contributors

JEROME H. BUCKLEY
Department of English and American Literature and Language
Harvard University

DONALD D. STONE
Department of English
Queens College, City University of New York

LISA RUDDICK
Department of English
University of Chicago

MONROE ENGEL
Department of English and American Literature and Language
Harvard University

THOMAS MALLON
Department of English
Vassar College

JOHN HILDEBIDLE
Literature Faculty
Massachusetts Institute of Technology

PHYLLIS ROSE
Department of English
Wesleyan University

ROBERT KIELY
Department of English and American Literature and Language
Harvard University

J. HILLIS MILLER
Departments of English and Comparative Literature
Yale University

RONALD BUSH
Division of the Humanities
California Institute of Technology

ROBERT COLES
Professor of Psychiatry and Medical Humanities, Harvard
  Medical School
Harvard University

BRUCE ROBBINS
   Section d'anglais
   Université de Lausanne

JUDITH WILT
   Department of English
   Boston College